# PATH THROUGH
## Scripture

# PATH THROUGH Scripture

## NEW INTERACTIVE EDITION

# MARK LINK, S.J.

TABOR® PUBLISHING

Allen, Texas

IMPRIMI POTEST
Bradley M. Schaeffer, S.J.

NIHIL OBSTAT
Rev. Glenn D. Gardner, J.C.D.

IMPRIMATUR
† Most Rev. Charles V. Grahmann

January 30, 1995

The Nihil Obstat and Imprimatur are official declarations that the material reviewed is free of doctrinal or moral error. No implication is contained therein that those granting the Nihil Obstat and Imprimatur agree with the contents, opinions, or statements expressed.


Calligraphy: Bob Niles
Maps: Bill Alger

ACKNOWLEDGMENT
Unless otherwise noted, all Scripture quotations, as well as the photograph on page 115, are from Today's English Version text. Copyright © American Bible Society 1966, 1971, 1976, 1992. Used by permission.

Send all inquiries to:
RCL • Resources for Christian Living®
200 East Bethany Drive
Allen, Texas 75002–3804

Toll free     877-275-4725
Fax             800-688-8356

Printed in the United States of America

**21090**    ISBN 0–7829–0470–X (Student Text)
**21091**    ISBN 0–7829–0471–8 (Resource Manual)

9  10  11  12  13  14      12  11  10  09  08  07

# NEW INTERACTIVE EDITION

*Path through Scripture* differs
from most books
that deal with presenting God's word.
Sharply focused, concisely written,
and graphically illustrated, each of
its 115 units follows a twofold format
that includes

- a *core* component and
- an *interactive* component.

First, the core component.

The core component focuses on the
*informational,* or *mind,* level of Scripture.
In other words, it deals with
*understanding* God's word.

Second, the interactive component.

The interactive component takes
an important step beyond the
informational, or mind, level of Scripture
by also focusing on

- the *formational,* or *heart,* level and
- the *transformational,* or *soul,* level.

In normal religious education parlance,
the book invites the reader into
a prayerful dialogue with the text
or a group in probing two important
dimensions of Scripture:

- the *value* dimension and
- the *faith* dimension.

In more conventional terminology,
the book deals with how Scripture

- enriches human life and
- invites openness to the gift of faith.

For facilitators and teachers of groups,
a detailed Resource Manual is available.

If the author has failed the scholars,
he begs their understanding.
If he has failed his readers,
he prays that another will succeed
where he has not.
If he has failed the Scriptures,
he trusts in a loving God's forgiveness.

Mark Link, S.J.

# CONTENTS

# I

# *World of Abraham*

## TIMELINE
*(APPROXIMATE)*
*B.C. = BEFORE CHRIST*

1900       Abraham

## BIBLE   *(KEY BOOK)*

Genesis

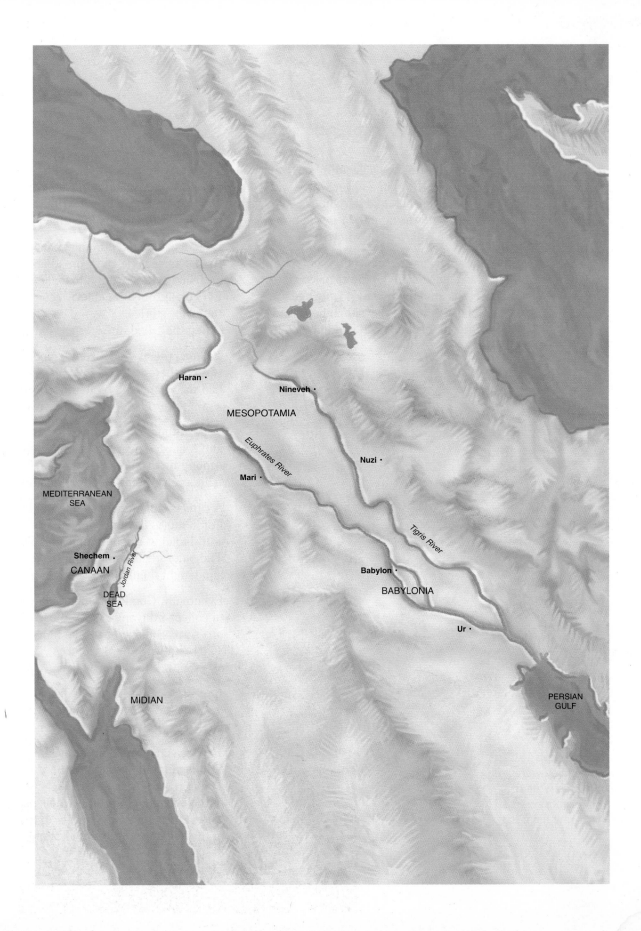

# CHAPTER ONE

# Scripture

## 1 Three Stages

Rapunzel was a beautiful girl who lived in a tower with a witch. The witch told her she was ugly. Since there was no mirror in the tower, Rapunzel believed the witch.

One sunny day a handsome young prince saw Rapunzel on the tower balcony. He was stunned by how lovely she was. To make a long story short, he rescued her from the evil witch and married her.

*S*cribes wrote with reeds, whose point was shredded to form a tiny brush.

Scribes followed strict rules when copying biblical manuscripts. For example, they were not permitted to write a word from memory— only a letter at a time.

This story and many others like it were communicated *orally* for centuries. One reason they weren't written down was that not many people then could read.

But education and printing changed that. As books became widespread and popular, *oral* storytelling went into decline. Eventually, only the elderly remembered the older stories. When they died, the stories would die too.

To keep this tragedy from happening, two brothers in Germany, the Grimms, had the old people recite the stories so that they could record and save them.

The brothers eventually found, edited, and recorded nearly a hundred stories. Among them were "Snow White," "Cinderella," and "Sleeping Beauty."

A similar situation existed in old Israel. For centuries, stories of God's dealings with Israel were communicated orally. The older generation memorized them and taught them to the younger generation.

Eventually, God inspired Israelite *scribes* to collect, edit, and record these stories on "scrolls" made of animal hide. The result was the Scriptures as we now know them.

And so Scripture developed slowly over centuries by three stages: life stage, oral stage, and written stage.

The *life* stage was the *live* event: God leading the Israelites out of Egypt. The *oral* stage was the *telling* of the event to children by their parents. The *written* stage was the *recording* of the event for future generations, like our own.

Ray Bradbury's sci-fi novel *Fahrenheit 451* describes a future when leaders destroy all sources of information to better control people. One day a friend tells Montag that a group of people have secretly memorized all of the world's greatest books.

*"It can't be," said Montag. "It is," replied Granger. "Some day the people will be called to recite what they know and we'll set it up in type."*

People ask, "How can vast parts of the Bible be passed on orally and accurately for centuries?" Jean Varenne can help here.

In *Yoga and the Hindu Tradition,* Varenne tells how young Brahmins, even today, memorize hundreds of pages of texts and perform such acrobatic feats of memory as reciting these texts backward, or saying every other syllable of them.

Record and share:
a. One thing you've committed to memory.
b. Your earliest memory (What age?).
c. Your most unforgettable memory.
d. Your most frightening memory.

2. Read or listen to Judges 8:28, Acts 8:26, Matthew 27:8, and Matthew 28:15.
a. What do the passages have in common?
b. How does this common trait point to the fact that each of these passages was passed on orally for an extended period before it was recorded?

3. Some people have a good knowledge of the Bible from previous courses. Others are not so fortunate. On a scale of 1 to 4 (1 = practically zero, 2 = poor, 3 = fair, 4 = good), how would you rate your knowledge of the Bible?

4. Take a few minutes to record:
a. The names of the two *main parts* into which the Bible is divided.
b. The name of the first book of the *first main part* of the Bible.

This scroll fragment was found in a cave and dates from before the birth of Jesus.

Stitch marks (right) show where scroll segments (made of animal skin) were joined and sewn.

Unlike English writing, Hebrew writing reads from right to left.

c. The number of books contained in the *second main part* of the Bible.
d. The number of Gospels and the names of the evangelists (gospel writers) who recorded them.
e. The name of the last book of the Bible.

5. Read or listen to Psalm 78:1–4. What clue does it contain concerning:
a. How ancient peoples passed it on?
b. What events, especially, it preserves?

6. What is one question you have about something in or related to the Bible?

## Three Stages

Why were stories like "Rapunzel" and "Snow White" not recorded at first? Why were they eventually recorded?

2. List and explain the three stages by which the Bible reached its present form.

3. Who were the scribes, and what gave rise to their profession?

# 2 Ancient Scrolls

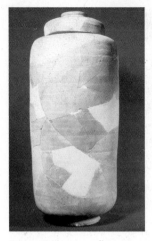

Some Qumran scrolls were found in jars.

**M**ost people think of the Bible as being just *one* single book. Actually, it is a *library* of scores of books that divide into two sections:

᛬ the *Old Testament,* which was written before the coming of Jesus, and
᛬ the *New Testament,* which was written after the coming of Jesus.

Surprisingly, the oldest copies of biblical books were found in 1947 at Qumran, on the northwest corner of the Dead Sea. They were written on leather scrolls, now known as the "Dead Sea Scrolls." Their discovery reads like a novel.

A young man was tending his goats. When one of them turned up missing, he went up a hillside in search of it.

Coming upon a large hole in the hillside, the young man threw a stone into the hole. When he heard something break inside, he panicked and ran away. The next day he returned with his cousin.

*Climbing through the hole and dropping to the floor of the cave, they first groped in darkness; but as their eyes grew accustomed, they made out some jars with lids. . . .*

*They opened one; it was empty. . . . They opened still another and from this one they took some hides that were rolled up and inscribed and wrapped in linen.*

Roland de Vaux, "The Qumran Story"

The boys' amazing discovery touched off a treasure hunt for more scrolls that might be hidden in other hillside caves

**S**ometimes hanging by ropes, work crews explored over 200 caves in the Dead Sea area.

Cave 4 (center opening) housed the biggest find: over 400 manuscripts.

Why didn't the scrolls rot or deteriorate in the caves?

of the Dead Sea area. The subsequent hunt produced these remarkable results:

🖐 Between the years 1947 and 1956, eleven caves yielded 800 documents (mostly in fragmentary form).
🖐 Some 200 were biblical writings that represented almost every book of the Hebrew Bible and were a thousand years older than our oldest copies of it.

Scholars think the scrolls belonged to Essenes (Jewish "monks") living in the desert at Qumran around A.D. 70.
The Essenes stashed the scrolls in the caves to keep them from being destroyed by invading Roman armies.

*P*opular Science magazine says that when the atom bomb mushroomed its message of death into the sky, many people speculated on the future uses of "atomic energy."
Few, if any, put Bible study on the list. Ironically, this is one of the first uses to which it was put.

A Chicago scientist used a Geiger counter to measure radioactivity from a scroll of the Book of Isaiah and dated it.
It turned out to be about a hundred years older than Jesus himself.
Remarkably, Jesus could have read from it in the episode described in Luke 4:16–21. Read aloud or listen to this episode in Luke.

Record and share what went on in:
a. Your mind as you read or heard it.
b. Jesus' mind, perhaps, as he read it.
c. The minds of Jesus' hearers, perhaps, as they listened to Jesus.

2. Concerning the dating of the Dead Sea Scrolls, *Popular Science* reported:

*It was strangely fitting that nuclear scientists, turning from war to peacetime research, should undertake the task of determining the age of an ancient transcript of the Book of Isaiah.*

Read aloud or listen to Isaiah 2:4–5. What did *Popular Science* have in mind?

3. Imagine you are a TV reporter preparing to interview a biblical expert upon the fiftieth anniversary of the finding of the Dead Sea Scrolls.

a. List three questions that your viewers might be interested in having the expert answer, and explain why.
b. Prepare a map of Palestine to show your viewers the location of Qumran with reference to the Dead Sea, the Sea of Galilee, the Jordan River, and Jerusalem.

4. In his book *What the Jews Believe*, Philip Bernstein says that during a fire in a synagogue, an Irish policeman rescued the Torah scroll from the ark. He gave it to the rabbi, saying proudly, "I saved your crucifix." Bernstein says, "Well, the Jews have no crucifix, but the policeman had the right idea."

a. What did Bernstein have in mind?
b. Research and share the meaning of *synagogue, scroll, ark, Torah,* and *rabbi;* give their approximate Christian equivalent. 🖐

*E*xcavated "monastery" at Qumran (shown) is helping to piece together the story of the "monks" who once lived here.

The hills surrounding the Qumran site are pock-marked with caves. The Dead Sea is visible in the background (left).

### Ancient Scrolls

*L*ist the two sections into which the "library" of the Bible divides.

2. When, where, and by whom were the oldest copies of the Bible found?

3. When, by whom, and from whom were the scrolls probably hidden in caves?

4. How many caves yielded how many biblical documents? How much older were these copies than those we had?

Egyptian papyrus from about 1600 B.C.

# 3  Inspired by God

*The Last Temptation of Christ* is a novel based on the life of Jesus. One scene portrays Matthew with a notebook open on his lap. Jesus enters and Matthew shows him the notebook, saying, "Rabbi, here I record your works."

After reading a few lines, Jesus turns and says, "Who told you these things?" Matthew replies, "The angel told me."

Jesus is shocked and asks, "What angel?" Matthew replies, "The one who comes each night I take up my pen to write. He dictates what I should write."

Christians have always believed that the Bible is *inspired* by God— even though they understand and express this belief in different ways.

How should we understand *inspiration?* We need to avoid two extremes.

First, we must not imagine that an angel or the Holy Spirit *dictated* the Bible word for word.
Second, we should not imagine that the role of the Holy Spirit was only that of spiritual "watchdog," keeping the human writers from error.

The earliest scrolls were made of papyrus.

These two Egyptians are gathering and splitting papyrus stalks to form a writing surface.

The biblical authors did not divide their work into chapters and verses. Scholars did this centuries later.

Why divide the Bible into chapters and verses?

6

Rather, we should picture the Holy Spirit
and the human writer as both
being actively involved.
We may describe "inspiration" this way:

Inspiration means the Holy Spirit
worked *in* and *through* the human writers
in such a way that they were empowered
to use their own talents and words
to communicate what God
wanted them to communicate.

Because the Bible is inspired,
it is free from religious error, that is,
*errors in matters related to salvation.*

But this does not mean it is free, also,
from scientific or historical error.
Nor is it free from them.

For example, Deuteronomy 14:7 says
hares chew cud, which is incorrect.
And 1 Samuel 31:4 says Saul killed himself,
but 2 Samuel 1:9–10 says
an Amalekite killed him.

*1*n *The Jewish Jesus,* Robert Aron
says that a biblical scribe had to
follow a set of very strict rules
in copying biblical scrolls:

*He must never write a word from his own*
*memory or without pronouncing it aloud.*
*Special care must be taken in writing*
*the divine names. Before each of these*
*the scribe must pronounce the formula:*
*"I intend to write the Holy Name."*
*If he forgets one single time,*
*the scroll is unfit to be read in public.*
*It must be entirely rewritten.*

a. Why pronounce each individual word?
b. Why pronounce the sacred formula?
c. Have members of your group try
copying on a chalkboard or newsprint
this passage from Matthew 28:19:
"Baptize them in the name of the Father,
the Son, and the Holy Spirit."
How far did the members get before erring?

2. Fred Smith was a biochemist and
an agnostic. One day, to satisfy a friend,
he attended church. He said later:

*I disliked the singing and the sermon,*
*but the following Bible passage touched me*

*J*esus, I've asked you
for a lot of help,
like the time I lost my
wallet . . .

*and became the seed of faith for me:*
*"If you confess that Jesus is Lord and*
*believe that God raised him from death,*
*you will be saved."*   Romans 10:9

Record and share:
a. One Bible passage or story that you like
especially, and explain why.
b. One Bible passage or story that you
have questions about, and explain why.

3. Compose a prayer asking God
to touch you, as Smith was touched.
During the week, pray it daily.
At week's end, report on:
a. How faithfully you prayed the prayer
on a daily basis.
b. How praying it affected you.

You might use the following prayer
as a model for your own prayer:

*Jesus, I've asked you for a lot of help,*
*like the time I lost my wallet,*
*my school ID, and my driver's license.*
*Now I'm asking for something*
*that I now see is far more important.*

*I'm asking you to touch me and heal me*
*of my resentment toward my dad.*
*I guess we just don't click. Heal him too.*
*Finally, Jesus, forgive me for hurting Amy.*
*Help me make it up to her.*

## Inspired by God

**H**ow might we
describe "inspiration"?
What two extremes
should we avoid in
trying to imagine how
God inspired the Bible
writers?

2. From what errors is
the Bible free? Give an
example of a scientific
error and a historical
error in the Bible.

3. Who divided the
Bible into chapters and
verses, and when?

# 4 Guided by God

Dead Sea Scroll fragment.

The biblical scroll was replaced by the biblical codex—a biblical manuscript in page form.

This 4th-century Greek codex of John's Gospel was found in a monastery at the foot of Mount Sinai.

in composing the Bible guided the Church in discerning which books are "inspired." This list of inspired books is called the canon of the Bible.

Catholic and Protestant churches agree on the New Testament canon, but not fully on the Old Testament canon. The reason goes back before Jesus' birth.

Between 300 B.C. and 150 B.C., the Old Testament was translated into Greek. This was because many Jews living outside Israel no longer spoke Hebrew.

The Greek translation was called the *Septuagint* ("seventy"), after the number of Jewish scholars legend says were involved in the project.

Christians (most of whom spoke Greek) adopted the Septuagint as their accepted Old Testament text. New Testament writers— like Matthew, Mark, Luke, and John— quoted from it over 300 times.

The Septuagint contained seven books— and parts of two books—that modern Jews omit from their official canon:

| | |
|---|---|
| Judith | Sirach |
| Tobit | Baruch |
| 1–2 Maccabees | Esther (long version) |
| Wisdom | Daniel (long version) |

A woman said, "Several ancient writings claim to be Gospels, for example, the Gospel of Thomas and the Gospel of James. How do we know which are inspired?"

Christians believe the same Holy Spirit who guided the human writers

Ancient Jews living inside Israel gradually distanced themselves from Greek-speaking Jews outside Israel— and from the Septuagint as well.

Decades after Jesus' ascension, Palestinian Jews adopted a new canon, omitting the books listed above.

Modern Jews and modern Protestants follow the later Palestinian listing; Catholics follow the Septuagint listing.

Around A.D. 400 Saint Jerome translated the Septuagint into Latin. The first complete English translation of the Bible came in the 14th century.

#4

The *New American Bible* translates the following passage from the Old Testament Book of Ecclesiastes in the following manner:

*Remember your Creator in the days of your youth, before the evil days come. . . . When the guardians of the house tremble . . . And the grinders are idle because they are few, and they who look through the windows grow blind; When the doors to the street are shut, and the sound of the mill is low.* Ecclesiastes 12:1, 3–4

What is Ecclesiastes talking about?

2. The *Good News Bible* translates the same passage from Ecclesiastes this way:

*Remember your Creator while you are still young, before those dismal days. . . . Then your arms, that have protected you, will tremble. . . . Your teeth will be too few to chew your food, and your eyes too dim to see clearly. Your ears will be deaf to the noise of the street.*

a. What is the difference between this translation of the Book of Ecclesiastes and the *New American Bible* translation?
b. List the pros and cons of each of the two translations of Ecclesiastes.
c. Which one do you prefer, and why?

3. Concerning the fact that Christians follow different canons, a girl said:

*Everybody agrees that not all books of the Bible are equal in importance. If we imagine the books of the Bible forming a series of concentric circles, the Gospels would be at the center. The lesser important books would ripple out from them. Christians should focus on the inner* circles *that unite us, not on the outer* ripples *that divide us.*

Evaluate her statement.

4. Record and share the point of each of these quotes:
a. "The Bible is alive, it speaks to me; it has feet, it runs after me; it has hands, it lays hold of me." Martin Luther

b. "Lay hold of the Bible until the Bible lays hold of you." William H. Houghton

c. "Most people are bothered by those passages in Scripture which they can't understand; but . . . I have noticed that the passages in Scripture that trouble me most are those I do understand." Mark Twain

*Guided by God*

**W**hat is the list of the inspired books of the Bible called? How is it determined?

2. What is the Septuagint? Who adopted it as their Old Testament Bible?

3. Why do Catholics list seven books more and longer versions of two other books in their "inspired list" than do Protestants? Name these nine books.

4. When was the first English translation of the entire Bible made? What is a codex?

# CHAPTER TWO

# Creation

## 5 Interpreting Scripture

How do you interpret this student's painting?

*1*n 1925, the state of Tennessee passed a law forbidding schools in the state to teach any theory that denies the biblical story of creation.

To test the constitutionality of the law, the American Civil Liberties Union asked a biology teacher, named John Scopes, to break the law by teaching the theory of evolution to his high school students. Clarence Darrow, a prominent criminal lawyer, agreed to defend him.

To offset Darrow's fame and prestige, the prosecution enlisted the services of the noted William Jennings Bryan, a former presidential candidate.

On July 10, 1925, the courtroom in the city of Dayton, Tennessee, was packed.

Darrow surprised everyone present by calling Bryan to the witness stand. Then he picked up the Bible and read:

*Evening passed and morning came—that was the first day.*

He asked Bryan, "Do you believe that the sun was created on the fourth day—as the Bible says later on?" Bryan answered with a resounding "I do!"

Then Darrow paused and asked Bryan, "Can you tell me how it was possible to have morning and evening on the first day if the sun wasn't created till the fourth day?" Snickers rippled across the courtroom.

Next Darrow turned a few pages and said, "Do you believe God punished the snake by making it to crawl—as the Bible says?" Bryan answered with another "I do!"

Then Darrow asked, "Can you tell me how snakes moved about before that?" Laughter swept across the courtroom.

Bryan exploded! "Your honor, this man, who doesn't believe in God, is using this court to ridicule him."

Darrow shouted out, "I object! I'm simply questioning your fool ideas that no thinking Christian believes."

**D**arrow (left) and Bryan (right) were the focus of attention in the Tennessee trial.

Scopes was convicted, fined $100, and released. Later, the Tennessee Supreme Court reversed the decision.

The Dayton drama ended on a tragic note, when Bryan collapsed and died in Dayton shortly after the trial.

The Tennessee trial had a carnival atmosphere. Preachers held forth on street corners, and peddlers hawked their wares wherever they could set up a table.

Here Darrow engages in a bit of theatrics to make a point for the jury.

The Tennessee trial drew people from all over. Because of the crowd and the July heat, several sessions were held on the courthouse lawn. The trial was called "The Monkey Trial."

Record and share:
a. Why you think the trial got this name.
b. Why you think the theory of evolution does/doesn't contradict the Bible.

2. Darrow asked Bryan, "Can you tell me how it was possible to have morning and evening on the first day if the sun wasn't created until the fourth day?" Record and share how you would answer this question.

3. *Inherit the Wind* is a well-known play by Jerome Lawrence and Robert Lee. It is based on the Tennessee trial and was made into a popular movie.

In Act 1, Scopes (Cates in the play) is in love with Rachael, the daughter of a fundamentalist preacher.

In Act 2, Rachael is called to the stand and forced to give damaging testimony against Cates, admitting that he told her that "God created man in his own image; but man, being a gentleman, returned the compliment."

In Act 3, Cates is convicted, fined, and released. A final scene shows Drummond (Darrow) packing the Bible and Darwin's *Origin of the Species* (pioneer study relating to the theory of evolution) side by side in his suitcase.

Record and share:
a. Why Rachael's testimony was "damaging."
b. What symbolism is contained in having Darrow pack the Bible and *Origin of the Species* side by side in his suitcase.

4. Imagine you are called to the stand to be a witness at the Tennessee trial. Darrow asks you, "Do you believe what the Bible says is true?"

Record and share your response. 

## Interpreting Scripture

Identify: Scopes, Darrow, Bryan, Darwin, American Civil Liberties Union, Dayton, *Origin of the Species.*

2. What verdict did the jury bring, and how did the Tennessee Supreme Court react to it?

3. What tragedy occurred shortly after the trial?

God's Home

waters above

moon
sun
stars

waters
below

earth's
foundation

Ancient Hebrew view
of the universe.

# 6 First Creation Story

The Bible portrays God creating the universe and everything in it over a period of six days. Each day is described in a similar poetic way:

*In the beginning, when God created the universe, the earth was formless and . . . in total darkness. . . .*

*Then God commanded, "Let there be light"—and light appeared.*

*Evening passed and morning came— that was the second day.*

*Then God commanded, "Let the water [be separated from the land]"—and it was done. [God] named the land "Earth," and the water . . . "Sea." . . . God was pleased. . . .*

*Evening passed and morning came— that was the third day. . . .*

**E**verything was engulfed in total darkness. . . .

Then God commanded, "Let there be light."

Genesis 1:2–3

*God was pleased . . . [and] separated the light from the darkness, and [God] named the light "Day" and the darkness "Night." Evening passed and morning came— that was the first day. . . .*

*Then God commanded, "Let there be a dome . . . [to separate the water above it from the water below it]"—and it was done. . . . [God] named the dome "Sky."*

*Then God commanded, "Let lights appear in the sky to separate day from night. . . ." God was pleased. . . .*

*Evening passed and morning came— that was the fourth day. . . .*

*By the seventh day God [was done]. . . . [God] blessed the seventh day and set it apart as a special day. . . . That is how the universe was created.*

Genesis 1:1–10, 13–14, 18–19; 2:2–4

And so the biblical author uses a poetic, repetitive style—much like the style found in many children's books.

The author uses this style of writing because he is addressing people who, like children, can neither read nor write.

A repetitive, poetic style of writing was ideal for *oral* teaching, because it was

- entertaining to listen to,
- easy to remember, and
- just as easy to repeat.

Reread or listen to the excerpts from the biblical story of creation on the previous page, and try to match each phrase below on the right with the correct description on the left.

| | | |
|---|---|---|
| ___ | Introduction | a. "Let there be" |
| ___ | Command | b. "Evening passed" |
| ___ | Execution | c. "God was pleased" |
| ___ | Reaction | d. "God commanded" |
| ___ | Conclusion | e. "It was done" |

Record and share your view of what the repetitive, poetic pattern of the creation story suggests about whether we should interpret the story literally.

2. Record and share:
a. What is being "separated" on each of the first four days.
b. The imagery of the second day.

3. *A child saw a tiny porcelain bear and asked, "How'd you get so lovely?" The bear said, "I wasn't always pretty. Once I was an ugly lump of clay.*

*"One day a lady put me on a wheel. She squeezed and poked me until I nearly passed out. 'Stop! Stop!' I cried.*

*"Next the lady put me in a furnace. She heated me hotter and hotter until I nearly burned up. 'Stop! Stop!' I cried.*

*"Then the lady put paint on me. She painted me over and over until I nearly choked. 'Stop! Stop!' I cried.*

*"Finally the lady stopped. When I looked into the mirror, I couldn't believe what I saw. And that's how I got lovely."*

Record and share:
a. How the style of the story of the creation of the bear is similar to the story of the creation of the world.
b. Why the story of the creation of the bear is told in this fashion.
c. What important lesson this story teaches.
d. An episode from your own life that taught you a similar important lesson.

4. Listen to Genesis 1:1–2:4a ("Creation"), prepared in advance by three people. After the reading, record and share:
a. A brief summary of the reading.
b. An idea or question that struck you during the reading.

*First Creation Story*

List and explain:
a. The fivefold pattern the biblical writer uses to describe each day of creation.

b. Three reasons why the pattern was ideal for teaching people in ancient times.

c. How clay tablets were made and inscribed.

# 7  Literal Interpreters

*How clearly the sky
reveals God's glory!*
Psalm 19:1

*[God's] eternal power
and [God's] divine nature
. . . are perceived in the
things that God has
made.*  Romans 1:20

Bible readers, for the most part, fall into two main groups: *literalists* (sometimes called fundamentalists) and *contextualists*.

*Literalists*, like William Jennings Bryan, interpret the Bible literally, saying, "It means exactly what it says!"

But not all literalists agree completely on how *literally* to interpret the Bible. For example, Jehovah's Witnesses say that you *may* interpret the word *day* as "era"—as in "Lincoln's day." Church of God members say you *must* interpret *day* to mean "24 hours."

Thus, following a literal "Bible calendar," Church of God members say that creation took place about 6,000 years ago.

People ask, "How can they say this, when science *proves* the planet Earth is millions of years old?" Literalists reply, "Read your Bible!"

*In the beginning,
when God created the universe,
the earth was formless and desolate.
The raging ocean that covered everything
was engulfed in total darkness. . . .*

*Then God commanded,
"Let there be light."*  Genesis 1:1–3

Literalists say the word *then* implies that planet Earth already existed before God said, "Let there be light." Therefore, the Bible is describing the *preparation* of Earth for habitation, not the actual *creation* of Earth.

Literalists answer Darrow's first question, #3 saying that the sun already existed but something prevented its light from reaching Earth. They add:

*Venus [blanketed by ultra thick clouds] illustrates what may have been the condition of its neighbor planet Earth up until the "fourth day."*
Watch Tower Bible and Tract Society

Literalists have a bigger problem trying to explain the presence of two creation stories in the Bible.

For example, the first story (Genesis 1:1–31) says that God created people last; the second (Genesis 2:4b–25) contradicts it, saying that God created people first. #4

𝒯he Book of Genesis contains two back-to-back versions of creation. The first story portrays God creating people last; the second story portrays God creating people first.

Record and share why you think the biblical editor was/wasn't aware of the contradictory nature of these versions, and, if so, why he placed both stories back-to-back anyway.

2. Disputes in biblical interpretation are as old as the Bible. For example, Peter says of Paul's letters:

*There are some difficult things in his letters which ignorant and unstable people explain falsely, as they do with other passages of the Scriptures.*
2 Peter 3:16

Early Christians deferred such disputes to church leaders. This way of settling them, however, ended for many Christians with the 16th-century Reformation, as this Protestant report notes:

*From that day on the misuse of the Bible has vitiated the spirit of Protestantism . . . and divided it into sects.*
Charles Morrison, "Protestant Misuse of the Bible"

Record and share:
a. Why you think Jesus would/wouldn't have provided a way to settle disputes.
b. How Matthew 18:16–20 and Acts 15 contain clues as to how Jesus seems to have intended disputes to be settled.

3. A student wrote this prayer as a response to the creation story:

*Thank you, Lord, for making trees, especially apple trees and orange trees. In spring they bloom and perfume the air. In summer they become rent-free motels for robins and sparrows and other birds. In fall their leaves put on a "color show" and then fertilize and enrich the soil. In winter they give us dead branches to brighten fireplaces and warm rooms.*

*Lord, fruit trees remind us why you made us—to serve you and others and make our world a better place to live in.*

Use the above prayer as a model and compose a similar one thanking God for one of the following: clouds, beaches, lakes, animals, friends. Illustrate it with a magazine photo.

𝒯hank you, Lord, for friends.

*A friend is someone who dances with you in the sunlight and walks beside you in shadows.*
Anonymous

*Without friends, the world is a wilderness.*
Francis Bacon

## Literal Interpreters

𝒟escribe the two main groups into which Bible readers fall.

2. How do some readers explain that creation took place about 6,000 years ago, when science proves the earth is millions of years old?

3. How do some readers answer Darrow's question about light appearing before the sun's creation?

4. If taken literally, how are the two creation stories contradictory?

15

# 8 Contextual Interpreters

Detroit Lions' linesman Mike Utley was paralyzed from the chest down during a 1991 NFL game. He courageously flashed a thumbs-up sign as he was wheeled off the field. That gesture became the team's symbol during the postseason playoffs.

Body-language experts tell us that the thumbs-up sign means different things in different cultures. Use it in a German bar and the waiter brings you a beer. Use it in Japan and the waiter brings you five beers. Use it in ancient Rome and you save a wounded gladiator's life.

The different "thumbs-up" meanings illustrate why contextualists insist that the context of a Bible image or story is often key to understanding its meaning.

Take the creation story. The context in which it was written sheds light on what the biblical writer intended to teach through it.

First, people of that time believed in many gods (polytheism). They worshiped the sun, moon, stars, and even animals.   Deuteronomy 4:16–19

Second, many people of that time believed creation happened by chance, as many people today still believe.

Third, many people of that time thought the human body was evil, because it seemed to war against what the human spirit considered right.

Finally, people of that time regarded the days of the week to be equal in importance. It is within this historical *context* that the Bible portrays God

**H**and gestures mean different things in different cultures.

They illustrate the importance of context in determining meaning.

- creating all things: sun, moon, etc.;
- creating according to a plan;
- declaring all creation to be "good";
- blessing the Sabbath, making it special.

And so the context of the creation story helps to clarify what the biblical writer intended to teach—namely, that

- God is one, not many;
- God created by plan, not chance;
- God created everything good, not evil;
- God made the Sabbath special.

#2

C B radio talk illustrates the importance of context. Given a CB context, certain expressions take on a meaning different from the one they normally have.
a. To illustrate, try to match each expression (left column) with its meaning in a CB context (right column).

| | | | |
|---|---|---|---|
| 3 | Drop the hammer | 1. | Gasoline |
| 5 | Portable parking lot | 2. | Passengers |
| 4 | Pregnant roller skate | 3. | Accelerate |
| 6 | Window washer | 4. | Volkswagen |
| 7 | Nap trap | 5. | Auto carrier |
| 1 | Motion lotion | 6. | Rainstorm |
| 2 | Seat covers | 7. | Motel |

b. What point about biblical interpretation does the above exercise illustrate?

2. In his book *Gestures: Do's and Taboos of Body Language Around the World,* Roger Axtell says the thumbs-up sign is one of many hand signs in use today. Which movie critics popularized it?

Team up with another group member and take four or five minutes to list as many hand signs as you can, explaining their meaning in a given context.

3. The world of nature—mountains, seas, galaxies, plants, animals— has always held a special place in world religions. With this in mind, explain the point of these quotes:

a. "Nature is an outstretched finger pointing to God."   Alan Hovhaness
b. "Earth is but a frozen echo of the silent voice of God."   Author unknown
c. "Earth's crammed with heaven, And every common bush afire with God; But only he who sees takes off his shoes; The rest sit round it and pluck blackberries."   E. B. Browning

4. Experimentation with nature raises questions about whether God intended us to do this sort of thing.

Is certain experimentation with nature like murder—something we can do but should not do?

For example, a clone is a child created from a body cell. It is a carbon copy of the person from whom it was taken.

By scraping your arm, you can get enough cells for a thousand clones. Some scientists think human clones will soon be possible.

Record and share why you think God did/didn't intend such experimentation.

G od is the Dancer . . . Creation is the Dance. . . .

Be silent and look at the Dance . . . a star, a flower, a fading leaf. . . .

And hopefully it won't be long before you see . . . the Dancer.
Anthony de Mello

*Contextual Interpreters*

List and explain four important facts about the context of the creation story that help clarify what the biblical writer wanted to teach through it.

2. List the four truths that the creation story teaches us, and tell why they were revolutionary.

# 9  Second Creation Story

The poet James Weldon Johnson portrays the "great God" kneeling down "toiling over a lump of clay." Slowly, the lump is transformed into a beautiful image and likeness of God.

This delightful scene introduces us to the second creation story in the Bible:

*The LORD God took some soil . . .*
*formed a man out of it . . .*
*[and] breathed life-giving breath*
*into his nostrils.*    Genesis 2:7

The second story raises a question: Why two creation stories?

Recall that large sections of the Bible were passed on orally for centuries. There were, apparently, two different "creation stories" or traditions. When the biblical editor was inspired to record these stories and traditions, he simply put them back-to-back.

The second creation story complements the first in two important ways.

First, it reveals the intimate union that creation set up between God and humans. It is a union that is even closer than that of a mother to her child. The prophet Isaiah expressed it this way:

*"Can a woman forget her own baby*
*and not love the child she bore?*
*Even if a mother should forget her child,*
*I will never forget you."*    Isaiah 49:15

Second, it reinforces the revelation that God gave humans power or dominion over the rest of creation.    Genesis 1:26

It portrays God bringing the birds and the animals to the human to be named.
Genesis 2:19

Naming something is a symbolic way of showing that the person naming it has power or dominion over it.

In summary, then, the second story of creation complements the first story in two ways:

- by revealing the intimate union between God and humans, and
- by reinforcing the revelation that God gave humans dominion over the rest of creation.

*[God] took some soil from the ground and formed all the animals and all the birds.*

*Then he brought them to the man to see what he would name them.*
Genesis 2:19

Agnostic - doesn't know
Athiest - doesn't believe in God

Anthropomorphism - attributing human characteristics to non-human realities

Second Creation Story

The creation story raises the question of evolution. Literalists reject evolution. Contextualists are open to its possibility. Here we need to keep in mind that evolutionists fall into two groups: *nontheists* and *theists.*

*Nontheists* do not see a *personal* God involved in the evolutionary process. They often speak of a "life force" at work, but not a personal God.

*Theists*, on the contrary, see the process intimately linked to a personal God. Surprisingly, Saint Augustine proposed something akin to evolution, suggesting that God could have created a "seed" from which everything else emerged.

Record and share:
a.  Why literalists must reject evolution.
b.  How contextualists can be open to it.
c.  Why Augustine's proposal does/doesn't contradict the biblical story of creation.

2.  Augustine's proposal anticipates the "big bang" theory that all matter was once condensed into a "fireball."

*The ball exploded, and all the matter has been expanding outward ever since. . . . Astronomers are still stumped by . . . where the original fireball came from. . . .*

*Scientists have not been able to come up with a better answer than that posed by many of the world's major religions. At one point matter was created.*
Ronald Kotulak, "Deadend for Expanding Universe?"

Record and share how:
a.  Augustine anticipates the "big bang."
b.  The "big bang" still points to a creator.
c.  "Big bang" backers might answer Darrow's first question to Bryan.

3.  Interview two people, asking them:
a.  Do you believe in evolution?
b.  If so, how do you explain the statement that God made "all kinds of animal life: domestic and wild"?   Genesis 1:24

4.  If God created everything good, how do you explain the presence of *physical* evil (sickness and death) and *moral* evil (sin) in the world?

How do you explain the presence of two creation stories? How does the second story complement the first?

2.  What did Augustine suggest concerning the way God created matter? Explain the difference between theistic and nontheistic evolutionists.

3.  Explain Mandell's way of dramatizing how big some stars are.

# 10  *Creation of Woman*

The second creation story ends by portraying God creating the first woman from the side of the first man.

NARRATOR      *Then the LORD God made*
*the man fall into a deep sleep,*
*and while he was sleeping,*
*he took out one of the man's*
*ribs and closed up the flesh.*
*He formed a woman out of the*
*rib and brought her to him. . . .*

MAN            *Here is one of my own kind—*
*Bone taken from my bone,*
*and flesh from my flesh.*
*"Woman" is her name because*
*she was taken out of man.*

NARRATOR      *That is why a man leaves*
*his father and mother*
*and is united with his wife,*
*and they become one.*

Genesis 2:21–24

Hebrew society, like many ancient ones,
was dominated by men.
Women were an oppressed minority.
They were valued primarily
as bearers of children—especially males:
warriors and workers.

Contextualists interpret the story
of God's creation of woman as a rejection
and correction of that social structure.

First, it repeats the important teaching
of the first creation story, which shows God
blessing humans—male and female—
with equal dignity. They share the same

- image and likeness,      Genesis 1:27
- power and dominion,     Genesis 1:26
- flesh and bone.          Genesis 2:23

Second, it portrays God calling them
to a union so equal and intimate that
they "become one."   Genesis 2:24

"Wherever you go,
I will go;
wherever you live,
I will live.

"Your people
will be my people,
and your God
will be my God.

"Wherever you die,
I will die,
and there is where
I will be buried."

Ruth 1:16–17

The intimacy of this union is akin
to that between God and humans.
They share God's own "life-giving breath."
Genesis 2:7
As a result, they are as close to God
as they are to their own breath.

And so contextualists interpret
the second creation story
as teaching two revolutionary truths.
God calls male and female to

- a dignity that makes them equal, and
- an intimacy that makes them one.

An ancient story concerns a young man who knocks at the door of a house. A voice from inside says, "Who is it, and what do you want?" The young man says, "It's Andrew. I've come to ask permission to marry your daughter." The voice replies, "You're not ready; come back in a year."

A year later the young man returns and knocks again. The voice says, "Who is it?" This time Andrew says, "It is us. We've come to ask permission to marry." The voice says, "Come in; you're ready."

Record and share:
a. Why Andrew is now ready.
b. Three things, especially, that a person should look for in choosing a life's mate.

2. "A wedding is an event, but marriage is an achievement." Anonymous
Commenting on this statement, someone observed:

*Many people get married with the notion that marriage is a treasure chest overflowing with gems: companionship, love, fidelity, thoughtfulness, intimacy.*

*The truth is, marriage is an empty chest. You find in it only what you put in it. Love and fidelity are not in marriage, only in people. Marriage is a treasure chest all right, but only for those who are willing to make it such.*

a. List six things you pray will be a part of your marriage someday, numbering them according to the importance you attach to them.
b. Ask a married person to do the same.
c. After the person finishes, share your list with him or her and discuss differences.
d. Record and share all your conclusions.

3. Compose a prayer to God, asking for the grace to find the right partner in life. Put it in an appropriate place and begin praying it daily. Here's an example:

*Lord, I'm not hoping for someone with money to burn, movie-star looks, and a sparkling personality. If he or she has these, it's icing on the cake.*

*What I am looking for is someone who can help me—and whom I can help— to become the kind of persons God made us to be. Amen.*

4. Read Genesis 2:4b–25 ("Partners"). After the reading, record and share:
a. A short summary of the reading.
b. One idea or question that struck you during the reading. ≶

*I love you not for what you are, but for what I am when I am with you.*
Roy Croft

## Creation of Woman

**W**hat was the status of women in many ancient societies?

2. Briefly describe the way the Bible portrays the creation of woman.

3. Explain the twofold interpretation that contextualists give to this story.

# CHAPTER THREE

# De-creation

## 11 Problem of Evil

*T*ime writer Lance Morrow says there should be a "Dark Willard." This "sick" newscaster would stand before TV cameras each morning to recite the morning "evil report."

On the wall behind Willard would be a big map with ugly blotches to show the places where "evil" defeated "good" that night: crime in America, floods in India, race riots in Africa.

"Dark Willard" raises a question: If God created everything good, how did evil enter our world? The Bible answers this question with a series of stories. We may call them "de-creation" stories— stories of how evil defeats goodness.

The stories start with a snake tempting Adam and Eve "to eat" something that God forbids them to eat, saying:

*"[God] knows that when you eat it,
you will be like God and know
what is good and what is bad." . . .
As soon as they had eaten it,
they were given understanding and
realized that they were naked.*     Genesis 3:5, 7

Contextualists interpret this story the way they do the creation story— as a *symbolic* story. The key to understanding it is the symbolism of the word *eating*.

Recall that the snake told Adam and Eve that if they *ate* from the tree,

**A**rchaeologists dug up this mural at Nineveh. Seven centuries older than Jesus, it illustrates an Assyrian king's boast:

*The heads of their warriors I cut off and formed into a pillar against their city wall.*

This violence caused one person to say:

*Man has been violent [from the start]. . . . Violence is forever.*

What do you say?

they would "be like God and know
what is good and what is bad."
The symbolism is this: *to eat* is *to know.*

*To eat* is a symbolic way of saying
the first couple *learned* "evil"
by becoming evil. They did evil.
They "tasted" it.
Since they were good and became evil,
they now *know* the difference
between good and evil.

And so the Bible answers the question
about how evil entered our world
by saying that it entered
through the sin of the first couple.

*A* sailor was assigned
to an artillery gun on a small ship.
He was given heat-resistant gloves
and told to catch the shell casings
that ejected from the gun after it fired.

The reason for gloves was that casings
are extremely hot after a shell is fired.
The reason for catching the casings
was to keep them from rolling around
the gun pit and endangering the gun crew.

a. Suppose you saw a sailor with gloves
holding a shell casing. Record and share
three ways you could learn or determine
if the casings were hot.
b. By which of these three ways
did the first couple learn what sin is
and how it impacts our lives?

2. James Farrell has a character
in his novel *Studs Lonigan* say:

*"I'd like to see God.
I'd like to tell him a few things.
I'd like to say, 'God, why did you
create men and make them . . .
live brief unhappy lives like pigs, and . . .
die disgustingly and rot?'"*

How might you answer Studs?

3. In Avery Corman's book *Oh, God!*
someone rebukes God for not lifting
a finger to help destroy the suffering
in the world. When God doesn't mount
any defense, the person says,
"So you've decided to just let us stumble

*W rong rules the land,
and waiting justice
sleeps.* Josiah Holland

along and never do a thing to help?"
God looks at the person and says:

*"Such a smart fella and you missed
the point. . . . I set all this up for you
and made it so it can work. Only the deal is
you have to work at it and you shouldn't
look to me to do it for you."*

a. What point is Corman making?
b. Why do/don't you agree with him?

4. Interview two adults and ask them
if they think evil *is* or *is not* more
widespread today than formerly.
Record and share their responses.

5. Select a second person to serve as
your coanchor and prepare
a five-minute "Dark Willard" report
for the group. You may use such props
as an overhead projector, a chalkboard,
or a newspaper. ♫

*Problem
of
Evil*

**W** hat do we mean
by the expression
"de-creation stories"?
How do contextualists
interpret these stories?

2. What is the Bible's
answer to this question:
If God created every-
thing good, where did
evil come from?

Explain the symbolic
way the Bible answers.

# 12 Self Alienation

Archaeology shows that ancients used *nakedness* as a symbol of defeat and disgrace. For example, stone slabs, found while digging up an ancient palace, show soldiers slain naked or being paraded naked through the city by their conquerors.

The biblical writer borrows this symbol and invests it with a spiritual meaning. He uses it to dramatize Adam and Eve's defeat and disgrace by the snake:

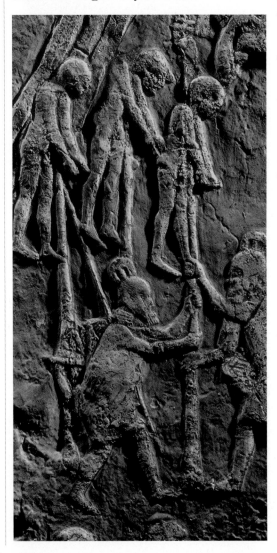

**N**akedness was a symbol of defeat and disgrace in ancient times.

This stone mural, unearthed at Nimrud, shows Assyrian archers shooting arrows past the impaled bodies of naked prisoners.

Assyrians were enemies of the Jewish people and are mentioned often in the Bible.
2 Kings 17–19

*As soon as [the man and the woman] had eaten [the fruit], they . . . realized that they were naked . . . and covered themselves.*   Genesis 3:7

Earlier the biblical writer said, "The man and the woman were both naked, but . . . not embarrassed."   Genesis 2:25

Embarrassment *after* sin (not there before it) symbolizes that sin destroyed something inside them. They now feel uncomfortable and guilty. They feel alienated from themselves.

In his book *The Seven Storey Mountain*, Thomas Merton gives us an example of such an "alienating" experience. After high school, he began living a wayward life. Then one night the realization of what he was doing hit him in a horrifying way. He writes:

*I was overwhelmed with a sudden and profound insight into the misery and corruption of my own soul. I was filled with horror at what I saw, and my whole being rose up in revolt against what was within me, and my soul desired escape . . . from all this with an intensity and an urgency unlike anything I had ever known.*

Adam and Eve had a similar alienating experience after their sin against God.

And so the *first* tragic effect of sin is alienation from *self*— a loss of one's inner peace and harmony.

Journalist Paul Horn observes that the main feeling you get today is that nearly everyone you meet is uptight in some way. He adds:

*Maharishi Mahest Yogi of India believes such a tense atmosphere and the wars that result from it could never happen in a world peopled by individuals at peace with themselves. He says, "For the forest to be green, the trees must be green."*

a. To what extent do you agree/disagree with Paul Horn's observation?
b. What link might there be between the way people feel today and the way the first couple felt after the first sin?
c. How do you account for this parallel?

2. Dr. Karl Menninger, dean of American psychiatry, wrote a surprising book called *Whatever Became of Sin?* Reviewing it, George Higgins observes:

*Dr. Menninger is bothered not only by individuals who refuse to acknowledge personal sin, but also by groups—even whole nations— who refuse to admit "collective sins."*

*Discrimination, war, polluting the environment, ignoring the poor . . . are some of the things that scare him.*

*He says that in "group sins," no single individual considers himself responsible or guilty.*

a. Explain the attitude in people today that bothers Dr. Menninger and the attitude in Adam and Eve after their sin.
b. To what extent would you say that all people are involved in some group sins?
c. What is the solution to these sins?

3. A young person said, "I know it sounds really weird, but I frequently pray best right after I sin. Even more weird is that I feel a desire to pray at that time."
a. How do you account for this experience?
b. How do you feel after you have sinned?
c. How do you account for your experience?

4. Sin can alienate us from ourselves so intensely that we want to be re-created by God. The psalmist prays:

*Wipe out all my evil.*
*Create a pure heart in me, O God,*
*and put a new and loyal spirit in me.*
*Do not banish me from your presence;*
*do not take your holy spirit*
*away from me.*
*Give me again the joy that comes*
*from your salvation.*   Psalm 51:9–12

Compose a similar prayer to God. 🔖

---

**G**ive me again
the joy that comes
from your salvation.
Psalm 51:12

## Self Alienation

**W**hat did nakedness symbolize in many ancient cultures, and where do we find evidence of this?

2. Explain how the biblical writer borrows this symbolism and invests it with a spiritual meaning.

3. What is the "first effect" of sin, and how does the biblical writer teach it?

# 13  God Alienation

*"The snake tricked me into eating it."*
Genesis 3:13

**W**hy does God remain so silent most of the time?

**T**he screenplay *The Seventh Seal* by Ingmar Bergman contains a scene in which a knight asks Death about his inability to communicate with God.

KNIGHT   *Why should God hide in the mist?*
*I want God to speak, to stretch
out his hand toward me,
reveal himself, and speak to me.*
DEATH   *But God remains silent.*
KNIGHT   *I call out to God in the dark
but no one seems to be there.*
DEATH   *Perhaps no one is there.*

(Slightly adapted)

This dialogue between cynical Death and the discouraged knight leads us to the *second* effect of sin. The Bible says:

*The Lord God called out to the man,
"Where are you?"
He answered, "I heard you in the garden;
I was afraid and hid from you,
because I was naked." . . .*

*God asked, "Did you eat the fruit . . .?"
The man answered,
"The woman . . . gave me the fruit. . . ."*

*[The woman said,]
"The snake tricked me into eating it."*
Genesis 3:9–13

Two important points emerge from this dialogue between God and the couple. First, it reaffirms the first effect of sin: alienation from *self.*

The dialogue portrays the first couple as being unable or unwilling to accept responsibility for their sin.
They make excuses and pass the buck. Adam passes it to Eve; Eve, in turn, passes it to the snake.

Second, the dialogue teaches us that the second effect of sin on Adam and Eve is to alienate them from *God.*

The biblical writer makes this point by showing that Adam and Eve are now uncomfortable in God's presence. They feel afraid of God.
They feel alienated and estranged.

And so the *second* tragic effect of sin is alienation from *God.*
It is estrangement from the loving God who created them and shared with them the divine image.   Genesis 1:27

T homas Merton says that after he realized the depth of the evil within him, he began to pray. He writes in *The Seven Storey Mountain*:

*And now I think for the first time
in my whole life I really began to pray—
praying not with my lips and
with my intellect and my imagination,
but praying out of the very roots
of my life and of my being,
and praying to the God I had never known,
to reach down towards me
out of his darkness and to help me
get free of the thousand terrible things
that held my will in their slavery.*

Describe in writing a time in your life when you prayed in a way similar to this.

2. E. Paul Hovey did an analysis of sin and came up with this conclusion:

*Sin has four characteristics:
self-sufficiency instead of faith,
self-will instead of submission,
self-seeking instead of benevolence,
self-righteousness instead of humility.*

a. Explain and give an example of each of these four characteristics.
b. Which one do you think your friends struggle with most? Explain.

3. Team up with a friend to compose a conclusion to the dialogue between the knight and Death; act it out for your group.

4. Saint Ignatius of Loyola proposes this meditation on the first sin. Find a quiet spot, make yourself comfortable, and try your hand at it. Spend a minute or so on each of the four points.

 Replay in your imagination what went on in the hearts of Adam and Eve after their sin, especially the anguish and pain they felt because of it.

 From a point high in the sky, visualize all the people who have ever lived parading by you. Consider how their sins have added to the suffering of the world.

 Stand appalled at what sin is— not only a rejection of God but also an instrument of suffering.

 Stand before Jesus on the cross and speak to him about your own sins.

When you have finished your meditation, record your thoughts on these points:
a. What have I done for Jesus in the past?
b. What am I doing for Jesus right now?
c. What ought I to do for Jesus in the future?

W hat have I done for Jesus in the past? What am I doing for Jesus right now? What ought I to do for Jesus in the future?

*God Alienation*

B riefly describe the conversation between God and the first couple after the first sin.

2. List and explain the two points that emerge from the dialogue between God and the first couple after the first sin.

# *14  Nature Alienation*

[The LORD] said to the woman,
    "I will increase . . .
        your pain in giving birth. . . ."
[And the LORD said to the man,]
"You will have to work hard and sweat
to make the soil produce . . .
until you go back to the soil from which
you were formed."    Genesis 3:16, 19

These chilling words of God introduce
the *third* tragic effect of sin.
It alienates the first couple from *nature*.

The harmony that once existed between
the first couple and the rest of nature
is now destroyed.

Even the bodies of the first couple
rebel against them, exposing them
to *physical* evil (suffering and death).
Thus *physical* evil
enters the world through *moral* evil (sin).

The first de-creation story ends with God
expelling the couple from the garden
and having a cherubim bar them
from the tree of life.    Genesis 3:2 (NRSV)

Archaeologists have shed light
on the tree of life and the cherubim.

The *tree of life* is a mythical *plant,*
thought to confer immortality (freedom
from death) on those with access to it.
We might compare it to the fountain
of youth that explorers hoped to find
in the "new world."

The *cherubim* is a mythical *beast*
with wings and a human head.
It was placed at entrances to buildings
to function as a kind of watchdog to keep
out unworthy intruders.

When we link these two symbols—
tree of life and cherubim—
we get the biblical writer's point.
It comes down to this.

Sin destroys the first couple's harmony
with the rest of God's creation.
They lose access to immortality and
become vulnerable to suffering and death.

Thus, sin (moral evil) opens the door
to suffering and death (physical evil).

And so the *third* effect of the sin of
the first couple is alienation from *nature.*

This sixteen-foot being
is identified as a
cherubim. It stood
guard at the outer
gateway of the
Khorsabad palace
of the Assyrian king
Sargon II (722–705 B.C.).

The cherubim's fifth leg
was added for artistic
purposes.

Viewed from the front,
the creature seems in
perfect symmetry.
Viewed from the side,
the leg gives the
impression of balance
and motion.

*T*eam up with a friend and come up with a fitting caption for this photo.

*A*lmost daily, the media run a report or story that reflects the alienation that exists between nature and the human race. For example, *Newsweek* ran a feature called "The Ten Biggest Challenges":

*Every minute an American frets about running out of landfills for garbage, six children— most in the developing world— die from drinking contaminated water.*

The report notes that when Americans got fed up with the pollution of the water in the U.S., clean-water laws got two-thirds of our rivers fit for drinking, swimming, and fishing.

Record and share:
a. The main point *Newsweek* is making.
b. Three other areas where turnarounds (like our water situation) are needed.
c. What might be a "first step" toward making these turnarounds.

2. Industrial wastes pour into the air to the point that our clouds produce acid rain, which pollutes lakes and destroys forests. Similar wastes erode the ozone layer, threatening life itself. We sometimes call this destruction of our planet *physical* de-creation. More tragic still is the destruction of ourselves by misusing our free will. We call it *spiritual* de-creation (sin).

a. What link do you see between physical de-creation and spiritual de-creation?
b. If you could make one suggestion for reversing the *physical* de-creation going on in our world, what would it be?
c. For reversing the *spiritual* de-creation?

3. Clip a picture from a magazine or a newspaper to illustrate one of these quotes:

a. "Don't blow it—good planets are hard to find."  Anonymous
b. "Don't make God a slumlord."  Robert Orben
c. "It is easier for us to be loyal to our club than to our planet."  E. B. White (adapted)

Appoint a committee to select the five most creative pictures.

## Nature Alienation

*W*hat is the third effect of sin, and how does the Bible teach it?

2. Explain (a) moral evil, (b) physical evil, and (c) how the latter entered the world.

3. Explain the light archaeologists have shed on the biblical images of the "tree of life" and the "cherubim."

4. What point does the biblical writer make through these symbols?

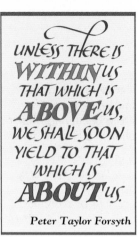

# 15 People Alienation

**M**arvin Gaye was a headline singer. His career started at age seven, when he began singing gospel songs in his father's church in Washington, D.C.

Unfortunately, a deep hostility developed between father and son.
As Marvin grew, so did the hostility.
Finally, on April 1, 1984, anger exploded into violence. Marvin's father shot his son. Gaye's biographer said of Marvin:

*He really believed in Jesus a lot, but he could not apply the teaching of Jesus on forgiveness to his own father. In the end it destroyed them both.*

David Ritz, *Divided Soul*

The Marvin Gaye story is a tragic echo of the biblical story of Cain and Abel. As these two family members grew, so did Cain's jealousy of Abel. Then one day it exploded into violence.

| | |
|---|---|
| CAIN | *Let's go out in the fields.* |
| NARRATOR | *When they were out in the fields, Cain turned on his brother and killed him.* |
| LORD | *Where is your brother Abel?* |
| CAIN | *I don't know. Am I supposed to take care of my brother? . . .* |
| LORD | *Your brother's blood is crying out to me from the ground. . . .* |
| NARRATOR | *Cain went away from the LORD'S presence.* |

Genesis 4:8–10, 16

The Cain and Abel story brings us to the *fourth* tragic effect of sin: alienation from *other people.*

Sin separates us from one another— even from members of our own family. Instead of living with them according to the harmony God intended, we do the exact opposite.

And so sin alienates us from

| | |
|---|---|
| ☙ self | awareness of nakedness, |
| ☙ God | hiding from God, |
| ☙ nature | pain and death, and |
| ☙ others | Cain's slaying of Abel. |

**G**aye's rendition of the national anthem at the 1983 NBA All Star Game was incredible.

The crowd got so caught up in his performance that they spontaneously began to clap in rhythm to his singing. Commenting on the crowd's reaction, Gaye said softly:

*Before I began singing that night, I asked God for the power to touch the souls of everyone present.*

*J*ournalist Arthur Snider filed a gloomy report some years ago of a meeting of anthropologists in Chicago. One speaker, Dr. Norman MacDonald, concluded:

*Man has been violent since his remote ape-like ancestors descended from trees. . . . Man being what he is, violence is forever. . . . [He] has insisted on developing more powerful weapons so that now . . . he can annihilate a planet.* Chicago Daily News

a.  On a scale of 1 (not at all) to 10 (totally), to what extent do you agree with Dr. MacDonald, and why?
b.  Do a survey of your group to see what its evaluation of MacDonald is.

2.  Find a headline and story dealing with physical or spiritual de-creation. Compose a prayer based on it. Make it three paragraphs long:

a.  Speak to God about it.
b.  Pray for those responsible.
c.  Pray for those hurt.

Here is an example.

*BLACKS GATHER*
*TO MOURN DEAD IN SOUTH AFRICA*

*JOHANNESBURG, SOUTH AFRICA—*
*Blacks gathered by the tens of thousands Friday to mourn their dead. . . . Witnesses said police broke up one ceremony with rubber whips and birdshot.*

PRAYER
*a.  Lord, why must people suffer so much in their native country? Why do we treat each other so cruelly? What can I do about all this?*

*b.  Lord, continue to move the hearts of people of all nations— including my own heart— to seek peaceful solutions to problems.*

*c.  Finally, Lord, give people who suffer injustices the courage to keep pursuing their rights, and the greatness of heart to forgive offenders.*

3.  Philip Henry reflected on the bitter reality of sin and concluded:

*Sins are like circles in the water when a stone is thrown into it; one produces another. When anger was in Cain's heart, murder was not far off.*

a.  Explain Henry's point.
b.  What was the sin circle in Gaye's life?
c.  What could be a sin circle in your life?

*People*
*Alienation*

*E*xplain in what sense the Marvin Gaye story is a tragic echo of the Cain and Abel story.

2.  List and briefly explain the four effects of sin that we have seen so far.

# 16 Alienation Spiral

The TV series *Roots* played to a record 130 million viewers. It dramatized Alex Haley's search for his African ancestry ("family tree"). It also sent many viewers to libraries to research their own family trees.

Genesis lists two family trees.

The first begins with Adam and ends with Noah.   Genesis 5:1–32

The second begins with Noah's son and ends with Terah, Abraham's father.   Genesis 11:10–26
Their purpose is twofold and symbolic. They allow the biblical writer

🔖 to leapfrog over history from Adam (father of all people) to Abraham (father of Hebrew people), and
🔖 to dramatize decreases in life spans, from Adam (who dies at age 930) to Abraham's father (who dies at age 205).

The decrease in life spans symbolizes a dramatic increase in sin. (Sin brings sickness and death; sickness and death decrease life spans.) The result is tragic.

| | |
|---|---|
| NARRATOR | *God looked at the world and saw that it was evil. . . .* |
| GOD | *[to Noah] I have decided to put an end to all people. . . . Build a boat [ark]. . . . Go into the boat with your whole family. . . .* |
| NARRATOR | *Rain fell on the earth forty days and nights. . . . It covered the highest mountains.* |

Genesis 6:12–14; 7:1, 12, 19

Literalists interpret this story as fact. That is why they sponsor expeditions to find Noah's ark, which the Bible portrays as coming to rest on Mount Ararat after the flood.   Genesis 8:4

Contextualists interpret the story as being symbolic. Some feel it is totally symbolic. Most think it is factual-symbolic.

It is *factual* in that the biblical writer bases the story on a flood tradition.

It is *symbolic* in that the writer uses the tradition to communicate an important religious truth: Sin leads to the destruction of ourselves and our world.

This clay tablet is 700 years older than Jesus.

One of a series of eleven, it contains the Assyrian version of the Epic of Gilgamesh, an account of an ancient Babylonian flood story.

Writing was done on soft clay with a triangular pen. The clay was then left to dry and harden in the sun.

Interest in locating Noah's ark reached fever pitch in 1974 when a U.S. Skylab photo showed a foreign object on Mount Ararat. But expeditions found nothing.

Recently Turkey restricted expeditions up the mountain, because it lies in a politically sensitive region.

Record and share:
a. How you feel about expeditions to find Noah's ark.
b. Why some people are so eager to locate concrete evidence of the ark.

2. One expedition to the upper levels of Mount Ararat uncovered a wood beam. The explorers were ecstatic, thinking it a remnant of the original ark. But carbon-14 dating showed that "the timber came from a tree chopped down around A.D. 700."

The large beam raised a further question: How did it get into the upper levels of Mount Ararat?

How do you think the beam might have gotten to the upper part of the mountain?

3. After meditating on the "de-creation" stories in Genesis, and after reflection on her own personal conversion, a woman wrote: "The experience of sin often results in the discovery of the path to light."

Record and share:
a. The woman's point.
b. Something from your own life that served as a "path to light."

4. With one or two people prepare a dramatic reading of Genesis 7 ("Riding out the Flood") and Genesis 8 ("The Dove Test").

Record and share:
a. A brief summary of each reading.
b. An idea or question that struck you during the reading.

5. Jesus refers to Noah and to the flood in Matthew 24:37–39.
a. What does Jesus say?
b. Doesn't his reference prove that the flood is factual? Explain.

6. Construct a brief family tree of your mother's or your father's side.

Record and share:
a. Where your ancestors came from.
b. The reason they came to this country, if you can learn the reason. ॐ

Why does the experience of sin often lead to the discovery of the "path to light"?

*Alienation Spiral*

Describe and explain the purpose of the two family trees in Genesis.

2. For what reason is God portrayed as deciding to destroy the earth with a flood?

3. How do contextual-ists and literalists differ in their interpretation of the flood story?

4. Identify:
a. Ararat
b. Epic of Gilgamesh
c. clay tablets

Tigris River

Euphrates River

**Tower of Babel** Ur ·

# *17 Alienation Climax*

The "de-creation" accounts end with the Tower of Babel story. It is portrayed as taking place after Noah's descendants repopulate the earth. The people say:

*"Let's build a city with a tower
that reaches the sky, so that we can
make a name for ourselves."*   Genesis 11:4

God confuses the speech of the people, and their "pride" project ends in failure. Then God "scattered them all over the earth."   Genesis 11:9

Archaeology sheds light on this story. The "tower that reaches the sky" refers to a *ziggurat* ("mountain peak") and was intended as a meeting place for gods and people.

Some Bible readers think the purpose of the Tower of Babel story is to explain the origin of nations and languages. But given the *context* of the "de-creation" stories, the biblical writer gives them a deeper purpose.

The writer uses the story to introduce us to the *fifth* effect of sin: alienation of *groups of people from one another.* Sin spawns prejudices and envy; and they, in turn, spawn divisions.

And so sin alienates us not only from self, God, nature, and other people (individuals), but also from other groups of people (nations and races).

When we finish reading the "de-creation" stories, we get this bleak impression. People, individually and collectively, are trapped in a giant whirlpool of sin. Every person is doomed to be caught in its all-engulfing destructive power.

This tragic "state" or situation is sometimes called the state of *original sin.* We may sum it up in this threefold way: The first sin of the first couple

- opens the door to evil in the world,
- flaws the human race, and
- dooms all to destruction.

**W**hen you say a situation or person is hopeless, you are slamming the door in the face of God.

Charles E. Allen

Given *people* as they are (sin-prone),
and given the *world* as it is (sin-filled),
neither can survive
unless God intervenes to save them.

ournalist Dorothy Thompson says
what frightens her about the Nazi
death camps is that "good" people
helped commit the crimes in the camps.
She explains:

*The physicians who
inoculated concentration camp victims
with malaria were prisoners
of the Nazis themselves. . . .
By assisting in the extermination
of their fellow prisoners, they
prolonged the lease on their own life.*

How does this chilling fact
illustrate the conclusion we draw
from the sin stories in Genesis 3–11?

2. The film *Lord of the Flies*
was based on William Golding's story
about a group of fourteen-year-olds.
They survive a plane crash at sea and
end up on a deserted island.
Without any adult guidance, they quickly
deteriorate into a group of savages.
J. D. Salinger takes just the opposite

approach in his book *Catcher in the Rye.*
It centers around Holden Caulfield,
an innocent, idealistic young person.

In time, however,
Holden's contact with adult society
destroys his innocence and idealism.

Explain which of these two statements
best sums up your overall view of people:

a. Down deep they are basically evil,
but society civilizes them.
b. Down deep they are basically good,
but society corrupts them.

3. Imagine the members of your group
got marooned (*Lord-of-the-Flies* style).
Why do you think you would/wouldn't
avoid the pitfall of the young people
in *Lord of the Flies?*

4. Explain these quotes and tell
how they relate to "de-creation":

a. "Adam ate the apple,
and our teeth still ache."   Proverb
b. A Milwaukee tailor chose an apple
as his trademark for his shop, saying,
"If it hadn't been for it,
what would I be doing today?"
c. "Sin is not hurtful because
it is forbidden, but it is forbidden
because it is hurtful."   Benjamin Franklin

**W**hat do you say?
Are we basically good
or basically evil?

*Alienation
Climax*

**H**ow has archaeology
shed light on our under-
standing of the Tower of
Babel story?

2. With what bleak
impression and conclu-
sion do the sin stories
leave us?

3. Briefly summarize the
threefold situation we
have in mind when we
speak of the *state of
original sin.*

# CHAPTER FOUR

# Re-creation

## 18  Call of Abraham

Mark Twain wrote a story
about a group of people who get
trapped in a hopeless situation.
It is like having them on a plane
ten feet away from crashing into a cliff.

Twain doesn't want these people to die,
but he doesn't know how to save them.
So he ends his story, saying,
"I can't save these people; if you think
you can, you are welcome to try."

Thousands of years ago the world
was in a hopeless situation.
Sin was destroying everything.
But God had a plan to save the world,
and that's what the Bible is all about.

We may think of the Book of Genesis
and its fifty chapters as being
like a stage play in three acts:

Act 1: *creation*      God creates   (1–2)
Act 2: *de-creation*   Sin destroys  (3–11)
Act 3: *re-creation*   God saves us  (12–50)

That brings us to "Act 3" and Abram.
With Abram's arrival, the Book of Genesis
changes sharply in content and style.

The *content* of "Act 1" and "Act 2"
deals with *prehistory* or protohistory—
the origin of the world and life on it.
The *style* used to narrate this content
is to present the reader with a parade
of easy-to-remember *symbol stories.*

Now all this changes dramatically.

The *content* now deals with *folk history,*
not prehistory or protohistory.
The *style* used to present it is to parade
before the reader a series of easy-to-remember
*folk stories,* passed on orally from generation
to generation.

"Act 3" begins with Abram and his wife,
Sarai, migrating from their birthplace
in Ur to the city of Haran in the north.
While in this city,
Abram experienced a "call from God":

*"Leave your country . . .
and go to a land [Canaan]
that I am going to show you."*   Genesis 12:1

This "call" initiates a pattern that repeats
itself over and over in biblical history.

Abraham is the first in
a long line of people
who have heard an
"inner call" from God.

In response, they leave
all and set out upon a
spiritual mission that
God reveals to them
only gradually.

Why does God act so
mysteriously? Why isn't
God's "inner call" more
clear?

Certain people experience an "inner call" from God to leave everything behind and to go forth on an unknown mission that God shows to them only gradually.

1 Imagine you are Abram. You tell an old relative that a "spiritual being" appeared and told you to leave Haran for a place that will be shown to you. This relative has seen you praying a lot lately and suspects that you might be going off the deep end.

With a friend, rough out together an imaginary conversation that might follow between you and the old relative. Act it out for your group.

2. Your close friend Jeremy is with you in a fast-food place. Suddenly he says:

*Pam, you're my friend. I respect you, and I trust your judgment more than I trust anyone else's. What I'm about to tell you sounds weird. For about two weeks now, I've felt that God is calling me, but I don't know to what. The idea scares me, but it won't go away. How can I be sure God is calling me— and to what?*

Record and share:
a. How you would answer your friend.
b. Whether you have ever felt called, as Jeremy does. Explain.

3. A college student made a retreat during spring break. He wrote to a friend a week later:

*While on a retreat I felt "called" to put God first in my life. I went into the chapel and promised God that I was going to try with all my heart. That gave me a real high. Then, a few days ago, I did something that no Christian should ever do. I'm totally devastated. Now I realize that nothing happened on the retreat. I only imagined that it did.*

Why would you agree/disagree with the college student's reasoning?

4. Chapters 12–50 of Genesis (re-creation) treat *folk-history* times (era of oral records). The Abram story deals with the era of oral records.

Record and share how this knowledge provides a clue as to how literally you should interpret this story.

5. Listen to a dramatic reading of Genesis 12 ("The Call"), prepared in advance by three people.

After the reading, record and share:
a. Two or three sentences that sum it up.
b. An idea or question that struck you during the reading. ❧

*It isn't a calamity to die with dreams unfulfilled, but it is a calamity not to dream.*
Benjamin E. Mays

*Call of Abraham*

List and briefly explain in what sense Genesis is like a stage play in three acts.

2. What do we mean by *prehistory* and *folk-history* times, and what kind of stories is used to narrate each?

37

# *19 Covenant with Abraham*

Abram eventually reached Canaan. The future lay shrouded in mystery. All he could do was wait for further word from God. Then one night it came:

GOD
> *Look at the sky*
> *and try to count the stars;*
> *you will have*
> *as many descendants. . . .*
> *Bring me a cow, a goat,*
> *and a ram. . . .*

NARRATOR
> *Abram . . . cut them in half*
> *and placed the halves*
> *opposite each other. . . .*
> *A flaming torch suddenly*
> *appeared and passed*
> *between the pieces. . . .*
> *The LORD made a covenant*
> *with Abram.*

GOD
> *I promise to give your*
> *descendants all this land.*
> Genesis 15:5, 9–10, 17–18

This ritual is called "cutting a covenant." Unlike people in modern times, who "sign a contract" or a treaty, ancient peoples "cut a covenant." The contracting parties walked between the halves of a divided animal.

The Bible preserves the ritual's meaning:

*"[They] made a covenant with me by walking between the two halves of a bull. . . . So I will do to these people what they did to the bull."* Jeremiah 34:18–19

Passing between the halves signified that the two parties would rather die a death as violent as that of the animal than break the covenant they have "cut."

In spite of God's covenant with Abram, however, he and Sarai remain childless. This causes them great anguish of heart. Then one day Sarai tells Abram

This art piece of stone and shell portrays daily life in ancient Ur, Abraham's birthplace.

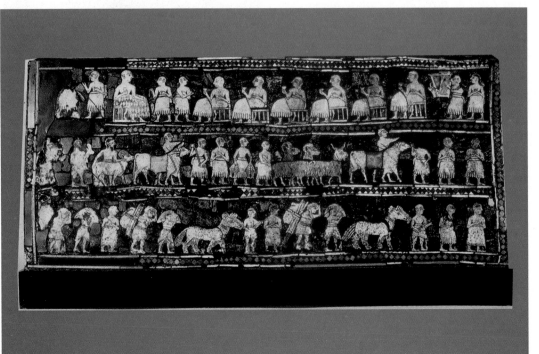

to have a child by Hagar, her maid.
Hagar bears Abram a son, Ishmael.

For centuries Sarai's behavior
confused many Bible readers.
Then archaeologists unearthed
clay tablets at Nuzi (in modern Iraq).

One of the tablets dated to Abram's time
and was a marriage contract.
It stated that a sterile wife had to provide
her spouse with a substitute wife
for childbearing, so that his name
and property could be passed on.

Sarai was simply carrying out
the marriage contract of the time.

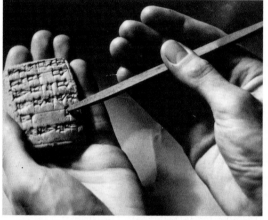

*A*fter World War II, workers found
the following inscription written
on the cellar wall of a bombed-out
house in Cologne, Germany.
It had apparently been written there
by a fugitive hiding from the Nazis.

*I believe in the sun*
*even when it is not shining.*
*I believe in love*
*even when I feel it not.*
*I believe in God*
*even when he is silent.*

Record and share:
a. Why you think so many people have
found this inscription so meaningful.
b. Why you would/wouldn't agree
with some people who think that God is
more silent today than ever before in history.

2. God promised Abram descendants,
but Abram and Sarai remained childless.
They were filled with confusion.

Imagine you are either Abram or Sarai.
One night you cannot sleep. You get up,
walk out into the starry night,
and tell God what is in your heart.
Above all, you ask God
why your faith is being tested so greatly.

Record and share:
a. What you would say.
b. What God might say in reply to you.

3. Explain the point of each of these quotes.
Give an example to illustrate each one,
if you can.

a. "When it comes to faith,
we need to avoid two harmful excesses:
excluding reason, and admitting nothing
but reason." Blaise Pascal
b. "Faith is like love; it cannot be forced."
Arthur Schopenhauer
c. "Some things have to be believed
to be seen." Ralph Hodgson
d. "Only if we learn to see the invisible
will we be able to do the impossible."
Frank Gaines (adapted)

4. "Cutting a covenant" is just one way
that people throughout history
have chosen to "formalize" agreements.
a. Why "formalize" agreements?
b. Why not just make them verbally?

This clay tablet is older
than Abraham. At first,
writing took the form of
pictures. It gave way to
"wedge" writing such
as you see here.

At first, the wedges
stood for ideas; later,
for a sound. For
example, at first, "foot"
stood for the idea
"walking." Later, it
stood for the sound
"foot," as in football.

*Covenant*
*with*
*Abraham*

**W**hat promise did God
make to Abram in the
context of "cutting a
covenant"? Explain the
significance of this ritual.

2. How has archae-
ology shed light on the
Sarah-Hagar episode?

3. How did wedge-
shaped (cuneiform)
writing evolve in
meaning?

Egypt's Anwar Sadat.

# 20  Mission of Abraham

*I*shmael's birth made Abram happy. It paved the way for God's promise for many descendants from Abram. Then came an enormously big surprise! God spoke to Abram again:

*"I am the Almighty God. . . .*
*Your name will*
*no longer be Abram, but Abraham. . . .*
*You and your descendants must all agree*
*to circumcise every male among you . . .*
*to show that my covenant with you*
*is everlasting. . . .*
*No longer call your wife Sarai. . . .*

A new *name* for a biblical person is, generally, the sign of a new vocation.

Abraham's new name fits his new calling. *Abram* means "exalted Father." *Abraham* means "father of many."

Sarai's new name, *Sarah*, means "princess" and fits her new vocation.

Abraham's *mark* is a sign of God's covenant with him and his descendants. It identifies them as belonging to a privileged group: God's *Chosen People.*

*T*his 14th-century icon portrays three heavenly visitors who announce that Sarah will bear a son.  Genesis 18:1–15

*Her name is Sarah. I will bless her,*
*and I will give you a son by her. . . .*
*You will name him Isaac."*
  Genesis 17:1, 5, 10, 13, 15–16, 19

This third encounter with God results in a new *name* and a *mark* for the father of God's new people.

*[And so Sarah] became pregnant*
*and bore a son to Abraham. . . .*
*Abraham named him Isaac,*
*and when Isaac was eight days old,*
*Abraham circumcised him.*  Genesis 21:2–4

After Isaac's birth, hostility erupts between Sarah and Hagar. Sarah prevails

**B**efore addressing the Knesset, Sadat attended Al Aqsa mosque, far right of Jerusalem's famous mosque with the "golden dome."

Beneath the dome lies a 40-by-60-foot rock. It is said to be the site where Abraham led Isaac to be sacrificed.

Later, David chose the site for the Temple.

on Abraham to dismiss Hagar and Ishmael. Abraham is saddened by this demand, but God consoles him, saying:

*"I will also give many children
to the son of the slave woman,
so that they will become a nation.
He too is your son."*  Genesis 21:13

To this day, Arab nations, such as Egypt, trace their ancestry back to Abraham through his son Ishmael. Abraham is their faith-father too.

**F**or centuries, the relationship between Arabs and Jews has been threatened by constant tension. The Camp David summit in the 1970s was a significant initiative to resolve this tension. Attending were Egypt's Anwar Sadat, Israel's Menachem Begin, and their U.S. host, Jimmy Carter.

*Time* magazine pointed out that Sadat's forehead bears a mark from touching the ground so often in prayer. It described Begin as a "man of Spartan tastes," who "rises at five to pray." Finally, Jimmy Carter teaches Scripture each Sunday at the church he attends.

a.  To what degree do you think the spiritual side of these leaders was a factor in the summit's success?
b.  Why do you think the media rarely presents the spiritual side of celebrities, preferring to dwell on their "unspiritual" side?
c.  List some TV shows that do this.
d.  Who do you think is most to blame for such shows: the media, the public, advertisers, or special-interest groups?

2.  Anwar Sadat is a hero in Arab-Jewish peace efforts. On November 27, 1977, he did something no previous Arab leader dared to do. He accepted an invitation to address the Knesset, the Israeli parliament. In the address, he noted that the day was *Id al-Adha,* an Islamic holy day commemorating Abraham's readiness to offer his son in sacrifice to God.

a.  Why do you think Sadat selected this day for the address? Why do you think he stressed it in his address?
b.  Explain why Jews, Christians, and Arabs revere Abraham.

3.  Imagine that a university invites a thousand Arab, Jewish, and Christian teenagers to use its facilities for a three-day "youth summit." You are on the committee to set up the agenda. List some events you would like to see scheduled, and explain why.

4.  Explain this statement by Alan Paton in his book *Cry, the Beloved Country:* "I have one great fear that one day when they are turned to loving, they will find we are turned to hating." Explain why you do/don't share his view. 🔊

*Mission of Abraham*

**E**xplain:
a.  The purpose of a biblical name change.
b.  How the name changes of Abram and Sarai reflected their new calling.

2.  What mark was assigned to Abraham and his descendants, and what purpose did it serve?

3.  How do Arab nations trace their ancestry to Abraham?

4.  What do Muslims celebrate on *Id al-Adha?*

Abraham prepares
to sacrifice Isaac.

# 21 Schooling of Abraham

Human sacrifice was not unusual in Abraham's time. Novelist James Michener mentions the ancient practice in *The Source.* He describes how the people of Makor adopted a new god, Melak, who demanded human sacrifice.

*[They adopted Melak]*
*partly because his demands upon them*
*were severe, as if this proved his power,*
*and partly because they had grown . . .*
*contemptuous of their local gods*
*precisely because*
*they were not demanding enough.*

It is within this historical *context* that God spoke to Abraham, saying,

"Take your son, your only son, Isaac. . . . Offer him as a sacrifice."  Genesis 22:2
Abraham was confused, but he obeyed.

| | |
|---|---|
| NARRATOR | *Abraham built an altar. . . . He tied up his son and placed him on the altar. . . . Then he picked up the knife to kill him. . . .* |
| ANGEL | *Abraham, Abraham! . . . Don't hurt the boy. . . . Now I know that you honor and obey God, because you have not kept your only son from him.* |

Genesis 22:9–12

Abraham's "test" reveals three things about the nature of faith:

First, faith involves great *trust.*
Abraham's heart rebels
at God's command to sacrifice Isaac.
He loves Isaac dearly.
Likewise, his mind rebels at the idea.
Hadn't God promised that through Isaac
he would have many descendants?
Sacrificing Isaac seemed cruel and dumb.
In spite of this Abraham trusted God.

Second, faith involves ongoing *struggle.*
Abraham learns there is no such thing
as "getting the faith" and never again
having to struggle with it.
Just when he thinks he "has the faith,"
it is tested to the breaking point.

Third, faith involves periodic *darkness.*
Abraham learns that faith is a lot like
the sun that shines in the sky.
Sometimes it shines so brightly that
we never think of doubting its presence.
Other times it disappears
so completely and for so long
that you wonder if it is still there.

The 17th-century Dutch artist Rembrandt spells out in living color God's command to Abraham:

*"Take . . . Isaac, whom you love so much, and . . . offer him as a sacrifice to me."*
Genesis 22:2

4. Michener says the people of Makor adopted Melak partly because his demands on people were great and partly because their local gods weren't demanding enough. Why would they want a "demanding god"?

5. A recent poll says many people today feel religion has been "watered down." As a result, people have gotten into the habit of not taking it seriously.

a. Why would you agree/disagree?
b. On a scale of 1 (not very) to 10 (very), how demanding would you say the teachings of Jesus are?

6. On a scale of 1 (not very) to 10 (very), how demanding do you feel these teachings of Jesus are?

___ "Turn the other cheek."   Matthew 5:39
___ "Love your enemies."   Matthew 5:44
___ "Carry your cross."   Matthew 16:24

7. An Old Testament person or event that points to a New Testament person or event is called a "type." Early Christians used types to show that Jesus was the one toward whom the Old Testament pointed. Read Genesis 22:1–8 (Isaac).

After the reading, record and share three ways that Isaac points to Jesus in a special way (is a "type" of him). ✎

*A* student said, "If God loves us, why does God want to test us? I wouldn't go about playing games with my friends by testing their loyalty." How would you respond to her?

2. Record and share your responses.
a. Did your faith ever seem to vanish or go behind a cloud for an extended period?
b. If so, can you recall what caused this lapse?
c. What is one thing about your faith that you sometimes question?
d. How do you resolve such questions, or are they still with you?

3. On a scale of 1 (low) to 10 (high), how strong is your faith
___ that God loves you, personally?
___ that Jesus is God's Son?
___ that Jesus sent the Holy Spirit to help you and guide you in your life?

A faith "blackout" can be very painful. A young person says in *The Devil's Advocate:*

*I groped for God and could not find God. I prayed to God . . . and God did not answer. I wept at night for the loss of God. . . .*

*Then, one day, God was there again. . . . I had never understood till this moment the meaning of the words "gift of faith."*
(Slightly adapted)

*Schooling of Abraham*

**H**ow does God test Abraham's faith?

2. List and explain three things that Abraham's test reveals about the nature of faith.

3. What is a "type," and how did early Christians use it?

# II

# *World of Moses*

## TIMELINE
*(APPROXIMATE KEY DATES)*
*B.C. = BEFORE CHRIST*

| | |
|---|---|
| 1770 | Israelites (in Egypt) |
| 1290 | Exodus |
| 1280 | Covenant |
| 1250 | Death of Moses |
| 1240 | Judges |

## BIBLE *(KEY BOOKS)*

| | |
|---|---|
| Genesis | Deuteronomy |
| Exodus | Joshua |
| Leviticus | Judges |
| Numbers | Ruth |

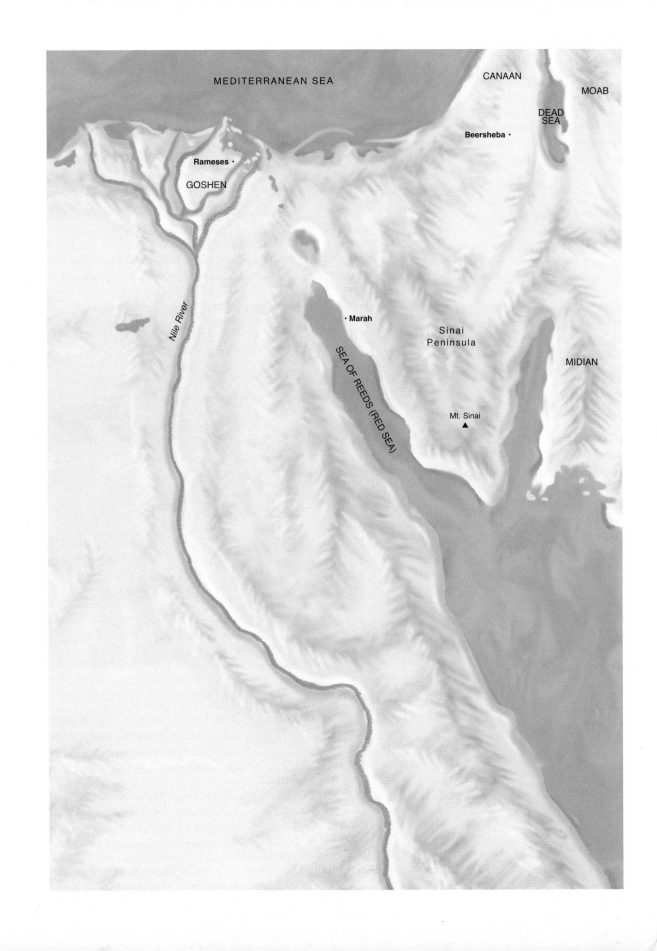

# CHAPTER FIVE

# Peoplehood

## 22  Isaac to Jacob

A tourist in Iran was watching students learning to weave rugs. After a while, she asked a student, "What happens if you make a mistake?" The student said, "Our teacher doesn't remove it; but finds a way to weave it into the *overall* pattern of the rug."

Isaac told Esau to kill an animal and prepare the special meal for doing this. Jacob overheard the conversation. When Esau departed, Jacob quickly prepared the proper meal, posed as Esau, and stole the blessing. This story illustrates two points.

Jewish youth observe traditions rooted in the faith of the ancient patriarchs (Abraham, Isaac, and Jacob).

God does something similar with people. Take the case of Isaac. When Isaac entered adulthood, he married Rebecca.

They had two sons: Esau and Jacob. One day Esau foolishly traded his firstborn birthright (double inheritance) to Jacob.
Genesis 25:31–33, Deuteronomy 21:17

Years passed and Isaac grew old and blind. He realized it was time to bless Esau and pass on to him his firstborn birthright. Ignorant of Esau's trade with Jacob,

First, it illustrates how God dealt with biblical people. God did not program them to be saints, nor treat them as puppets. God gave them the same free will that God gives us.

When they acted foolishly or sinned, God simply "wove" the new situation, created by foolishness or sin, into the pattern of salvation.

Second, it illustrates the Jewish belief in the power of the spoken word

when uttered in important situations.
Once uttered, it cannot be revoked.
It is like an arrow shot from a bow;
it cannot be "unshot."

This explains why Isaac could not revoke
the blessing when he learned
what Jacob had done.    Genesis 27:30–41

When Esau discovered what had happened,
he plotted to kill Jacob, but Jacob fled.

*A*close friend confides to you
that she feels a lot like Esau.
She did something stupid, regrets it,
and wants to remedy the mistake
and put God back into her life.
But she doesn't know where to begin.
What advice would you give her?

2.  J. Peter Schineller tells how his nephews
were playing together. Soon the youngest
began monopolizing a toy.
The oldest intervened and said
with surprising tact and gentleness:

*"It's our turn!*
*You have to let us play with it."*
*"I don't want to, and I don't have to."*
*"You have to and you know you have to. . . .*
*You promised!" "Well, OK," he said.*
*My youngest nephew knew*
*he was trapped. . . . He knew*
*in his child's wisdom that a promise*
*is something special . . . and not just*
*any old word.*    Review for Religious (adapted)

a.  How does this episode help us
appreciate Jewish belief in the power
of the spoken word?
b.  What does Schineller mean by saying
of his nephew "in his child's wisdom"?
c.  What do you think happens to this
"wisdom" as people grow older?

3.  Every spoken word sparks an "emotional
response" (infinitesimal perspiration).
A psycho-galvanometer can measure it.

Rank the three words in each group
from 1 (lowest) to 3 (highest)
according to the response they trigger
in the average person in an average setting.

| Group A | Group B | Group C |
| --- | --- | --- |
| ___ dance | ___ (your name) | ___ white |
| ___ kiss | ___ friend | ___ blue |
| ___ love | ___ money | ___ green |

a.  How and why might these responses
vary greatly, depending on who speaks
them and in what setting?
b.  How might the emotional "turn-on"
power that words have provide an insight
into Jewish belief about the power
of the spoken word in certain settings?

4.  Read or listen to a reading of
Genesis 25:27–34 ("The Trade") and
Genesis 27:1–45 ("The Crisis").

After the reading, record and share:
a.  Two or three sentences that sum up
the point of the reading.
b.  A thought or question that occurred
to you during the reading. ๛

*H*e knew in his
childhood wisdom that
a promise is something
special.

*Isaac*
*to*
*Jacob*

*W*ho were the sons of
Rebecca and Isaac, and
how did the younger
son acquire the
firstborn rights?

2.  How did the
younger son go about
getting the firstborn
blessing? Why didn't
his father retract the
blessing?

3.  How did Esau react
when he learned what
had happened?

# 23 Israelite Forerunners

*J*acob fled and headed for Haran.
One night he came to a holy place
and decided to pitch camp there.
He built a fire and fell asleep.

NARRATOR    *[Jacob] dreamed that
he saw a stairway reaching
from earth to heaven,
with angels going up
and coming down on it.
And there was the LORD
standing beside him.*

GOD    *I am the LORD, the God
of Abraham and Isaac. . . .
I will give to you
and to your descendants
this land . . . and through you
and your descendants
I will bless all the nations.*

Genesis 28:12–14

Jacob settles in Haran.
Later he returns to the dream site.
Again, he experiences God's presence.

GOD    *Your name is Jacob, but from
now on it will be Israel. . . .*

NARRATOR    *Then God left him. . . . [Jacob]
named the place Bethel.*

Genesis 35:10, 13, 15

The stories of Abraham, Isaac, and
Jacob take the form of *folk history.*
Unlike modern history, it preserves
the past in colorful stories
that can be easily remembered.

*Folk history* is real history.
It preserves tribal traditions.
For example, a Hebrew child might ask,
"Why are we called Israelites?
Why do we pilgrimage to Bethel?"

And so, just as biblical *prehistory*
deals with such important revelation
as the origin of the world and evil,
biblical *folk history*
deals with such things as the origin
of tribal traditions and customs.

In time, Jacob (Israel) returns to Canaan.
There he has twelve sons, forerunners
of the twelve tribes of Israel (Israelites).
Joshua 13–19

Jacob (Israel) loves his son Joseph best,
because he is the son of his old age.
This makes Joseph's brothers so jealous
that they sell him as a slave to traders,
who take him to Egypt.    Genesis 37

*T*hese unusual houses
are located near Haran
(in southern Turkey).

Abraham lived in
Haran before going
to Canaan. Jacob
also fled to this city
from Esau.

Some think that the
houses in Abraham's
time may have
resembled these
beehive-shaped houses.

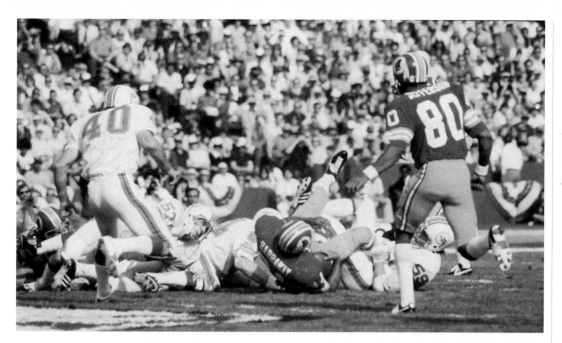

Where did the name "Hail Mary pass" come from?

The stories of Abraham, Isaac, and Jacob are examples of *folk history.* It preserves the past in easy-to-remember stories. Among these are the so-called *origin stories.*

a. Why would origin stories be especially important to groups like Israel?
b. Team up with another person and make a list of modern "origins" that people often ask about, such as

❧ why a long, last-second football pass is called a "Hail Mary pass."
❧ how the seventh-inning stretch started.
❧ how "toasting" at banquets began.

c. Do a composite list of "origins" collected by other teams in your group and answer as many as you can.
d. Team up with another person to do detective work on these origin stories.

2. Scholars debate the meaning of the name *Israel.* Some suggest it means "let El rule" or "let El shine." *El* is one of several Hebrew words used to refer to God.

a. Team up with another person and list as many biblical names as you can that end in the letters *el.*
b. Make a composite list of all the words the group compiled.

3. In *The Power within You,* Pat Williams says Joseph was the butt of the first "good news/bad news" jokes in history.

Read or listen to a dramatic reading of the following, prepared in advance by four people.

a. *Good news:* Joseph is his father's favorite child.   Genesis 37:1–11
*Bad news:* Joseph's jealous brothers sell him into slavery.   Genesis 37:12–36
b. *Good news:* A high Egyptian official buys and befriends Joseph.   Genesis 39:1–6
*Bad news:* The official's wife frames Joseph and gets him jailed.   Genesis 39:7–23

4. TV lecturer Bishop Fulton Sheen said, "Jealousy is the tribute that mediocrity pays to genius."

a. What is Bishop Sheen's point?
b. How is his remark especially true in the case of Joseph and his brothers?

5. Imagine you are a school counselor and a student admits to being jealous of a brother or a sister because of parental favoritism. What advice would you give the student? ❧

*Israelite Forerunners*

What happened during Jacob's first stay at Bethel? His second stay?

2. With the origin of what things does prehistory deal? Folk history?

3. How many sons did Jacob have, and to what are they the forerunners? Why was Joseph Jacob's favorite son? How did Joseph become an Egyptian slave?

4. What do the letters *El* designate in Hebrew?

MEDITERRANEAN SEA
CANAAN
DEAD SEA
GOSHEN
Pithom
Great Pyramid
RED SEA
Mt. Sinai
MIDIAN
EGYPT
Nile River

# 24  Israelites to Egypt

Joseph was sold to Potiphar, an officer of the Egyptian king. The officer's wife was attracted to him. When he ignored her, she accused him falsely, and he was imprisoned.

Soon Joseph won fame interpreting dreams. When the king heard of Joseph's ability, he asked him to interpret two dreams. Joseph obliged, saying:

*"The two dreams mean the same thing. . . . There will be seven years of great plenty. . . . After that . . . seven years of famine."*
Genesis 41:25, 29–30

Joseph impresses the king deeply, is freed, and is put in charge of storing grain during the "years of plenty." World famine strikes, and the brothers of Joseph are among those who come to Egypt to seek grain.

After testing them to see if they have changed, Joseph reveals himself to them. He invites them to bring his father and all their relatives to Egypt. They settle in Goshen and prosper.

Archaeologists have unearthed records to show that in Joseph's time dream interpretation was a respected art. They also document long-term famines. One record reads, "For the past seven years . . . there is a shortage of food."

The Book of Genesis ends abruptly with the death of Joseph.

The Book of Exodus begins with a reversal of fortune for the Israelites. A new Egyptian king comes to power. Fearing the growth of the Israelites, he enslaves them and orders that all newborn males be put to death at birth.

The Sphinx was over 1,000 years old when Joseph came to Egypt.

The sculpture measures seven stories high and extends the length of a football field.

It is into this terrifying era
of Israelite history that Moses is born.
He is saved from death by his mother,
who hides him in reeds along a river.
Pharaoh's daughter finds the basket
while bathing in the river.
She adopts Moses and raises him
as her own son.     Exodus 2:1–10

When Moses grows older,
he becomes aware of his Hebrew origins.
One day, after seeing an Egyptian beat
a Hebrew slave, he kills the Egyptian.
Even though Moses enjoys considerable
favor in Pharaoh's family, killing an Egyptian
is a deadly crime for a Hebrew.
Fearing for his life, Moses flees to Midian.
There he becomes a shepherd.

*J*oseph told his repentant brothers,
"[Don't] blame yourselves
because you sold me here.
It was really God who sent me ahead
of you to save people's lives."   Genesis 45:5

a.  What point in the story about students
learning to weave rugs (page 46)
does this passage illustrate?
b.  Record and share a time when "bad news"
turned into "good news" for you.

2.  Dreams are often the source
of religious revelation in the Bible.
Dreams have also been the source
of scientific revelation. For example,
physicist Niels Bohr (1885–1962)
got the idea for his atom model
from a dream. Mozart, Einstein, and Poe
also got ideas from dreams.

a.  Describe in detail the two dreams
Pharaoh had and how Joseph
interpreted them.   Genesis 41
b.  For what reason might God choose
to speak to people in dreams
rather than in awake moments?
c.  Recall a dream that you had that you
have never forgotten. Prepare to share it.

3.  The Greek historian Herodotus
records a number of "birth legends"
not unlike that of Moses.
A narrow escape from death at birth

is often a folk-history device
to show that the "blessing of the gods"
is upon the child.
Some scholars think that Moses' escape
falls into such a folk-story category.
Folk-history device or not, the story
of Moses' birth (Exodus 2:1–10) has a real
warmth and naturalness about it.
What are some examples of this?

4.  Read or listen to a dramatic reading
of Genesis 44:1–34 ("The Missing Cup"),
prepared in advance by two people.

After the reading, record and share
your feelings about what Joseph did.
For example, do you think he acted
rightly? Explain. ✑

*R*ameses II (shown) has
been identified as the
probable pharaoh
(king) who oppressed
the Israelite people.

*Israelites
to
Egypt*

*H*ow did Joseph end
up in prison in Egypt
and get the attention of
the king? How did the
Israelites end up living
in Egypt?

2.  List two examples
of how archaeology
supports details of the
Joseph story.

3.  Describe the
situation of the Hebrews
in Egypt when Moses
was born. How was he
saved, raised, and
educated?

> *Earth's crammed
> with heaven,
> And every common
> bush afire with God;
> But only he who sees
> takes off his shoes;
> The rest sit round it
> and pluck blackberries.*
> ◆
>
> Elizabeth Barrett Browning

# 25 Leadership of Moses

One day Moses was tending sheep. He noticed a nearby bush on fire. This was not so unusual. Dry bushes occasionally caught fire in the hot Sinai sun, but this bush didn't burn up. Moses went over to see why. As he approached it, a voice said:

GOD    *Take off your sandals, because you are standing on holy ground. I am the God of your ancestors. . . . I am sending you to the king of Egypt so that you can lead my people out of his country.*

MOSES    *I am nobody. How can I go to the king and bring the Israelites out of Egypt?*

GOD    *I will be with you. . . .*

MOSES    *When I go to the Israelites and say . . . "The God of your ancestors sent me to you," they will ask me, "What is his name?" So what can I tell them?*

GOD    *I am who I am. You must tell them:*

*"The one who is called I AM has sent me to you."*
Exodus 3:5–6, 10–14

Moses returns to Egypt a changed man. Nine times he confronts Pharaoh (king). Nine times Pharaoh shouts, "No!"

Each refusal triggers a "plague": the Nile turns bloody; frogs fill the land; gnats swarm like dust; boils infect and kill animals.   Exodus 7–10

But Pharaoh will not budge.

Then God instructs Moses to prepare the Israelites for the tenth and final plague: the death of all firstborn males.   Exodus 12:12

They are to sacrifice a lamb and smear its blood on their houses— a sign for the "angel of death" to spare ("pass over") that house.   Exodus 12:23

Then they are to eat the lamb, whose blood has saved their firstborn. This joyful celebration becomes known as the *Passover* and is still celebrated.

When Moses returned to Egypt, he saw a sight like this.   Exodus 5:7–19

His Hebrew brothers were reduced to slavery, making bricks under the hot Egyptian sun.

The wall painting is from the tomb of an Egyptian king and dates to Moses' time.

The last plague "breaks the camel's back." Pharaoh calls Moses and shouts:

*"Get out, you and your Israelites! . . . Take your sheep, goats, and cattle, and leave."* Exodus 12:31–32

*D*wight Moody said, "I find it significant that when God decided to free the Israelites from Egypt, God chose a man with a speech defect— not a powerful army." Exodus 6:12
a. What is Moody getting at?
b. What important message might Moody's statement contain for our time?

2. The phrase "I am who I am" brings us to God's personal name. Spelled *YHWH* (Hebrew has no vowels), we translate it into English as LORD. Some interpret it to mean "I cannot be named or defined." At one point in history, Jews ceased to pronounce God's name out of fear. In its place, they said *Adonai* ("Lord"). Thus its true pronunciation became lost.

Medieval scholars decided it should be pronounced *YaHoWaH*, or *Jehovah*. Modern scholars, with resources at their disposal, pronounce it *YaHWeh*, or *Yahweh*. The significant thing is not how to pronounce it, but that God revealed it. To tell others your name is to enter into a personal relationship with them.

a. Explain what is meant by a personal relationship with someone. With God.
b. How can someone develop such a God relationship?

3. Moses asked God, "How can I go to the king and bring the Israelites out of Egypt?" God answered, "I will be with you." Exodus 3:11–12
If Moses thought he would have smooth sailing with God on his side, he had another think coming. Pharaoh responded to Moses' demands by making the Israelites work harder. As a result, the Israelites ignored Moses.

Moses complained to God, "Even the Israelites will not listen to me, so why should the king? I am such a poor speaker." Exodus 6:12

a. Why do you think God let this happen?
b. What lesson does it contain? Explain.

4. *Everyday Life in Bible Times,* by the National Geographic Society, suggests the plagues were natural, explaining:

*Silt and microbes redden the Nile in flood. . . . Floodlands breed gnats and mosquitoes. . . . Frogs breed. . . . As frog swarms die, vermin breed on the carcasses. Pests such as the screwworm fly inflame skin of man and beast.*

a. What do you think of the suggestion?
b. Why does/doesn't it undermine the account of the plagues in the Bible?

*T*he Israelites were forced into slave labor, building Egyptian cities. Exodus 1:11

The beauty of these cities can be glimpsed from these pillars of the Temple of Amun at Karnak along the Nile.

Dating from near the time of the Israelites, the temple is so big that it would swallow Saint Patrick's Cathedral in New York City.

*Leadership of Moses*

*H*ow is God's name:
a. Spelled in Hebrew?
b. Expressed in English?
c. Pronounced today?
d. Interpreted by some?

2. What was the tenth and final plague? How did God tell Moses to prepare for it?
Under what name is this event celebrated to this very day?

# 26 Exodus from Egypt

The Israelites had barely departed when Pharaoh regretted that he had freed them. He ordered his army to pursue them. When the Israelites discovered this, they were terrified. Then the LORD said to Moses:

*"Hold out your hand over the sea. . . ."*
*So Moses held out his hand over the sea,*
*and at daybreak the water returned*
*to its normal level . . .*
*and covered the chariots, the drivers,*
*and all the Egyptian army. . . .*
*On that day*

These young people walked twenty miles to participate in an outdoor Mass by the Holy Father outside Denver in the 1990s.

The Israelites must have presented a similar image marching into the Sinai wasteland, where they would encounter God.

*"Lift up your walking stick*
*and hold it out over the sea.*
*The water will divide,*
*and the Israelites will be able to walk*
*through the sea on dry ground." . . .*

*The water was divided,*
*and the Israelites*
*went through the sea on dry ground,"*
*with walls of water on both sides.*

*The Egyptians pursued them. . . .*
*The LORD . . . made the wheels*
*of their chariots get stuck, so that*
*they moved with great difficulty. . . .*
*The LORD said to Moses:*

*the LORD saved the people of Israel . . .*
*and they had faith in the LORD*
*and in his servant Moses.*

Exodus 14:16, 21–28, 30–31

The Bible calls the place where Moses and the Israelites crossed *yam suph.* Usually translated "Red Sea," it can also be translated "Reed Sea." This latter translation suggests that the place was a swamplike area, typical of lake regions.

The Bible seems to support this when it says of the Egyptians, "The LORD . . . made the wheels of their chariots get stuck."

Whether the "walls of water" were
an actual tidelike phenomenon
or a poetic flourish is debated.

There is *no* debate, however,
that the important point is not *what*
happened, but *why* it happened.

It is an affirmation of Israel's faith
that it was Yahweh
who delivered them from Egypt.

*A* mother asked her six-year-old
what things he learned
in Bible class that day.
"Well," he said, "our teacher told us how
God saved the Israelites at the Red Sea.
Moses' engineers built a pontoon bridge
over the water. After everyone crossed,
they saw the Egyptian tanks coming.

"In a flash, Moses radioed headquarters.
Bombers came, blew up the bridge,
and saved the Israelites."

"Bobby," said his startled mother,
"is that really how your teacher
told the story?"
"Well, not exactly, but if I told it
the way she did, you'd never believe it."

Do you think this story points up
a real problem children have
when it comes to the Bible? Explain.

2. An ancient Jewish legend says
that when Moses held his walking stick
over the waters of the Red Sea,
as God commanded, they didn't divide.
Not until the first Israelite stepped
into the sea did the miracle take place.

a. What is the point of the legend?
b. How does the point hold relevance
for people who are trying to change
our world today?

3. *Newsweek* magazine (10/11/76)
has a story and photos of the mummy
of Rameses II, who opposed Moses.
Team up with a friend and report back
to the group on it.

4. For many Israelites,
their first real "God experience" came
when God rescued them at the Dead Sea.
Record and share the first time you had
what might be called a "God experience."
Here is one student's response:

*My first God experience
occurred in my sophomore year in school.
One night I was ice-skating with
some friends on a lagoon off a big lake.*

*For some strange reason,
I left my friends and skated out
all alone into the darkness of the lake.
The moon was bright, and there was
about half an inch of snow on the ice.*

*All of a sudden I got this great feeling.
I remember thinking,
"This must be what heaven is like."
When I returned to my friends,
I didn't tell them what happened,
because they wouldn't have understood.*

*A*n Egyptian king is
portrayed driving one
of his chariots.

It is probably not unlike
the royal chariots that
got bogged down in the
mud while pursuing the
Israelites.

### Exodus from Egypt

*B*riefly describe:

a. What happened at
the Red Sea.
b. How else we may
translate the Hebrew
term for "Red Sea."
c. Why this translation
fits better with what the
Bible says.

2. What is the key
point underlying the
description of the Red
Sea event and what it
affirms?

55

# CHAPTER SIX

# Covenant

## 27 Journey to Sinai

Imagine you are being held hostage on the edge of a hostile wasteland. One night you escape and enter it. You have no idea where safety lies or where to find water and food.

This is the situation of the Israelites after they crossed the Red (Reed) Sea and entered the Sinai desert. Then three amazing things happened.

The first thing was the appearance of a "pillar of cloud" to guide the Israelites by day and a "pillar of fire" to guide them by night.   Exodus 13:22

Since the Sinai desert contains ancient volcanoes, now inactive, some people ask, "Could they explain the two pillars? Smoke coiling upward from a volcano could resemble a pillar of cloud by day and glow like a pillar of fire by night."

The second amazing thing to happen was the appearance of quail, settling on the Israelite camp and providing the Israelites with food.   Exodus 16:13
Again, people ask, "Could this be linked to an event like the one described in *National Geographic Magazine?*"

*Every year great migrations of quail wing their way across the Mediterranean and Red Seas en route between Europe and Africa. Even today Bedouin in the Sinai peninsula catch the exhausted birds after their long flight over the water.*

The third amazing thing to happen was the appearance of *manna,* which means "What is it?"   Exodus 16:15

Again, people ask, "Could it be linked to the sap that oozes from certain desert shrubs when insects puncture them? Once exposed to the air, the sap dries into a sweet, flaky food." You will find Bible readers on both sides.

And so the question arises: How do we interpret these events? Were they

- *true miracles* worked by God,
- *ordinary events* that God used in an extraordinary way, or
- *literary symbols* expressing Israel's faith that God protected and guided

[*T*he LORD] *touches the mountains, and they pour out smoke.*
Psalm 104:32

People living in areas of the northern Sinai capture quail in these nets as the hungry, weary birds make their yearly migration from Europe to Africa.

the Israelites on their desert journey? This much is certain. As the Israelites looked back on their flight from Egypt and their journey across the desert, they realized they could not have made it without God's special help.

*T*he psalmist says of Israel:
*By day [God] led them with a cloud
and all night long with the light
of a fire. . . . [God] sent down birds,
as many as the grains of sand
on the shore.* Psalm 78:14, 27

Bible readers interpret these events in one of three ways:
- *miracles* that God performed,
- *ordinary events* that God used in an extraordinary way, or
- *symbol stories* that affirm Israel's faith that God helped the Israelites in their desert journey.

Which interpretation do you prefer? Why?

2. Imagine you are an Israelite musician. Moses asks you to prepare entertainment around the campfire one night.
Select two teams to prepare different "rap-style" versions of the following:

*Let all things now living
a song of thanksgiving*

*to God our Creator triumphantly raise;
Who fashioned and made us,
protected and stayed us. . . .*

*His banners are o'er us,
his light goes before us,
A pillar of fire shining forth in the night:
Till shadows have vanished
and darkness is banished,
As forward we travel
from light into Light.* Anonymous

3. John Newman published the following under the title "The Pillar of Cloud."

*Lead, kindly Light, amid the encircling
gloom, / Lead thou me on;
The night is dark, and I am far from home;
Lead thou me on.
Keep thou my feet; I do not ask to see
The distant scene; one step enough for me.*

*I was not ever thus, nor prayed that thou
Shouldst lead me on; / I loved to choose
and see my path; but now
Lead thou me on. / I loved the garish day,
and spite of fears, / Pride ruled my will:
remember not past years.*

a. Explain the following images: "kindly Light," "encircling gloom," "distant scene," "one step."
b. What is the second stanza saying?

*W*hat three events took place to help the Israelites in the desert?

2. What are three ways to interpret these events?

3. What one thing did the Israelites realize "for certain" as they looked back on their journey across the desert?

57

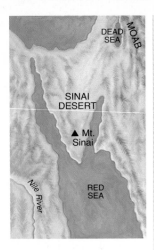

# 28 Encounter with God

Historians scratch their heads:
"How did a band of ex-slaves, with
neither organization nor education,
change the course of human history?"
For this is what the Israelites did.

The only explanation that makes sense
is the one the Israelites themselves gave.

At a mountain in the Sinai desert
they encountered God,
who covenanted them and gave them
a new identity and a new destiny.

GOD      *[I] brought you here to . . .*
*be my chosen people, . . .*
*and you will serve me*
*as priests. . . .*

NARRATOR    *On the morning*
*of the third day . . .*
*a thick cloud appeared*
*on the mountain, and . . .*
*the people . . . trembled. . . .*
*The LORD . . . called Moses*
*to the top of the mountain.*
       Exodus 19:4–6, 16, 20

Then God presents Moses
with these Ten Commandments:

*[1.] Worship no god but me. . . .*
*[2.] Do not use my name for evil. . . .*
*[3.] Keep [the Sabbath] holy. . . .*

*[4.] Respect your [parents]. . . .*
*[5.] Do not commit murder.*
*[6.] Do not commit adultery.*
*[7.] Do not steal.*
*[8.] Do not accuse anyone falsely.*
*[9.] Do not desire [another's wife]. . . .*
*[10.] Do not desire [another's property].*
       Exodus 20:3, 7–8, 12–17

*Moses wrote down*
*all the LORD's commands. . . .*
*The next morning, he built an altar. . . .*
*[After sacrificing cattle,*
*he read the commands to the people.]*

*[Then, he poured blood*
*on the altar and on them, saying,]*
*"This is the blood*
*that seals the covenant which*
*the LORD made with you."*    Exodus 24:4, 8

God's covenant with the Israelites
reflects the treaty format of that day,
in which a powerful king
pledged favors to a weaker king.
In turn, the weaker king pledged
total allegiance to the powerful king.

*T*radition says this is
where God covenanted
with Israel:

*I, the LORD, . . .*
*brought you here. . . .*
*You will be*
*my chosen people.*
       Exodus 19:4–5

And so God's covenant with the Israelites transforms them from a band of ex-slaves into a nation of people with

🖎 a new *identity* (God's people) and
🖎 a new *destiny* (priestly people).

Jewish writer Will Herberg describes God's covenant with Israel this way in his book *Jewish Existence and Survival:*

*Israel is not a "natural" nation; it is, indeed, not a nation at all like the nations of the world.*

*It is a supernatural community, called into being . . . by God's special act of covenant, first with Abraham . . . [then] with Israel collectively. . . . Apart from the covenant, Israel is nothing.*

Explain Herberg's point.

2. Commenting on Herberg's observation, an anonymous writer said:

*Apart from Christianity and Islam, who owe their origin, in part, to Israel, no other religion began as did Judaism. It did not spring from nature, as others did, but from an encounter with God, at a specific point in time and at a specific point on the planet.*

a. How does Christianity owe its origin, in part, to Israel?
b. Research and share Islam's origin.

3. The commandments are like ten titles of ten chapters in a book.

They identify ten categories of morality (right and wrong conduct).
Each category, however, needs explanation and expansion. For example, "Respect your [parents]" needs explanation (What is respect?) and expansion (Respect extends beyond parents).

Explain each of these quotes, and decide under which commandment each falls.

a. "Capital punishment is . . . wrong as a cure for crime, as charity is wrong as a cure for poverty."  Henry Ford
b. "The best thing a dad can do for his kids is love their mother."  Anonymous
c. "In one generation movies went from silent to unspeakable."  Doug Larson (adapted)

d. "Better be hated for what you are than loved for what you pretend to be."  Anonymous

4. Briefly explain:
a. How did Jesus summarize the Ten Commandments?  Matthew 22:34–40
b. Which of the Ten Commandments fall into Jesus' summary categories? 🖎

My father didn't tell me how to live; he lived and let me watch him do it.
Clarence Kelland

*Encounter with God*

**W**hat makes Israel totally unlike all other nations of the world?

2. List the Ten Commandments.

3. Describe how Moses presented the covenant and the commandments and what new destiny and identity they gave the Israelites.

> The Sabbath
> kept Israel
> ✡
> better than Israel
> kept
> the Sabbath.
>
> Author unknown

# 29  New Life & Worship

God's covenant with the Israelites at Mount Sinai introduced them to two revolutionary changes: a new *worship style* and a new *life style*.

The first change was a new *worship style*. It grew out of the Ten Commandments.

Moses put the two stone tablets, on which the commandment were written, in a sacred box called the Ark of the Covenant. He placed the Ark in a sacred Tent behind a sacred curtain.   Exodus 25:8, 26:1–36 As soon as Moses put the Ark there, a remarkable thing happened:

Over the centuries, this ram's horn *(shofar)* sounded the call to worship on major Jewish festivals.

It is still used in many synagogues on the eve of Yom Kippur ("Day of Atonement").

*[A] cloud covered the Tent and the dazzling light of the LORD's presence filled it. . . . The Israelites moved their camp to another place only when the cloud lifted from the Tent.*   Exodus 40:34, 36 *It was called the Tent of the LORD's presence.*   Exodus 33:7

And so the first focus of Israel's new worship style became the Tent of the LORD's presence (future Temple). "Anyone who wanted to consult the LORD would go out to it."   Exodus 33:7

The second focus of Israel's new worship style was a series of religious celebrations. These included the Passover and Yom Kippur.   Exodus 12:1–17, Leviticus 16:20–22

The Passover celebrated God's freeing of Israel from slavery in Egypt to be the Chosen People, through whom God would take a giant stride forward in the "re-creation" of the world.

Yom Kippur celebrated the Israelites' desire to repent and to atone for their failure to live out their calling.

The second change that the covenant introduced to Israel was a new *life style*. It was based on the Ten Commandments.

The Israelites saw the commandments as freeing them "from" their own ignorance and passion and freeing them "for" a life of love and service.

Only in this light can we appreciate this beautiful prayer of the psalmist to God:

*How I love your law! . . . Your word is a lamp to guide me and a light for my path.*   Psalm 119:97, 105

*We have grown in numbers, wealth, and power as no other nation has grown.*

*But we have forgotten the God . . . that made us.* Abraham Lincoln

On Good Friday, April 5, 1985, 8,000 disc jockeys across the world played the song "We Are the World" at the same time. They did this to dramatize the unity of the human family and to focus attention on starving family members in Africa.

Why is a ritual (civil or religious) more effective in moving people to act than a verbal statement?

2. The Israelites performed an unusual ritual on Yom Kippur. The high priest (representing the nation) placed his hands on a goat's head and confessed over it the people's sins. Then the goat was driven off into the desert. Leviticus 16:20–22

Can you discover the meaning of these ritual acts?
a. Placing hands on the goat's head.
b. Confessing the people's sins over it.
c. Driving it off into the desert.

3. President Abraham Lincoln made this proclamation in 1863:

*We have grown in numbers, wealth, and power as no other nation has grown. But we have forgotten God. . . . It behooves us, then, to humble ourselves before the offended Power, to confess our national sins. . . . I designate and set apart Thursday, the 30th day of April, 1863, as a day of national humiliation, fasting, and prayer . . . that the united cry of the Nation will be heard on high.*

Why do/don't you think it would be appropriate for a modern president to make such a proclamation?

4. Seeking God's forgiveness reminds us that we should forgive others the way that we ask God to forgive us. Explain the point of these quotes:

a. "Forgiving an enemy sets a prisoner free and that prisoner is me." Anonymous
b. "Doing an injury
puts me below my enemy;
revenging an injury
puts me even with my enemy;
forgiving an injury
puts me above my enemy." Author unknown

5. Recall someone who has injured you. After sharing what the person did to you, compose a prayer asking God to help you forgive him or her from the heart. End by asking God to give the person a special blessing. (Why do this?) ❧

## New Life & Worship

**B**riefly explain:

a. The two changes that the covenant introduced into Israel.
b. Israel's view of the Ten Commandments.

2. Identify:
a. Ark of the Covenant
b. sacred Tent
c. sacred curtain
d. Passover
e. Yom Kippur
f. shofar

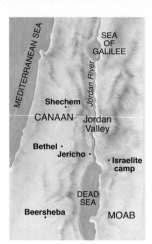

# 30 *Teaching & Testing*

Moses and the people stayed at Mount Sinai for about a year. Then they set out across the desert for the land that God had promised them. The desert into which they traveled was made up of three regions:

- stretches of dry sand, where little or nothing could actually grow;
- expanses of rock, with a few springs of water;
- semiarid land, with just enough vegetation to feed sheep and goats.

This harsh landscape became the theater in which the next highly important years of Israel's history were enacted. Almost from the start, problems arose both from *within* and from *without*.

From *within*, the Israelites grew weary and began to complain to Moses, saying:

*"Our strength is gone. There is nothing at all to eat— nothing but this manna."*  Numbers 11:6

Next, rebels began to challenge the leadership of Moses.  Numbers 16:3–14

From *without*, foreign kings refused to let the Israelites and their flocks pass through their lands.  Numbers 20:14–21

But with God's help, Moses managed to hold things together and survive both threats.

Finally, after forty years of testing, the Israelites emerged from the desert and pitched camp on the plateau of Moab.

Stretching out below them—as far as the eye could see—was the Promised Land.

*F*rom a plane, the Jordan River looks like a giant snake coiling downhill.

Eventually it empties into the Dead Sea. Lowest body of water on earth, the Dead Sea has six times the salt content of the ocean.

The worst swimmer on earth can't sink in it.

About the size of Vermont and the latitude of Georgia, the heart of the land was a ten-mile-wide fertile valley.

Over the western ridge of the valley was the Mediterranean Sea, with its elegant, white-sand beaches. At the north end was the Sea of Galilee, a fisherman's dream of paradise. Sixty-five airline miles due south was the Dead Sea. Linking these seas was the Jordan River.

To the desert-weary Israelites, the Promised Land was a breathtaking, spectacular sight.

Harry Truman was president at the end of World War II. He had a lot of hard calls to make. Truman refused to let popular opinion influence his decisions, saying, "How far would Moses have gone if he had taken a poll in Egypt?"

When should/shouldn't a leader be influenced by popular opinion?

2. Explain the point each of these quotes makes about leaders.

a. "The nations will find it very hard to look up to the leaders who keep their ears to the ground."   Winston Churchill
b. "People want to know how much you care before they care how much you know."   James F. Hind
c. "You can't lead anyone any further than you have gone yourself."   Gene Mauch

3. A modern Bible reader said, "The trouble with people today is that they want to get to the Promised Land without struggling through the desert."

What did the person mean? What motivates you to keep struggling through the desert?

4. Explain how these quotes relate to motivation, and give an example to illustrate your explanation.
a. "If you think you can, you can. If you think you can't, you're right."   Mary Kay Ash
b. "God doesn't want our deeds; God wants the love that prompts them."   Teresa of Avila
c. "The greatest treason: to do the right deed for the wrong reason."   T. S. Eliot

5. Read Numbers 21:4–9 ("The Pole"). What event in the life of Jesus does this episode remind you of? Explain.

6. Read John 3:14–17 ("The Cross"). How do the story of "The Pole" and the words of Jesus illustrate these words of Saint Augustine?

*In the Old Testament the New Testament lies concealed; in the New Testament, the Old Testament lies revealed.* ☙

The Sinai desert has an "other-world" look.

Rugged mountain peaks soar 8,000 feet above a desert floor carpeted with rocks.

It is a region suited more for gazelles and wild goats than for human beings.

No wonder the Israelites complained and rebelled against Moses.

*Teaching & Testing*

**L**ist and describe the three regions of the desert into which the Israelites went.

2. List and explain the two sources that threatened the Israelites' existence in their desert journey.

3. Briefly describe the Promised Land.

63

# 31 Journey's End

Moses gathered the people to talk to them in final preparation for entry into the Promised Land. He explained how their desert sojourn was a time of testing and teaching:

*Like an eagle teaching its young to fly, catching them safely on its spreading wings, the LORD kept Israel from falling."*

Deuteronomy 32:9–11

Like Moses' own time in the desert, the Israelites' time in the desert served as a schoolroom. It taught them about their infidelity and weakness and about God's fidelity and power.

The Book of Deuteronomy ends with the death of Moses, saying:

*The LORD buried him in a valley in Moab, opposite the town of Bethpeor, but to this day no one knows the exact place of his burial.*   Deuteronomy 34:6

It is one of the ironies of history that great leaders like Moses, who fight so valiantly for causes, often die without enjoying the results of their struggles.

The death of Moses concludes the Jewish *Torah,* the name given to the first five books of the Bible:

- Genesis,
- Exodus,
- Leviticus,
- Numbers, and
- Deuteronomy.

These five books form the foundation upon which the rest of the Bible is built.

*Who are you?*
*Where have you been?*
*Where are you going?*
Carl Sandburg

*"Remember how the LORD your God led you . . . through the desert these past forty years, sending hardships to test [and] . . . teach you that you must not depend on bread alone to sustain you, but on everything that the LORD says."*
Deuteronomy 8:2–3

*[Then Moses recited this song.]*
*"Jacob's descendants he . . . found . . . wandering through the desert. . . .*
*He protected them and cared for them. . . .*

Astronaut Jim Irwin describes in his book *To Rule the Night* how he prepared mentally for his *Apollo 15* moon voyage:

*I would go to the beach. . . . I enjoyed sleeping out there . . . completely alone.*

*I'd get up in the early morning, and
go for a dip or go for a run on the beach.
I have always been a sun worshiper.
And there was real peace and quiet,
lying there on the beach and listening
to the breakers and the seagulls.*

a.  How did Moses prepare the Israelites
for their entry into the Promised Land?
b.  Why prepare mentally for something?
c.  Where is your favorite spot for
getting away from things and thinking?
d.  How hard is it for you to be alone,
without a radio or TV?
e.  Why do/don't you think it might
be good to do this occasionally?

*I sit on a rock . . . and say to myself,
"Who are you, Sandburg? Where have
you been, and where are you going?"*

Record your own responses to Sandburg's
three questions. Why are they important?

3.  A "desert experience" may occur
accidentally. Keith Miller describes
such an experience in his book
*A Taste of New Wine.*
It occurred when he broke his neck
in an auto accident in a remote area.

*I lay there an hour and a half
for the ambulance. . . . As I prayed
I had a strange feeling of peace. . . .*

2.  People still go "into the desert"
to find God—and themselves.
It usually takes the form of a "retreat."
Poet Carl Sandburg expressed the value
of such an experience this way:

*[We] must get away . . .
to experience loneliness. Only those
who learn how to live with loneliness
can come to know themselves and life.
I go out there and walk and . . .
I listen to the sounds of loneliness.*

*I thought to myself,
"What a shame to find out so late in life
that this kind of peace is a reality." . . .
I realized at that moment . . .
there was Something very personal,
very real, which was more important
than anything else I had ever known.*
Keith Miller, *A Taste of New Wine*

How do you explain (a) Keith's feeling
of peace, (b) his last sentence? ✑

## Journey's End

**H**ow did Moses
prepare the people for
entry into the Promised
Land?

2. What role did Moses
say the desert hardships
of the Israelites played?

3. With what event does
the Torah end? List the
five books of the Torah.
Why are these books so
important?

# III
# World of David

## TIMELINE
*(APPROXIMATE KEY DATES)*
*B.C. = BEFORE CHRIST*

| | |
|---|---|
| 1030 | Saul |
| 1010 | David |
| 970 | Solomon |
| 922 | Division |
| 722 | North falls |
| 587–539 | South exiled |
| 168 | Maccabees |
| 63 | Romans |
| 37 | Herod |

## BIBLE *(KEY BOOKS)*

| | |
|---|---|
| 1–2 Kings | Jeremiah |
| 1–2 Chronicles | Ezekiel |
| Psalms | Jonah |
| Proverbs | Job |
| Song of Songs | Ecclesiastes |
| Amos | Daniel |
| Hosea | 1–2 Maccabees |
| Isaiah | |

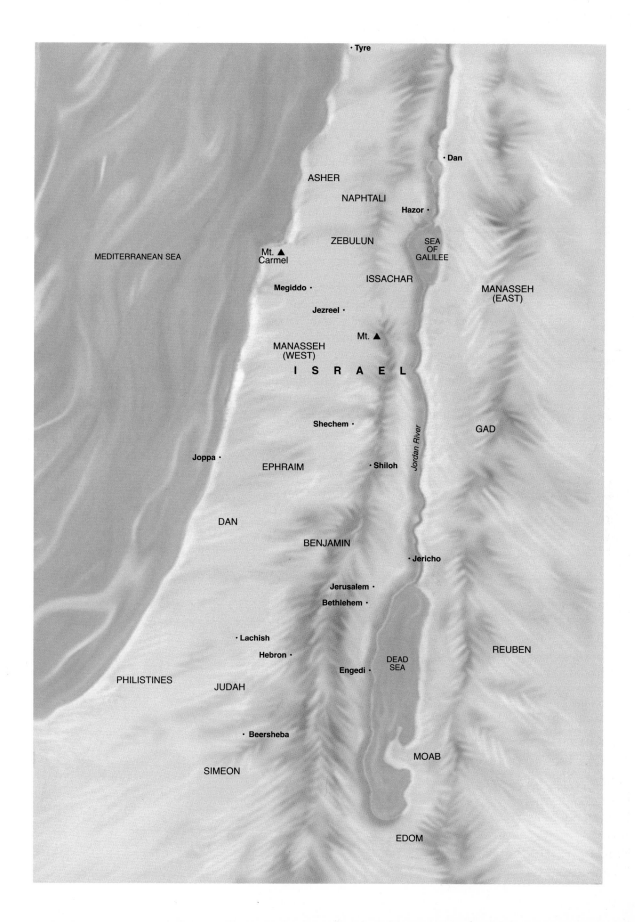

- Tyre

ASHER

NAPHTALI

- Dan

Hazor -

ZEBULUN

SEA
OF
GALILEE

Mt. ▲
Carmel

MEDITERRANEAN SEA

ISSACHAR

MANASSEH
(EAST)

Megiddo -

Jezreel -

Mt. ▲

MANASSEH
(WEST)

I S R A E L

Shechem -

GAD

Jordan River

Joppa -

EPHRAIM

- Shiloh

DAN

BENJAMIN

- Jericho

Jerusalem -

Bethlehem -

- Lachish

REUBEN

Hebron -

Engedi -

DEAD
SEA

PHILISTINES

JUDAH

- Beersheba

MOAB

SIMEON

EDOM

Ostracon (broken pottery used as a writing surface).

# CHAPTER SEVEN

# Nationhood

## 32 Into the Land

Joshua assumed leadership of Israel. Immediately he organized the crossing of the Jordan River into the Promised Land. The priests led the way, carrying the Ark of the Covenant. "As soon as they stepped into the river, the water stopped flowing." Joshua 3:15

This remarkable report prompts us to ask, "Could the stoppage be explained by an earthquake, similar to the one in 1927, which killed hundreds and blocked the Jordan for a day?"

Whatever the explanation, the main point of the report is to affirm the Israelites' belief that God was with them— as God was with their ancestors at the crossing of the Red Sea.

*O God . . . your people did not conquer the land with their swords; . . . it was by your power . . . , by the assurance of your presence.*
Psalm 44:1, 3

Next, Joshua prepares to attack Jericho.

*The LORD said to Joshua . . . "March around the city seven times while the priests blow the trumpets. . . . The city walls will collapse."* Joshua 6:2, 4–5

Joshua obeys and the walls collapse. Again, we might ask, "Could an earthquake explain this, also? Archaeology clearly shows that earlier in Jericho's history an earthquake did crumble its walls."

After Jericho falls, the Israelites destroy everything in the city. Such mass killing, called "the ban," was not uncommon in biblical times. Although it shocks us, we need only recall the Nazi holocaust of the Jews. This does not justify "the ban," but it does sober our outrage.

We can say this much. The ban reveals Israel's limited understanding of God at this time:

A tell is a mound or hill concealing the remains of a buried ancient city.

Archaeologists have excavated a number of tells dating from Joshua's invasion of the Promised Land.

One of the first things they look for in a tell is pottery. It has been called the "alphabet of archaeology." Why?

- God orders wars,
- God takes Israel's side,
- God destroys Israel's enemies.

Only with the passage of time does this primitive portrait of God undergo dramatic modification by the prophets.

Finally, Joshua attacks other cities, secures the land, and divides it among the twelve Israelite tribes.

A college teacher said to her class, "Faith is less likely to proceed from miracles than miracles from faith." Explain her point. Give an example.

2. The Book of Joshua is listed as a "historical book" in most Bibles. But it is not historical in a modern sense. First, its battle stories are simplified and the time between them is telescoped. This is typical of oral communication.

But there is a second reason for simplifying and telescoping. The editor of Joshua wanted to make sure we didn't miss the point of the book: God, not Joshua's armies, is responsible for the takeover of the Promised Land.

a. Why would simplifying and telescoping be typical in oral communication?
b. How would simplifying and telescoping tend to stress the point of the book?

3. The Israelites of Joshua's time had no idea of an afterlife in which people were rewarded and punished. They assumed God rewarded and punished in *this* life and regarded themselves to be God's instrument to punish evil people.

Explain where and how we find this idea reflected in the Book of Joshua.

4. The God of the Book of Joshua is a "national God" who orders battles and takes sides. It required centuries for Israel to appreciate these words of Saint Augustine:

*It is easier to say what God is not than to say what God is. . . . Nothing we know is like God. If we could conceive of God, we would conceive of something other than God.*

Explain the point of these quotes:
a. "When a savage ceases to believe in his wooden God, this does not mean that there is no God, but only that the true God is not made out of wood."
Leo Tolstoy
b. "The atheist staring from his attic window is often nearer to God than the believer caught up in his own false image of God."   Martin Buber

5. Read Joshua 9 ("The Deception"). It is a truly entertaining story.
a. What phrase in the story indicates that it was handed on orally for a long time?
b. How does the story illustrate Israel's respect for the spoken word?

Pottery allows archaeologists to date the layers of a tell with high accuracy. Its design and shape puts it in a definite period of history.

*Into the Land*

Briefly describe:
a. the Jordan crossing.
b. the fall of Jericho.
c. the ban.
d. Israel's view of God in the Book of Joshua.
e. the book's "main point."
f. in what sense the book is/isn't historical.

2. Evaluate the theory that an earthquake explains the "miracles" of the Jordan and Jericho.

3. What is a tell? Why is pottery valuable?

# 33 Era of the Judges

**W**hat happens when a leader dies without a successor? This happened to the Israelites when Joshua died. Without a leader, they floundered, drifted from the covenant, and turned to false gods.

When this happened, God corrected them by letting their enemies defeat them. Then the Israelites returned to their senses, repented, and came back to God.

We find this pattern repeating itself over and over in the Book of Judges. We might compare it to a play in four acts: (1) Israel sins, (2) God corrects, (3) Israel repents, (4) God forgives.

Here is an example to help illustrate the pattern followed in Judges:

ACT 1  *The people of Israel sinned against the LORD. . . .*

ACT 2  *So the Lord let them be conquered by Jabin, a Canaanite king [of Hazor]. . . .*

ACT 3  *Then the people of Israel cried out to the LORD. . . .*

ACT 4  *Deborah . . . was serving as a judge for the Israelites. . . . She sent for Barak. . . . Deborah said to Barak, "Go! The LORD . . . has given you victory. . . ." So Barak went. . . . That day God gave the Israelites victory over Jabin.*
Judges 4:1–4, 6, 14, 23

The name *Deborah* introduces us to charismatic leaders called judges. They are not black-robed figures who sit in courtrooms and try cases.

Rather, they are gifted natural leaders who surface from time to time

**T**he stone slab shown here was discovered during the excavation of a Canaanite temple at Hazor.

The hands are raised to the Canaanite moon god, Ba'al Hammon.

Deuteronomy 4:19 warns the people of Israel about worshiping the moon, sun, or stars.

to defend Israel, uphold her honor, and lead the people back to God.

Not all the judges are saintly people. They are products of their time. God uses them in spite of their sins. Among the other judges are Gideon, Jephthah, and Samson.   Judges 6–8, 11, 13–16

The role of judges, therefore, is to provide some degree of leadership from the death of Joshua to the Era of the Kings. The Era of the Judges extends roughly from 1240 B.C. to 1040 B.C.

*A*ctor Johnny Depp told *Rolling Stones* that he broke into places, stole, and did drugs. He said, "Eventually, you see where it's headed and you get out."

Ballerina Gelsey Kirkland took cocaine and was anorexic and bulimic. She saw where she was headed, got out, returned to the stage, and danced to rave reviews in *Romeo and Juliet.* She now teaches ballet.

Actor James Dean was given a ticket for speeding two hours before the accident that snuffed out his young life.

Which of these celebrities mirror the Israelites in the Book of Joshua? Why? What is your theory about why some people see where they are headed and get out, while others do not?

2. Explain the point of these quotes and how they relate to the above discussion.

a. "Of all human acts, repentance is most divine. The greatest of all faults is to be conscious of none."   Thomas Carlyle

b. "Through sin do we reach the light." Elbert Hubbard (slightly adapted)

c. "If necessity is the mother of invention, discontent is the father of progress."   David Rockefeller

3. Read or listen to these excerpts from the story of the judge Jephthah: Judges 10:6–17; 11:1–6, 29–40.

a. How does the story illustrate the fourfold pattern of Judges?

b. List two striking features of the story.

c. What lesson might these features contain for your own personal life?

4. Take a few minutes to review your life, especially your ongoing relationship with God.

*R*epentance is not self-regarding, but God regarding. It is not self-loathing, but God loving.   Fulton J. Sheen

*Who repents sin is almost innocent.*
Seneca

a. To what extent does it mirror the "four-act" pattern found in Judges?

b. On a scale of 1 (we're strangers) to 10 (we're close friends), evaluate your present relationship with God.

5. Compose a prayer to God about your present relationship.

*Era of the Judges*

*I*dentify:
a. judges and their role
b. Deborah
c. Gideon
d. Samson

2. Briefly describe the fourfold pattern that the Israelites followed repeatedly in the Book of Judges.

3. Give the approximate dates of the Era of the Judges.

# 34 Era of the Kings

Shown here are four great personalities of the Bible. Each holds a symbol that is a clue to who the person is.

Identify the person and tell why the artist chose the symbol. For help see: Genesis 22:1–12, Numbers 21:6–9, 1 Samuel 7:7–13.

When the Era of the Judges ended, Israel was a shipload of passengers adrift on the sea without a captain. The Bible says of this leadership void, "Everyone did whatever they pleased." Judges 21:25

Into this leadership void stepped Samuel. (Two books of the Bible bear his name.) Samuel anointed Saul Israel's first king.

Saul started brilliantly, but success turned his head and he drifted from God. 1 Samuel 15:10–11 He ended up as one of the tragic figures of Old Testament history.

As the star of Saul fell from the sky, the star of a young shepherd named David rose above the horizon. 1 Samuel 16:1–13 David succeeded Saul as king. Under his inspired leadership, Israel began its "years of lightning."

David made Jerusalem his political and religious capital. He brought the Ark of the Covenant to Jerusalem and laid elaborate plans to build a beautiful temple to house it.

One night, however, the LORD told him that the honor of building the temple would fall to Solomon, his son, adding:

*"You will always have descendants, and I will make your kingdom last forever. Your dynasty will never end."* 2 Samuel 7:16

This covenant promise to David is one of the milestones in the Bible. It begins a series of promises known as the "messianic prophecies." They point to a messiah ("anointed one") from David's line, whose kingdom (God's) will never end.

And so as God's covenant changed Abraham and Israel, it now changes David. We may sum up the changes this way:

Abraham is given
- a new identity: *chosen person,* and
- a new destiny: *father of many.*

Israel is given
- a new identity: *chosen people,* and
- a new destiny: *priestly people.*

David is given
- a new identity: *chosen king,* and
- a new destiny: *Messiah's ancestor.*

David made Jerusalem his capital and arranged to build within it a magnificent temple.

Today, Jerusalem still retains a special biblical flavor about it.

David, a young shepherd, was skilled in the slingshot, the only defense shepherds had against large wild animals.
He skyrocketed to fame one day when the Philistine and Israelite armies were preparing to clash in battle.

A giant warrior, Goliath, stepped from the Philistine ranks and challenged any Israelite soldier to a prebattle duel.
When no soldier accepted, the young shepherd stepped forward.

Read 1 Samuel 17:41–18:16. Record the reaction of the following to David:

a. Goliath
b. the Philistine army
c. Jonathan
d. Saul's officers and men
e. women of Israel
f. Saul

2. A movie opens with a gunman stalking Hitler. He gets him in focus and pulls the trigger. "Click!" The gun is empty.

The gunman smiles and disappears.
The rest of the movie is a flashback explaining the story behind the episode.
The gunman never intended to kill Hitler.
He merely wanted to prove that he could.

Read 1 Samuel 26, in which David does something similar to Saul. Do you think David did it for a similar reason? Explain.

3. David spared Saul's life because he respected the office of kingship, even though he disliked Saul.

Explain the distinction David made between office and person.
Explain why this distinction is important to keep in mind, especially today.

4. David decided to build a temple when he realized he lived in a cedar house and the Ark of the Covenant (symbol of God) was kept in a tent.   2 Samuel 7:2
David believed that the temple should be the most beautiful structure in the city.

Some people today think the opposite.
They complain about beautiful churches, saying this money should go to the poor.
How do you feel about this, and why?

5. Saul's jealousy increased steadily.
One day David had to flee for his life.
Saul and a small army pursued him.
When Saul pitched camp for the night, David and a friend did something brave.

Read 1 Samuel 26 and record:
a. what they did and
b. what David's action says about him. 🖎

*Era of the Kings*

What crisis threatened Israel at the end of the Era of the Judges?

2. Identify:
a. Samuel
b. Saul
c. David
d. Solomon
e. messianic prophecies
f. Jerusalem

3. List and briefly explain the new identities and destinies that God gave Abraham, Israel, and David through covenants.

73

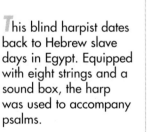

> The
> Book of Psalms
> is more a
> school of prayer
> than a book
> of prayer.

# 35 Israel's Soul Book

**D**avid is credited with authoring the Book of Psalms. Actually, he probably wrote only a few of its 150 psalms. Ancients commonly credited authorship to a person who inaugurated or promoted an important literary project.

The Book of Psalms was Israel's prayer book and hymnbook.

As its *prayer book,* it gives us a glimpse into Israel's soul. We see how the people prayed to God in times of doubt, sorrow, and joy.

As its *hymnbook,* it gives us a glimpse into Israel's heart. We see how the people worshiped God, especially in two settings.

**T**his blind harpist dates back to Hebrew slave days in Egypt. Equipped with eight strings and a sound box, the harp was used to accompany psalms.

The *first setting* was around the campfire, where the people gathered when the work of the day was finished.

A musician began by strumming a musical instrument; and the people— especially the children— began clapping, dancing, and singing. The words of the song would go something like this:

*Listen [to the marvelous things]. . .*
*our ancestors told us.*
*We will not keep them from*
*our children; we will tell [them]. . .*
*about the LORD's power and*
*his great deeds.*   Psalm 78:1, 3–4

The *second setting* in which the Book of Psalms played a key role was in the Temple worship, especially on Jewish holy days.

Use of the psalms in Temple worship was elaborate and exciting. Temple worship included instrumental music, song, and dance. It involved a chorus, dancers, musicians, and the whole congregation.

Psalm 150 gives us an insight into how elaborate Temple worship was. The psalm takes only seconds to read but took, perhaps, an hour to perform.

To catch its spirit, imagine a director inviting each music group to praise the LORD in its unique way:

*Praise [the LORD] with trumpets.*
*Praise [the LORD] with harps and lyres.*
*Praise [the LORD] with drums and dancing.*
*Praise [the LORD] with harps and flutes.*
*Praise [the LORD] with cymbals. . . .*
*Praise [the LORD], all living creatures!*
                                    Psalm 150:3-6

*S*ome people see a similarity between ancient psalms and some modern songs. Display on a chalkboard or overhead the lyrics to a modern song, and explain in what sense it qualifies as a modern psalm and in what sense it does not.

2. Explain the point of each of these quotes, and tell why you agree/disagree with it.

a. "Give me the making of the songs of a nation, and I care not who makes its laws." Andrew Fletcher
b. "To sing is to pray twice." Author unknown
c. "Where words fail, music speaks." Hans Christian Andersen

3. Tradition divides psalms into praise, wisdom, royal, lament, thanksgiving psalms.

❧ *Praise* psalms concern God's glory and frequently begin "Praise the Lord."
❧ *Wisdom* psalms concern human conduct and often begin "Happy are those."
❧ *Royal* psalms concern the king, who is a symbol of the coming Messiah.
❧ *Lament* psalms are "songs of woe" about a bad situation: "I am like a lonely bird on a housetop."
❧ *Thanksgiving* psalms express thanks.

Copy the following psalm excerpts: 30:11–12, 32:1–2, 38:9–11, 45:1–3, 103:1–2. List the psalm type each excerpt is and the words that give the clue to the type.

4. Psalm 1 begins: "Happy are those who reject the advice of evil people, who do not follow the example of sinners."

Using these lines as your model, compose your own modern psalm. Use a magazine picture to illustrate it. Here is an example:

*Happy are those*
*who choose not to copy their homework,*
*who do not cheat.*
*They are like athletes who stay in shape.*

*Copiers aren't like that at all.*
*They are not prepared*
*when the time of testing comes.*

*Those who do their own homework*
*have nothing to fear.*
*Copiers have everything to fear.*

If you need a start on your psalm, here are two suggestions:

a. *Happy are those*
*who don't resort to ridiculing others,*
*who do not make fun of them.*
b. *Happy are those who don't*
*pretend to be more than they really are,*
*who don't brag about themselves.* ❧

*G*od sent
*His singers upon earth*
*With songs*
*of sadness and mirth,*
*That they might touch*
*the hearts of men*
*And bring them back*
*to heaven again.*
Henry Wordsworth Longfellow

*Israel's Soul Book*

**W**ho is credited with authoring the Book of Psalms, and why?

2. Explain:
a. How the Book of Psalms gives us a glimpse into Israel's soul.
b. How it gives us a glimpse into Israel's heart.
c. Two settings in which Israel used the psalms to worship.
d. Five types into which tradition divides the psalms, describing each briefly.

# 36 Israel's Wisdom Books

**S**olomon became king
after his father, David, died.
Shrewd in politics and finance,
he made Israel strong and wealthy.
But power and prosperity took their toll
on Solomon. His early idealism
gave way to decadence.    1 Kings 8, 11

Because Solomon was gifted
with great wisdom by God, he is credited
with authoring three wisdom books:

- Proverbs,
- Song of Songs,
- Ecclesiastes.

**S**ome entries in the
Book of Proverbs were
designed to prod
people into meditating
on everyday "mysteries":

*an eagle flying in the
sky, a snake moving
on a rock, a ship finding
its way over the sea,
and a man and a
woman falling in love.*

Proverbs 30:19

First, consider the Book of Proverbs.
Every nation has its proverbs.
Cervantes describes a proverb as
"a short sentence based on long experience."
Lord Russell describes it as
"the wisdom of many and the wit of one."
The purpose of Israel's Book of Proverbs
is to teach the young, especially,
"how to live intelligently and
how to be honest, just, and fair."    Proverbs 1:3
For example, one proverb reads:

*If you refuse to listen to the cry
of the poor, your own cry for help
will not be heard.*    Proverbs 21:13

Second, consider the Song of Songs.
It takes the form of a love poem.
A sample excerpt from it reads:

*Come then, my love;
my darling, come with me.*

*The winter is over . . .
the flowers are in bloom.
This is the time for singing;
the song of doves is heard. . . .
Figs are beginning to ripen. . . .
Come then, my love;
my darling, come with me.*
Song of Songs 2:10–13

Some scholars speculate that the poem
was used as part of a marriage rite.
The groom's love for his bride
symbolizes God's love for Israel.

Thus the poem has two levels of meaning.
On the surface,
it describes the love of two people.
At a deeper level,
it describes God's love for Israel.

The Book of Ecclesiastes
is a different kind of "wisdom literature."
We will discuss it later.

$E$very nation has its own book or list of favorite proverbs. Explain the point of the following proverbs of the following nations:

RUSSIA   *Pray to God but continue to row to the shore.*

CHINA   *Fool me once, shame on you; fool me twice, shame on me.*

ITALY   *The same fire that burns the straw, purifies the gold.*

GREECE   *When the fox cannot reach the grapes, he says they are sour.*

SPAIN   *Who loses the right moment loses all.*

U.S.   *Whoever is his own doctor has a fool for a patient.*

2. *Poor Richard's Almanac* by Benjamin Franklin is an example of early American wisdom literature. Explain the point of each of these proverbs from the Almanac.

a. "Fish and visitors stink after three days."
b. "We are taxed twice as much by our idleness, three times as much by our pride, and four times as much by our folly."
c. "Who is good at making excuses is seldom good for anything else."
d. "If we could have half our wishes, we would double our trouble."
e. "A plowman on his knees is higher than a gentleman on his legs."

3. Israel's Book of Proverbs is a collection of short, easy-to-remember sayings about everything from helping the poor to staying sober. Many entries in the book are brief and poetic in form; others are longer and prose in form. Here is an example of each:

*When you give to the poor, it is like lending to the LORD, and the LORD will pay you back.*   Proverbs 19:17

*Don't let wine tempt you, even though it is rich red, and it sparkles. . . . The next morning you will feel as if you had been bitten by a poisonous snake.*

This limestone tablet was found at Gezer in Palestine and dates to the time of Solomon.

It contains a "ditty" for teaching children the seasons of the year and the activity proper to each: planting, hoeing, harvesting, and feasting.

*Weird sights will appear before your eyes, and you will not be able to think or speak clearly. You will feel as if you were out on the ocean, seasick, swinging high up in the rigging of a tossing ship. "I must have been hit," you will say . . . "but I don't remember it. . . . I need another drink."*   Proverbs 23:31–35

a. Why do/don't you think this advice about drinking is effective teaching?
b. How a scale of 1 (not very) to 10 (very), how serious a problem is drinking among your friends? Explain.

*Israel's 9 Wisdom Books*

$W$hat was good about Solomon? Tragic?

2. List three books credited to Solomon. Why him?

3. List the purpose of the Book of Proverbs.

4. List the two levels of meaning of the Song of Songs.

# CHAPTER EIGHT

# Division

## 37 Two Nations

*The ancient city of Dan leaped into the headlines in the 1980s when this clay image of a masked musician was unearthed there.*

*The city was named after Dan, one of Jacob's (Israel's) twelve sons, forerunners of the twelve tribes.*

*The famous judge Samson was from Dan.*
Judges 13:2

**N**ative Americans in South Dakota were once forced to live in dire poverty.
The reservation had no employment, and the nearest public transportation was thirty miles away.
People wanted to work but couldn't.

Tragic situations like this explain why people sometimes turn to violence to try to right the wrongs of injustice.
This happened in Israel after Solomon died and his son, Rehoboam, took the throne.

Solomon had taxed the people heavily in money and manpower to support his building projects.
Thus, when Rehoboam became king, the ten northern tribes, led by Jeroboam, banded together to change this.     1 Kings 12:1–24
But their pleas fell on deaf ears.

And so in 922 B.C., the twelve tribes split into two rival nations:

- Israel in the north and
- Judah in the south.

To keep people in the north from going south to worship at the Temple in Jerusalem, the North set up religious centers at Bethel and Dan.
This planted the seeds of religious disunity and idolatry.

The seeds germinated and sprouted when, years later, Ahab became Israel's king.
He married a pagan princess, Jezebel, who openly promoted the cult of the pagan storm god, Baal.

Because Baal was supposed to be in charge of the fertility of flocks and fields, he appealed to Israelite farmers—especially when Yahweh seemed to ignore their prayers in times of drought.

Baal ministers exploited the situation, telling Israelite shepherds and farmers:
"Yahweh is a desert god, not a farm god."
The result was tragic, fueling the flames of

- religious disunity and
- religious idolatry.

Into this critical situation stepped a group of spiritual giants called *prophets*.
With their appearance a new era dawned in the history of God's people.

The people in the north petitioned King Rehoboam to treat them more considerately than did his father, Solomon. Rehoboam told them he would give them his answer in three days.

NARRATOR    *King Rehoboam consulted the older men who had served as his father Solomon's advisors.*
KING        *What answer do you advise me to give these people?*
OLD MEN     *If you want to serve this people well, give a favorable answer. . . .*
NARRATOR    *But he ignored the advice . . . and went instead to the young men who had grown up with him. . . .*
YOUNG MEN   *Tell them, "My father . . . beat you with whips; I'll flog you with bullwhips!"*

1 Kings 12:6–8, 11

Why do you think the men in each group advised King Rehoboam as they did? How do you decide when you should take a gentle approach with someone and when you should take a harsh approach?

2.  Record and share the point of each of these quotes. Give an example to illustrate each, if you can.

a.  "Who accepts evil without protesting against it is really cooperating with it."
Dr. Martin Luther King Jr.

b.  "Apathy is the glove into which evil slips its hand."    Bodie Thoene

c.  "When the eagles are silent, the parrots begin to jabber."    Winston Churchill

d.  "When Jesus came to Birmingham, they simply passed him by. They never hurt a hair of Him, they only let Him die."    G. A. Studderd-Kennedy

3.  To what extent do you agree/disagree with the following?

a.  "If you are suffering from someone's injustice, forgive them from the heart, lest there be two bad people."    Saint Augustine

b.  "Fight all error, but do it with good humor, patience, kindness, and love. Harshness will damage your own soul and spoil the best cause."    John of Kanty

The Israelites met Yahweh in the desert. Now many of them lived as farmers.

Some Israelites were seduced by pagan neighbors to exchange their "desert" God for a "farm" god.

Such a "farm" god was Baal, shown here, ready to hurl a lightning bolt.

*Two Nations*

What happened to Israel after Solomon died? Why?

2. What action planted what seeds of religious chaos under what king? When and how did the seeds sprout?

3. Why did some Israelites find the cult of Baal appealing, and with what tragic results?

4. What new era dawned as a result of this?

79

Jehu pillar.

# 38 Era of the Prophets

ourists entering Palestine by the seaport of northern Haifa can see Mount Carmel from the ship. At Mount Carmel, the prophet Elijah and 450 prophets of Baal held a contest to determine the "true God."

The Baal prophets began the contest by placing a young bull on an altar. Then they prayed to Baal, the "storm god," to strike the bull with lightning and set it ablaze. When nothing happened, Elijah taunted them.

ELIJAH    *Pray louder! . . .*
          *Maybe Baal's sleeping. . . .*
NARRATOR  *The prophets prayed louder*
          *and cut themselves . . .*
          *but no answer came. . . .*
          *[Then Elijah took over.]*
ELIJAH    *O LORD, the God of Abraham,*
          *Isaac, and Jacob, [answer] . . .*
          *so that this people will know*
          *that you, the LORD, are God. . . .*
NARRATOR  *The LORD sent fire down, and*
          *it burned up the sacrifice. . . .*

*The people . . . exclaimed,*
*"The LORD is God."*
1 Kings 18:27–29, 36–39

This story of Elijah and other stories like it   (1 Kings 17, 19) serve an important twofold purpose. They teach the people that they should

- worship Yahweh alone and
- have faith in Yahweh, as Elijah did.

Elijah's colorful ministry ends abruptly when he is taken to heaven in a "chariot of fire."   2 Kings 2:11

Symbolic or not, this striking story of Elijah's exit from earth gives rise to the belief that he will return.
Malachi 4:5, Matthew 17:12

Elisha continues Elijah's ministry. Like his teacher Elijah, he is credited with great wonders, even raising the dead.   2 Kings 4:32–37

And, like Elijah, Elisha is remembered and eulogized by none other than Jesus.   Luke 4:25–27

Elisha ended the kingly line from which Ahab came. He anointed as king a military leader named Jehu.
2 Kings 9:1–13

During Jehu's reign, mighty Assyria began bullying weaker nations. Jehu survived by paying "protection money."

The Jehu pillar belonged to the Assyrian king, Shalmaneser III. This blowup of the pillar's second panel identifies Jehu and says, "I received from him silver, gold, and javelins."

Many Jews put an "Elijah chair" at the seder (Passover) table. They pray this will be the year Elijah returns to proclaim the coming of the promised Messiah.    Malachi 4:1–5

What did Jesus say about the return of the prophet Elijah?    Matthew 17:12–13

2.  God sent Elijah to a poor widow and her son to ask for food during a great famine. They gave him all they had, thinking they would now "starve to death."    1 Kings 17:12
The two containers from which the food was taken miraculously refilled and remained full throughout the famine. Jesus recalled this story.    Luke 4:25

"When Elijah heard it, he covered his face with his cloak."    1 Kings 19:12–13

What clue might this story hold for you in your search for God today? Explain.

4.  Some people report having had an "Elijah experience" of their own. That is, they have sensed God's presence in a powerful way. A young person from Boston writes:

*I was at World Youth Day '93 in Denver. There were hundreds of thousands of kids from all over the world. All of a sudden during one of the Masses I was caught up with the presence of God. I wanted to hug everybody,*

The modern harbor and city of Haifa as seen from Mount Carmel, where Elijah challenged 450 prophets of Baal.

a.  What point does this story make?
b.  How does Jesus make the same point in Matthew 6:24–34?
c.  How relevant is the point for today?

3.  One day Elijah was told that God was going to pass by. Suddenly a great wind began to blow, but God was not in it. Then there was a violent earthquake, but God was not in it. Next there was a great fire, but God was not in it either. Finally there was a "soft whisper."

*even people I didn't know. It was eerie. I was not the only one who felt it. Many around me did also. The effect of this experience was to deepen our faith in God and in our ability to change our world.*

a.  What suggests that the young person's experience was, indeed, of God?
b.  Record and share the closest thing to an "Elijah experience" you have ever had.

*Era of the Prophets*

What twofold purpose did the Elijah stories serve for the Israelites?

2. What gave rise to the belief that Elijah would return? Who succeeded him?

3. How are Elisha and Jehu linked? What data on Jehu have archaeologists found?

# 39 Writing Prophets

Decades ago an eastern city lady asked a remote western motel clerk about the weather for the next day. The clerk had no information. A Native American guide, sitting nearby, heard her and said, "Rain! Much rain!"

The next day, it poured rain. Awed by the guide's accuracy, the lady inquired again the next day. "Blue sky! Cold air!" he replied. Again, the prediction was right on target. The next night, the lady consulted him again. "Dunno!" he replied. "Radio broke!"

The prophets were much like that guide. Their message was not their own either. It came from a higher source: they were spokespersons for God.

The prophets fall into two groups: *nonwriting* prophets, like Elijah, and *writing* prophets, like Isaiah. They are called "writing" because their prophecies are recorded in books bearing their name.

The *writing* prophets may be divided further into two groups: *major* (long writings) and *minor* (short writings).

The four major prophets are:

Isaiah Ezekiel
Jeremiah Daniel

The twelve minor prophets are:

Hosea Jonah Zephaniah
Joel Micah Haggai
Amos Nahum Zechariah
Obadiah Habakkuk Malachi

Included among the *prophetic* writings are two other books (linked to Jeremiah): Lamentations and Baruch.

Prophets and kings are often like the two rails of a train track.

One of the greatest "writing prophets" was Isaiah. This "page" from the Isaiah scroll found at Qumran bears this beautiful prophecy:

*The Sovereign LORD is coming. . . . He will . . . gather the lambs together and carry them in his arms.*
Isaiah 40:10–11

Stitching forms the pages into a scroll. Scribal corrections appear in margins and above the seventh line.

Where you find one, you find the other. This is because one of the prophet's job was to council and confront the king. But more importantly, the prophet's job was to council and confront the people.

And so we may describe the prophets this way: *As spokespersons for God, they counciled and confronted both the people and the king.*

The prophet Nathan is an example. He counciled David about God's promise, and he confronted David about sin.
2 Samuel 7:1–17, 12:1–12

Theologian Martin Buber describes the role of the prophet in these challenging terms: "The prophet is appointed to oppose the king, and even more: history."

Record and share how the authors of the following statements oppose history in a way reminiscent of how the ancient prophets opposed it.

a. "Those who make peaceful revolution impossible will make violent revolution inevitable." John F. Kennedy

b. "Ours is a world of nuclear giants and ethical infants." General Omar Bradley

c. "Some of us die by shrapnel. Some of us go down in flames; but most of us perish inch by inch, playing at little games." Anonymous

2. Philip Yancey was on a plane, reading *Night* by Elie Wiesel. In an article titled "Fire," Yancey writes:

*It's . . . about Elie's teenage years . . . in German concentration camps. . . .*

*The Jews of Elie's town first heard of the German holocaust through a man named Moche [who had lived in the town, was taken by the Nazis, machine-gunned, and left for dead].*

*Over and over Moche told the story. The Jews refused to believe him. . . .*

*"They take me for a madman," Moche would whisper, and tears like drops of wax would flow from his eyes.*

a. How does Moche's experience illustrate what Jesus said about prophets? Luke 4:24
b. Can you give examples of people who might be classified as "modern prophets"? Explain.

3. Someone described a prophet as someone who comforts the disturbed and disturbs the comfortable.

Explain how each of these quotes "comforts" or "disturbs," and try to illustrate your response with an example.

a. "Problems are big when people aren't." Anonymous
b. "You can't turn back the clock, but you can wind it up again." Bonnie Pruden → comfort
c. "Whenever you find yourself on the side of the majority, it is time to pause and reflect." Mark Twain

One of the jobs of the Holy Father is to "council and confront" the modern world.

It is a thankless job. At times he must feel the way Supreme Court Justice Earl Warren did when he said:

*Everything I did in my life that was worthwhile I caught hell for.*

## Writing Prophets

How do writing and nonwriting prophets differ?

2. Into what two groups do writing prophets divide? Name four prophets who fall into each group.

3. How can the prophets be described? Illustrate your response, using Nathan as an example.

*Give*
someone a fish,
and you feed
them for a day.

*Teach* them
to fish, and
you feed them
for a lifetime.

*Author unknown*

# 40  Israel Says "No"

A cartoon shows a bearded old man holding a sign that reads: "Repent! The end is near!" Behind him, rockets crisscross the sky. The caption reads: "Have you noticed? No one's laughing at him anymore!"

The prophets were often treated like that. At first, they were ridiculed when they confronted the people. Take Amos.

with the approval of King Jeroboam, drives him out of town.  Amos 7:12

And so Amos returns to Judah, but not before making the same point that the New Testament writer John would repeat centuries later:

*If we say we love God,*
*but hate others, we are liars.*  1 John 4:20

This wall mural from an Assyrian palace at Numrud shows soldiers of King Tiglath Pileser III (745–727 B.C.).

He harassed Israel and Judah and is mentioned several times in the Bible.  2 Kings 15:29

His successor, Shalmaneser V, began the attack that led to Israel's destruction.

2 Kings 18:9

God called Amos from his farm in Judah to be the first writing prophet to Israel. He was sent to the temple of Bethel to confront the northern kingdom about social injustices toward the poor. Pointing a bony finger at the rich and powerful, God says through Amos:

*"They trample down the weak . . .*
*and push the poor out of the way."*  Amos 2:7

And to those who sing loudly to God on the Sabbath but oppress God's poor the rest of the week, Amos shouts:

*[God says,] "Stop your noisy songs. . . .*
*Instead, let justice flow like a stream,*
*and righteousness like a river."*  Amos 5:23–24

The reaction to Amos is predictable. The priest of Bethel, Amaziah,

Amos is followed by the prophet Hosea. Little is known of him except that he weds an unfaithful wife but stays faithful to her—much as God wedded and stayed faithful to Israel.
Hosea 3:1–5

Hosea takes a more tender approach. He reminds the Israelites of what God has done for them in the past. Speaking for Yahweh, Hosea says:

*"When Israel was a child, I . . .*
*called him out of Egypt as my son.*
*But the more I called to him,*
*the more he turned away from me."*
Hosea 11:1–2

But neither Amos's bluntness nor Hosea's tenderness moved Israel.

A growing number of young people are working as volunteers on summer work projects for the needy.

List reasons why such projects are attracting both young and old.

Someone has pointed out that if we shrink the population of the world to 1,000 people, 60 of these people will control half the world's wealth and will own 15 times more possessions than the world's average person.

Of the remaining 940 people, 60 will eventually die from starvation. Half of their infants will die at a young age, and the other half will be crippled mentally or physically.

a. As one of the 60 people who control half of the world's wealth, how do you, an American teenager, feel about this situation in the world?
b. As a starving teenager in a third-world country, how might you feel?
c. What solution would you suggest?

2. "Give someone a fish, and you feed them for a day. Teach someone to fish, and you feed them for a lifetime."

a. How does this principle apply to helping the poor?
b. What about those poor who are too old, sick, uneducated, or crippled "to fish"?

3. How do the following statements relate to the situation in our world?

a. "Lisa," coaxed her mother, "thousands of starving children would give anything for the food you won't eat." Lisa replied, "Name one!"
b. Pat shouted, "Lord, how can you stand by and let such injustice exist? Why don't you do something?"
c. Under "Dog" in the yellow pages of the Evanston, Illinois, phone directory, an ad for a "Pet Motel" listed these services for pets of vacationing owners:

*Deluxe and imperial suites*
*FM music in every room*
*Senior citizens' care plan*
*Daily cookie breaks*
*Beauty salon*

4. A fourth-century Christian bishop named Basil told wealthy Christians:

*The food you have stored away*
*belongs to the hungry;*
*the unworn garment in your closet*
*belongs to the naked;*
*the gold you have hidden away*
*belongs to the poor.*

a. What would be the reaction if a bishop said that today?
b. Why this reaction?
c. What action might be taken to create a more positive reaction?

## Israel Says "No"

Who was Amos, and why was he an unlikely choice for the job God called him to do?

2. List two abuses Amos addressed. Explain how the leaders of Israel responded to his message.

3. Who followed Amos, and how did his approach differ from that of Amos? What was the response to his message?

# 41 Day without Brightness

I n *The Power and the Glory,* Graham Greene describes a priest living in Mexico during a time of violent religious persecution. Fear of being caught takes its toll on him. He becomes an alcoholic, is caught, and is sentenced to death.

The morning of his execution, he wakes with an empty brandy flask in his hand. He tries to pray but is too confused.

Then he notices his shadow on the wall. As he stares at it, tears roll down his cheeks. He is not afraid to die but is disappointed because he has to go to God empty-handed. At that moment he'd have given anything to be able to live his life over again.

Such a moment came for Israel. In spite of Elijah and Elisha, in spite of Amos and Hosea, the North did not change. And so a day of judgment dawned, a day without brightness.     Amos 5:20

In 722 B.C. the Assyrians conquered Israel. What the prophets had tried to avoid now came to pass.

Most of the people were led away and never heard from again. Historians dub them Israel's "lost tribes."

A few inhabitants, however, were permitted to remain behind. But their fate fell under a shadow. They intermarried with the Assyrians who occupied the land.

This drew down upon them the contempt of Jews in the south. The Samaritans, as they were called, were never again respected by most Jews.

Shock waves rumbled through Judah when the Jews heard of Israel's fate. But they did not panic, thinking smugly that no such tragedy could befall them. They said, "Aren't we of David's line? Aren't we the heirs to God's promise of an unending kingdom?"

Ironically, Judah soon drifted into the same evils that befell Israel:

- idolatry,
- religious formalism (going through the motions of worship), and
- exploitation of the poor.

This destroyed palace, in Samaria, dates back to the time when the Assyrians conquered the North.

The palace belonged to King Ahab and his pagan wife, Jezebel.

Hundreds of pieces of carved ivory, found at the site, witness to the beauty it once had.
1 Kings 22:39

c. How do Luke 10:25–37, Luke 17:11–19, and John 4:1–10, 39–41 reflect Jesus' attitude toward Samaritans?

2. A woman dreamed an angel took her to church. The organ played, but no music was heard. The choir sang, but no song sounded. The people moved their lips, but no words came out. The woman asked, "Why don't I hear anything?"

a. What do you think the angel said?

b. How is the woman's dream related to the situation that developed in Judah?

c. How can you keep this from happening in your own life?

3. Andrew Young, former ambassador to the United Nations and mayor of Atlanta, and close friend of Martin Luther King Jr., says King "never closed a speech without quoting either Jeremiah, Isaiah, or Amos." Read or listen to Amos 2:6–3:2 ("Injustice"), and explain why King often quoted Amos.

4. A student council held an "insight day." It began with a film on the third world. Next, students broke into groups of six and picked colored tickets from a box. Then three dollars (lunch money) was collected from each student. Finally, a discussion of the film followed. The discussion was sluggish.

At noon the students went for lunch. Red tickets got a pizza, fries, and a shake. White tickets got a candy bar and a small soft drink. Blue ones got a small bag of popcorn. After the meal the groups resumed discussion. It was almost wild.

a. Take three minutes to record your reaction to the "insight day."

b. Explain how an "insight day" might shed light on the situation in Judah after the fall of Israel—and how it relates to the situation in our world. ✎

Assyrians were master strategists. After conquering a nation, they took thousands of the citizens, deported them, and replaced them with foreigners.

This happened when they defeated Israel. Those left behind (Samaritans) slowly intermarried with the foreigners. This infuriated Jews in the south (Judah), who saw this as compromising Jewish faith and identity.

a. Why do you think the Assyrians uprooted and deported conquered peoples?

b. How do John 8:48 and Luke 9:51–56 reflect Jewish-Samaritan hostility?

This Samaritan high priest stands on Mount Gerizim, a Samaritan holy place.

The number of Samaritans has gone from an estimated 40,000 in Jesus' day to a few hundred today.

*Day without Brightness*

What happened in Israel in 722 B.C.? What fate befell most of the people?

2. What fate eventually befell the remainder of the people, and why wasn't Judah moved by all this?

3. List the three evils into which Judah, ironically, drifted in the years ahead.

# 42 Day of Warning

No prophet is more admired by Jews and by Christians than Isaiah. Called "prophet of God's holiness," he began his ministry with this vision:

ISAIAH  *I saw the Lord.*
*He was sitting on his throne,*
*high and exalted. . . .*
*Flaming creatures . . .*
*were calling . . . "Holy, holy,*
*holy! The LORD Almighty*
*is holy! . . ."*
LORD  *Whom shall I send? . . .*
ISAIAH  *I answered, "I will go!*
*Send me!" So he told me*
*to go.*  Isaiah 6:1–3, 8–9

Isaiah confronts the people of Judah and the king of Judah, saying:

*"You are stained red with sin,*
*but I will wash you as clean as snow. . . .*
*If you defy me, you are doomed to die.*
*I, the LORD, have spoken."*  Isaiah 1:18, 20

One of Isaiah's warnings to Judah takes the form of a parable expressed in song:

*Listen while I sing . . .*
*of my friend and his vineyard: . . .*
*He dug the soil and cleared it of stones. . . .*
*He waited for the grapes to ripen,*
*but every grape was sour.*
*So now my friend says . . .*
*"Is there anything I failed to do for it?*
*Then why did it produce sour grapes*
*and not the good grapes I expected?"*
Isaiah 5:1–4

Isaiah's warnings go unheeded.
Soon it becomes clear that
only a shock will get Judah to reform.
It comes in 701 B.C.

Assyrian armies under Sennecherib
march in battle array toward Jerusalem.
When they reach the city walls,

they pitch camp and prepare for battle in the morning.

As night falls and the moon comes out, King Hezekiah and all of Jerusalem crouch terrified inside the city walls. The next morning, when the sun rises, they can hardly believe their eyes. The powerful Assyrians are pulling out.

After they depart, Jewish patrols go out and find the Assyrian campsite littered with bodies: a plague had struck it.
2 Kings 19:35, Sirach 48:21

You would think this narrow escape would shock Judah into reform! But it doesn't.

This baked-clay prism was unearthed in the ancient palace of Sennacherib in Nineveh. A section of it reads:

*As for Hezekiah . . .*
*I laid siege to forty-six of his strong cities . . .*
*and captured them. . . .*
*I shut him up in Jerusalem . . . like a bird in a cage.*

Sennacherib omits telling why he didn't attack Jerusalem.

Reread Isaiah's vision, quoted on the previous page.
a. What keeps you from volunteering to serve God as readily as Isaiah did?
b. Compose a brief prayer that deals with your desire to serve God. (You may wish to use the prayer below as a guide in composing your own prayer.)

*Lord,*
*I know that you created me and*
*gave me my talents for a purpose.*
*I know that Jesus died for me*
*and called me to complete his work.*
*I know that the Holy Spirit*
*wants to help me carry out the work*
*for which I was created and called.*
*But something keeps blocking me.*
*What is it, Lord?*
*Why can't I say yes to you*
*as generously as the prophet Isaiah did?*

2. Explain the following statements, using the prayer above to illustrate your explanation.
a. "In prayer it is better to have a heart without words than words without a heart."  John Bunyan
b. "The value of persistent prayer is not that God will hear us, but that we will finally hear God."  William McGill

3. Reread Isaiah's "parable in song," quoted on the previous page.

a. Who is Isaiah's "friend"?
b. Who does the vineyard stand for?
c. What point is Isaiah making?
d. Why do you think he used a "parable" to make his point, and why did he "sing" it rather than say it?

4. Team up with a friend and prepare a rap-style rendition of this poem excerpt:

(1) *The Assyrian came down*
      *like a wolf on the fold,*
(2) *And his cohorts were gleaming*
      *in purple and gold. . . .*
(3) *Like the leaves of the forest*
      *when Summer is green,*

(4) *That host with their banners*
      *at sunset was seen;*
(5) *Like the leaves of the forest*
      *when Autumn hath blown,*
(6) *That host on the morrow*
      *lay withered and strown. . . .*
(7) *And the might of the Gentile,*
      *unsmote by the sword,*
(8) *Hath melted like snow*
      *in the glance of the Lord!*
                              Lord Byron

a. What event is the poet describing?
b. What *progressive* imagery does the poet use? Why do you think he chose it?
c. Explain the imagery and meaning of lines 6–8. ❧

*Lord, I know you created me and gave me my talents for a purpose.*

*I want to say yes, as Isaiah did, but something keeps blocking me.*

*What is it, Lord? Why do I find it so hard?*

*Day of Warning*

Describe Isaiah's call to be a prophet.

2. The armies of what nation and what king threatened to destroy Judah? How was Judah saved, and what effect did this have on changing Judah?

3. Describe the archaeological find that confirms biblical accounts of Hezekiah and Sennacherib.

# 43 Day of Decline

**T**ragedy struck when Hezekiah died and his son Manesseh became king. Manesseh ruled over thirty years and was one of Judah's worst kings. The Second Book of Kings says of him, "He practiced . . . magic and consulted fortunetellers." 2 Kings 21:6

No tears were shed, therefore, when Manesseh died and the throne passed to Josiah, an eight-year-old boy. Josiah grew up to be remarkable.

Early on, he remodeled the Temple. During the work, an old book of the law was found. When it was read to Josiah, he tore his clothes "in dismay" and ordered an immediate reform. 2 Kings 22:11

An array of prophets backed him: Nahum, Zephaniah, Habakkuk, Jeremiah.

Of these, Jeremiah was the giant. Like Josiah, he was called at a young age. At first he protested that he was too young. But God had other plans. Jeremiah said:

*The LORD reached out, touched my lips, and said to me . . . "I give you authority over nations."* Jeremiah 1:9–10

Reform begins and proceeds well. Then tragedy strikes: Josiah is killed, leaving Jeremiah standing alone, like a solitary tree in a great desert. He stations himself outside the Temple and warns the people:

*"Change the way you are living. . . . Be fair in your treatment of one another. . . . Stop worshiping other gods."* Jeremiah 7:5–6

Pointing his finger in the direction of Babylon, Jeremiah warns, "Your enemies are coming." Jeremiah 13:20 But the people ignore his words. Finally the time comes when Jeremiah must pass sentence on those he loves.

Enraged, the people throw him into a pit. Brutal treatment like this wounds Jeremiah's sensitive nature. Once again, he protests to God:

*LORD, you have deceived me. . . . You have overpowered me. . . . I am ridiculed and scorned all the time because I proclaim your message. . . . Curse the day I was born! Forget the day my mother gave me birth! Curse the man who made my father glad by bringing him the news, "It's a boy! You have a son!"* Jeremiah 20:7–8, 14–15

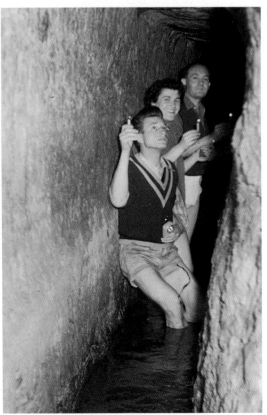

**H**ezekiah built this secret tunnel hastily to provide water for Jerusalem just before armies surrounded it.

Two teams worked toward each other. Clearly visible is a slight jog where the two teams met.

The tunnel is mentioned in three places in the Bible. 2 Kings 20:20, 2 Chronicles 32:30, Sirach 48:17

*I*magine this fantasy situation.
You are a TV reporter
in Jeremiah's time.
After Jeremiah is thrown into the pit,
you are assigned to interview him.
You arrive at the pit and overhear him
complaining out loud to God.     Jeremiah 20:7–18
You get it all on tape.

Use the exclusive tape as a point
of departure for your interview with him.
(Team up with someone and reenact
the interview for your group.)

2.  Prayer is not only speaking to God
from your heart, but also listening to God
speak to your heart.
Take Jeremiah's complaint to God.
Reread it (previous page) and compose
a response that God might make
to Jeremiah. Here is an example:

*Jeremiah, what makes you think*
*I don't see and understand*
*the brutal treatment you are receiving*
*on my account from your neighbors?*
*I look with love on you*
*sitting in the darkness of your pit.*
*I do understand how you feel*
*in the depths of your wounded heart.*

*But think of it this way, Jeremiah.*
*The trials you are suffering in this life*
*are as a drop of water*
*compared to the ocean of joy*
*I have stored up for you in eternal life.*
*Trust me, Jeremiah! Trust me!*

3.  Explain the following statements,
and illustrate each with an example.

a.  "God will help us when we ask for help,
but in a way that will make us
more mature, more real,
not in a way that will diminish us."
Madeleine L'Engle

b.  "Christians need ten minutes of prayer
each day, except when they are very busy.
Then they need twenty minutes."     Anonymous

*T*he prophet Jeremiah.

4.  Both King Josiah and Jeremiah
were called by God at a young age.
Interview a priest, a deacon, or a religious
brother or sister.
Here are some questions to ask:

a.  How old were you when God called you?

b.  What form did your call take?

c.  To what extent did you resist the call,
at first, as did Jeremiah?

d.  How happy are you with your call now?

## Day of Decline

*W*ho succeeded
Hezekiah, and what
kind of king was he?

2. What "spiritual giant"
worked with Josiah to
reform Judah, and how
was the "call" of each
somewhat similar?

3. What happened to
Josiah? Concerning what
nation did Jeremiah
warn the people, and
what response did they
make to him?

4. Describe a legacy of
Hezekiah that is referred
to in three places in the
Bible and that still exists.

91

# CHAPTER NINE

# Rebirth
## 44 Day of Drums

The "Eternal Light" (*Ner Tamid*) burns continuously before the curtain of the ark in this synagogue in Cologne.

The two tablets above and behind the light contain symbols of the Ten Commandments.

Jeremiah's warnings became bitter reality. In 597 B.C. Babylonian armies attacked and conquered Judah, carrying off key officials and skilled workers.   2 Kings 24:16

But the city and the Temple survived. The king and the people viewed their "miraculous" survival as a sign of God's special protection.

But Jeremiah took a different view. He saw the Babylonian attack as a warning from God. If Judah ignored the warning, terrible things would happen.   Jeremiah 22:5

Judah did ignore the warning and terrible things did happen. The Babylonians returned in 587 B.C. and destroyed Jerusalem.   Jeremiah 39:1–10

The survivors divide into three groups, each meeting with a different fate.

First, there were the very poor, who were left behind to grub for themselves.

Second, there were the escapees, who fled to Egypt, Jeremiah among them.

Third, there were soldiers and the citizens who were skilled in arts and crafts. They were led off as prisoners to Babylon.

And so the focus of the Israelite history shifted from Jerusalem to Babylon.

Some of the exiled prisoners drifted from their faith and adopted Babylonian beliefs and ways. Others remained faithful to God and, in many cases, underwent a deep conversion.

The faithful remnant began to meet each Sabbath to pray and study God's word. Out of these meetings emerged two unexpected blessings.

The first was a new worship place, eventually called the synagogue. Primarily a *place of instruction,* it differed from the Temple, which was primarily a *place of sacrifice.*

The second blessing that emerged
was the written word of God.
Scribes begin to record God's word,
previously passed on mostly orally.

And so as faithful Jews reached up to God,
God reached down to them.

Teenaged Joni Eareckson
was totally paralyzed by a diving
accident. She became a skeleton
covered with jaundiced skin.
Joni turned to the Book of Lamentations,
a description of destroyed Jerusalem.
The words seemed directed right to her:

*All night long she cries. . . .*
(Joni: "Oh, God, how true.")
*He sent fire from above . . .*
*and left me in constant pain. . . .*
(Joni: "Diving accident, paralysis.")
*He has left my flesh open and raw. . . .*
(Joni: "Bedsores.")
*I am a prisoner with no hope of escape.*
(Joni: "In bed for a year.")  1:2, 13; 3:4, 7

Joni wrote:

*My studies in the Scriptures*
*began in earnest now. I'd visualize*
*Jesus . . . saying . . . "I am with you. . . ."*
*I discovered that the Lord Jesus Christ*
*could indeed empathize*
*with my situation. On the cross . . .*
*He was immobilized, helpless."*  Joni

Today, Joni remains totally paralyzed;
but she is an acclaimed artist (holds the pen
in her teeth), has starred in a movie,
and is a much sought-after speaker
for youth groups.

Record and share:
a.  What two things in Joni's story
struck you most and why?
b.  What determines whether tragedy
makes a person better or bitter?
c.  In what sense is Joni an example
of the words of Helen Keller
(who was blind, deaf, and dumb):
"I thank God for my handicaps,
for through them, I have found myself,
my work, and my God"?

2.  Sometimes people don't see the value
of a handicap or tragedy until much later.
For example, Golda Meir, former Israeli
Prime Minister, wrote:

*I was never a beauty. There was a time*
*when I was sorry about that. . . .*
*It was only much later*
*that I realized that not being beautiful*
*was a blessing in disguise.*

Why do you think Golda considered
not being beautiful a blessing in disguise?

3.  Explain these quotes and the valuable
message each holds for our world.

a.  "It is the crushed grape
that yields the wine."  Anonymous
b.  "How else but through the broken heart
May the Lord Christ enter in."  Oscar Wilde
c.  "From the standpoint of eternity,
my body is only a flicker
in the time span of forever."  Joni Eareckson

Clay tablets, known
as the "Babylonian
Chronicles," describe
Babylonia's conquest
of both Assyria and
Judah.

This tablet confirms
2 Kings 24:10–17.
It reads:

*In the seventh year in*
*the month of Kislev, the*
*king of Babylon . . .*
*besieged Judah. . . .*
*He captured the city and*
*seized the king. . . . He*
*appointed there a king*
*of his own choice.*

## Day of Drums

When and by whom
was Jerusalem eventually
destroyed?

2. Describe the archaeo-
logical find that confirms
the biblical account of
Jerusalem's fall to the
Babylonians.

3. In what two ways did
the Jews react to their
exile to Babylon?

4. List and explain two
unexpected blessings
that resulted from the
exile and captivity in
Babylon.

# 45 Years of Waiting

Today, the ancient city of Babylon
has been excavated
from a sandy grave.
For the first time in centuries,
the sun shines on its ancient ruins.

Through the city's famous Isthar Gate,
proud Babylonian armies
used to parade their trophies of war.
Through this same gate walked Ezekiel,
the first of two great prophets to Judah
during their Babylonian exile.

Ezekiel was brought up in Jerusalem, and
it was there that he received God's call.
His ministry divides into two periods:

🕯 before the fall of Jerusalem and
🕯 after the fall.

*Before* the fall, Ezekiel was a *disturber,*
warning the people about
their complacency over their situation.

*After* the fall, he was the *comforter,*
prophesying the eventual restoration
of the king (Ezekiel 34:23), the people
(Ezekiel 37:14), and the Temple (Ezekiel 43:5–7).

New Testament writers see Jesus
fulfilling these three prophecies.

| king | Jesus is the Good Shepherd, the *eternal king* (John 10:11); |
|------|----------------------------------------------------------------|
| nation | Jesus sends the Holy Spirit, who forms his followers into a *holy people* (Acts 2); |
| Temple | Jesus' followers become God's new *living temple* (1 Corinthians 3:16–17). |

But the New Testament and Jesus
were far beyond the horizon in the future.
All that faithful Jews could do now
was wait in darkness by a candle of hope.

The second prophet of the Babylonian exile
was "Second Isaiah,"
so-called by many because he prophesied
in the spirit of "great" Isaiah.

Eventually his writings were appended
to those of "great" Isaiah
and called the Book of Consolation (40–55).

The following passage echoes its spirit:

*Those who trust in the LORD for help*
*will find their strength renewed.*
*They will rise on wings like eagles;*
*they will run and not get weary;*
*they will walk and not grow weak.*
Isaiah 40:31

German archaeologists discovered and excavated ancient Babylon in the early 1900s.

This painting by Eckhard Unger is a faithful reproduction of the grandeur that the city once had.

*Those who trust in the LORD for help will find their strength renewed. They will rise on wings like eagles.* Isaiah 40:31

ob Richards was a U.S. Olympic pole-vault champion. One of his favorite memories concerns Olympic vaulter Fred Hanson, who was worried because he was behind.

Fred paused momentarily to read a letter in which his dad reminded him that he could mount up with wings of eagles. Inspired by the word of "Second Isaiah" and trusting in his dad's counsel, Fred soared across the next crossbar.

a. Why was the image that Fred's dad chose especially appropriate?
b. Why do/don't you think it is right to take a Scripture passage originally intended for Jewish exiles in Babylon and apply it to your own life?
c. Record and share a time when God used another person, like Fred's dad, to channel grace to you.

2. Ezekiel foretold the restoration of three pillars of Judaism that were eclipsed during their exile. Identify and explain:
a. The images (below) that Second Isaiah used to foretell them.
b. How the New Testament portrays Jesus to be their final and intended fulfillment.

§ *[The LORD] set me down in a valley covered with bones. . . . He said,*

*"Prophesy to the bones. . . ." While I was speaking . . . the bones began to join . . . [and] came to life.* Ezekiel 37:1, 4, 7, 10
§ *"I will rescue my sheep and . . . give them a king . . . and he will take care of them."* Ezekiel 34:22–23
§ *I saw . . . the dazzling light of the presence of the God of Israel. . . . [It entered] the Temple [and filled it] with the glory of the LORD.* Ezekiel 43:2, 5

3. The Babylonians were star watchers. They dated events by recording on clay tablets the position of stellar bodies when the event took place. As *Time* magazine notes, however:

*Tracing astronomical motions backward for more than 2,000 years is forbiddingly time consuming. . . . [Enter the computer.] Scholars . . . are already hard at work . . . [and may soon] check the dates of such events as Nebuchadnezzar's deportation of the Jews . . . perhaps, to the very hour, Babylonian Standard Time.*

Some people wonder if, perhaps, it was a part of God's plan and mercy to have science support Scripture at a time when some people needed support of this nature.
What are your thoughts about this? §

## Years of Waiting

List: (a) the two eras into which the ministry of Ezekiel divides and Ezekiel's role in each; (b) the three pillars of Judaism that Ezekiel prophesied would be restored.

2. Explain in whom and how the New Testament saw these prophecies reach ultimate fulfillment.

3. Explain: (a) why "Second Isaiah" is so called; (b) what chapters in "Great Isaiah" contain his prophecies and what name we give them.

# 46 Day of Joy

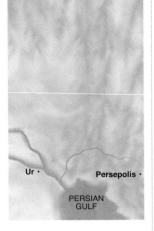

*As a deer longs for a stream . . .
so I long for you, O God. . . .
When can I go and
worship in your presence?*   Psalm 42:1–2

For five decades Jews sat in darkness,
hoping and praying.
Then one day, rumors began to circulate.
The armies of King Cyrus of Persia
were marching across the land,
piling up victory after victory.

"Is it possible!" Jews wondered.
Would the armies of Cyrus invade Babylon?
Would Cyrus be the instrument
by which Yahweh would reassert
a saving presence in Israel's history?
As the rumors mounted,
so did the hopes of the excited Jews.

Finally, Second Isaiah sang out:

*"Comfort my people," says our God. . . .
"They have suffered long enough. . . ."
To Cyrus the LORD says . . .
"I appoint you to help my servant Israel,
the people that I have chosen. . . .
I will send victory . . . like rain;*

*the earth . . . will blossom with freedom
and justice."*   Isaiah 40:1–2; 45:1, 4, 8

And so after long years of waiting,
God is about to act decisively,
just as God did for the Jews' ancestors
long ago in Egypt.
The exiled Jews will cross the desert
in a "new exodus."
Second Isaiah sings joyfully:

*"Prepare . . . a road for the LORD!
Clear the way in the desert for our God!"*
                                        Isaiah 40:3

Finally, the great day dawns.
Cyrus invades Babylon, and the city falls.
An ancient record, the "Cyrus Cylinder,"
says he entered the city "as a friend."

Immediately Cyrus issues a proclamation
giving Jews permission to go home
to rebuild their city and Temple.   Ezra 1:3
It is too fantastic to be true.
The joy of the Jews reaches fever pitch.
The psalmist recalls the great moment:

*It was like a dream! How we laughed,
how we sang for joy!*   Psalm 126:1–2

This clay cylinder,
unearthed in Babylon
by archaeologists, says:

*I am Cyrus. . . .
I entered Babylon as
a friend. . . . My
numerous troops walked
around in peace.*

The cylinder agrees
with 2 Chronicles
36:22–23 and
Ezra 1:1–4.

Cyrus II died in 530 B.C. His son, Cambyses II, took over and eventually committed suicide.

Darius, an army general, seized the throne, reigned about 35 years, and built a magnificent palace, called Persepolis ("Persian city").

Two centuries later the armies of Alexander the Great wrecked and looted Persepolis (shown).

Before his conversion in A.D. 389, Saint Augustine wanted to change. Using Isaiah's imagery ("Fill every valley; level every mountain"  Isaiah 40:4), he resolved to fill every "valley of lust" and level every "mountain of pride." But he couldn't. Then one day a voice said, "Take and read."

Augustine opened the Bible and read: "Take up the weapons of the Lord Jesus Christ, and stop paying attention to your sinful nature."  Romans 13:14 Augustine said, "Suddenly my heart became flooded with light . . . leaving me with a profound peace."

Record and share:
a.  Why God sometimes seems to let us struggle before answering our prayers.
b.  Why Augustine's "Bible roulette" is not recommended for the average person.

2.  "Second Isaiah" is famous, especially, for his "Suffering Servant" prophecies (42:1–7, 49:1–6, 50:4–9, 52:13–53:12).  One reads:

*"Because of our sins he was wounded. . . .*
*We are healed*
*by the punishment he suffered. . . .*
*Like a lamb about to be slaughtered . . .*
*he never said a word. . . .*
*He was put to death*
*for the sins of our people."*  Isaiah 53:5, 7–8

For a remarkable reference to this prophecy, read Acts 8:26–38. Roughly, how many years before this reference was this prophecy spoken?

3.  On Easter, two discouraged disciples were returning home to Emmaus. Jesus intercepted them, but they didn't recognize him. They told him about the death of the one they thought might be the promised Messiah.

*Jesus said to them . . . "Was it not*
*necessary for the Messiah to suffer*
*these things and then to enter his glory?"*
*And Jesus explained to them what was*
*said about himself in all the Scriptures,*
*beginning with the books of Moses*
*and the writings of all the prophets.*
Luke 24:25–27

Where does Jesus identify himself in this passage as the "Suffering Servant"? Why do you think many people— including the disciples—failed, at first, to connect Jesus to these prophecies?

4.  Jesus speaks of the "books of Moses" and "all the prophets." Team up with another person and list as many books of Moses and prophets as you can.  ✎

*Day of Joy*

How long did the Jews "sit in darkness" in faraway Babylon?

2. What prophet foretold what leader would free the Jews from exile?

3. Identify:
a. Cyrus II
b. Cyrus Cylinder
c. "Suffering Servant Prophecies"
d. Darius
e. Alexander the Great

# 47 Call to Refocus

A Starlifter plane, filled with American POWs from Vietnam, touched down on a runway in 1973. A huge crowd surged forward, chanting, "Welcome home, welcome home!"

No such welcome greeted the Jewish POWs returning from Babylon to the destroyed city of Jerusalem. Years of rebuilding—under leaders like Ezra and Nehemiah and prophets like Haggai and Zechariah—lay ahead.

Top priority was given to the Temple. Neighbors offered to help the returnees, but their offer was rejected.    Ezra 4:2–3 Angered, the neighbors turned hostile and hindered rather than helped the Jews. Nehemiah 4:16–18

Further problems developed when farm crops failed the first year back.

Enthusiasm died, and the returnees turned inward, pitying themselves. They forgot they were chosen to be God's instruments for re-creating the world that sin had "de-created."

Into this critical situation stepped two writing prophets: Malachi and Jonah.

The Book of Jonah, especially, stands out. Literalists interpret it *factually.* Contextualists interpret it *symbolically,* as a kind of book-length parable.

In the book God orders Jonah to go to Nineveh to preach repentance to the people. Jonah can't believe his ears. The Ninevites are enemies and sinners. They should be smashed, not saved. So he flees from God on a ship to Spain.

The prophet Nahum called Nineveh, capital of Assyria, a "murderous city" that inflicts "endless cruelty." Nahum 3:1, 19 Small wonder Jonah didn't want to preach there.

Assyria's military might was legendary. The archers (shown) were a key part of the Assyrian army.

This wall mural was found at Nineveh in the 209-room palace of Sargon II, who is mentioned in Isaiah 20:1.

A storm washes Jonah overboard.
He is swallowed by a great fish
and spit up on a deserted beach.
God appears again and repeats the order:
"Preach to the Ninevites!"
Jonah obeys and the Ninevites repent.

The point of the Jonah story is clear.
It confronts the people of Judah
and reminds them that God is concerned
about all people, not just Jews.

The Book of Jonah
reveals a new universalism concerning
God's saving activity in human history.
God is not a "tribal" God for Judah alone,
but the "universal" God for all peoples.

One day a young woman
became terribly frustrated
during a Bible-sharing session.
She said passionately and bluntly:

*I don't blame Jonah for not wanting
to preach to the Ninevites. There are
people today I'd like to see smashed.
They don't deserve to be saved.*

a. How common is such a feeling,
and what might be said about it?
b. Toward whom do you sometimes
feel hostile and why?
c. How do you deal with hostile feelings?

2. One day Jesus was preaching.
Some people were looking for a sign
from Jesus, but he refused, saying:
*"[As] the prophet Jonah was a sign
for the people of Nineveh,
so the Son of Man will be a sign
for the people of this day. . . .
On the Judgment Day the people
of Nineveh will stand up and accuse you,
because they turned from their sins
when they heard Jonah preach."*   Luke 11:30, 32

Record and share:
a. In what sense Jonah was "a sign."
b. In what sense Jesus "will be a sign."
c. Why Jesus' reference to Jonah
is/isn't proof, necessarily,
that the Book of Jonah should be
interpreted literally rather than
as a book-length parable.

3. Psychologist Abram Maslow says
most people flee responsibility.
He demonstrated his point one day
by asking students at Brandeis University,
"Which of you hopes to become
a governor or a senator?"

The students responded by joking around,
until he asked, "If not you, who?"

a. Why do/don't you agree with Maslow?
b. What is one responsibility you are,
perhaps, fleeing right now? Explain.

4. The French communist publication
*Paix et Liberte* wrote:

*The Gospel is a more powerful weapon
than our Marxist view of the world,
but we shall conquer you in the end.
How can anyone believe in
the all-surpassing value of this Gospel
if you do not practice it, if you do not
spread it, if you sacrifice neither your time
nor your money for this purpose?*

Write a brief letter to the editor of *Paix et
Liberte*, giving your answer to the question
posed in the last sentence. 

The students responded
by joking around,
until he asked,
"If not you, who?"

**Call to Refocus**

Name: (a) two leaders
and two prophets who
guided the returnees
upon their return from
exile; (b) two problems
that blocked the
rebuilding process.

2. Retell the Jonah story,
and explain the "new
universalism" it reveals
concerning God's saving
activity.

> There is
> no such thing
> ~~as darkness;~~
> only
> a failure
> to see.
> ❖
> Malcolm Muggeridge

# 48 Shattered Dreams

*These are the words
of the Philosopher, David's son,
who was king in Jerusalem. . . .
I have seen everything done in this
world, and I tell you it is all useless.
It is like chasing the wind.*

Ecclesiastes 1:1, 14

This is a good description
of the way that Jews felt in the years
following their rebuilding
of Jerusalem and the Temple.

The Book of Ecclesiastes
mirrors the heart of a Jew
waiting for further revelation from God.
For example, Jews had little or no idea
of reward or punishment in an afterlife.
They assumed
God rewards and punishes in *this* life.
But this doesn't always happen. Why?

This is the question
that is raised in the Book of Job.
(*Job* is pronounced "jobe," as in "robe.")

Judah's "isolation"
years ended when
Alexander swept across
the East and became
the ruler of the largest
empire ever headed by
one man.

The Roman historian
Plutarch says that
Alexander's joy of
victory was sobered
when he read on the
tomb of Cyrus II:

*O man, whoever you are
and wherever you came
from—for I know you
will come—I am Cyrus,
son of Cambyses, who
gave the Persians their
empire. Do not begrudge
me this tiny plot of earth
where my body rests.*

Alexander died in his
30s. Three of his
generals split his vast
empire.

They were invaded and controlled
by one powerful nation after another.
This pawnlike existence jolted
their pride and shattered their dreams
of someday being a glorious nation
with a powerful king of their own.

Their discouragement and confusion
is reflected in the Book of Ecclesiastes.
It contains none of the sure-footed
wisdom of the Book of Proverbs.
And that's where its value lies.

Job was a super-good man
who spent his life doing good.
Job was a saint if ever there was one.
Then tragedy after tragedy befell him.
Job could not understand why.

After he had probed all possibilities
without an answer, a storm blew up.
Out of the storm came God's voice,
asking Job a series of questions:

*"Was it you, Job,
who made horses so strong? . . .*

*Does a hawk*
*learn from you how to fly? . . .*
*Does an eagle wait for your command*
*to build its nest?"*   Job 39:19, 26–27

Gradually the point dawns on Job:
His own wisdom falls so short of God's
that it's folly to challenge God's fairness
or God's wisdom.
To challenge them is to be a fool,
not a person of faith.

*A*n angel was carrying a torch and
a bucket. Someone asked the angel,
"What do you plan to do with those?"
The angel said, "I'm going to burn the
mansions of heaven and put out the fires
of hell. Then we'll find out who loves God."

a. What is the angel's point?
b. What percentage of your motivation
for obeying God is bound up with fear
of punishment? Hope of reward? Love of God?

2. Job asked, "If God rewards and punishes
in this life, why do good people suffer?"
One answer Jews gave was that these people
suffer because of the sins of their parents.
a. In what sense is this true? Not true?
b. Can you guess the other two reasons
Jews gave for why good people suffer?

3. Ezekiel 18:19–20 teaches that God
does not punish us for the sins of parents,
but many Jews still clung to this error.
For example, someone asked Jesus
about a blind man: "Whose sin
caused him to be born blind . . .
his own or his parents'?"   John 9:2
Research and explain Jesus' answer.

4. A teacher gave this assignment to students:
"Describe a time you suffered
and what helped you most to bear it."
One student wrote:

*I suffered greatly after my mom's death.*
*I missed her terribly. Then one day I saw*
*a card under the glass top of my dresser.*

*I noticed it the first time a few weeks*
*before mom went to the hospital,*
*but I didn't bother to read it then.*
*Now I pulled it out and read:*

*"For ev'ry pain we must bear,*
*For ev'ry burden, ev'ry care,*
*There's a reason.*

*"For ev'ry grief that bows the head,*
*For ev'ry teardrop that is shed,*
*There's a reason.*

*"For ev'ry hurt, for ev'ry plight,*
*For ev'ry lonely, pain-racked night,*
*There's a reason.*

*"But if we trust God, as we should,*
*It will turn out for our good;*
*God knows the reason."*   Author unknown

*As I sat there, I could picture my mom,*
*before going to the hospital, coming into*
*my room and slipping the card under*
*the glass, as if to say to me, "It's all right,*
*Jon. Don't worry; he knows the reason."*

a. Explain the student's point and how it
illustrates the point of the Book of Job.
b. Record and share a time you suffered
and what helped you most to bear it.

*[*The LORD *said,] Was it*
*you, Job, who made*
*horses so strong . . . ?*

*They eagerly paw the*
*ground in the valley; they*
*rush into battle with all*
*their strength.*
      Job 39:19, 21

### Shattered Dreams

**E**xplain how
Ecclesiastes mirrors the
mind of Judah collec-
tively and of Jews
individually.

2. What question does
the Book of Job raise;
what answer does it
give?

3. Who was Alexander,
and what happened to
his vast empire when he
died at an early age?

# 49 Call to Trust

*S*uddenly a human hand . . . began writing on the plaster wall . . . where the light . . . was shining most brightly. . . . The king . . . was so frightened that his knees began to shake.   Daniel 5:5–6

The king's "wizards and astrologers" could not read the writing. So the king sent for Daniel, who deciphered it.

*P*eople who play God are dangerous. Such a person was Antiochus IV, a Syrian king, whose armies marched into Judah around 175 B.C. A lover of Greek culture, he believed that he was an incarnation of the Greek god Zeus and called himself *Epiphanes* ("god-manifest"). Jews dubbed him *Epimanes* ("madman").

Antiochus tried to effect a cultural revolution in Judah by ordering Jews to adopt Greek ways. Result? A religious persecution ensued that shook Judah to its roots. The Book of Daniel addresses this horrendous situation. It divides into two major sections:

 stories about a young Jew, Daniel, who remained faithful to God during the Babylonian exile, and
 visions that God gave to Daniel.

Typical of the *stories* is the one about Daniel's appointment to serve in the palace of the king. He was bright and was liked by the king— to the envy of Babylonian officials.

Aware that Daniel prayed to God daily, the officials connived to have the king pass a law forbidding prayer of this kind. Of course, Daniel ignored the law. Result? He was thrown to the lions, which refused to touch him. The point of the story is to assure persecuted Jews that God would save them, as God saved Daniel in the lions' den.

Typical of Daniel's *visions* is one in which he sees

*One like a son of man coming,*
*on the clouds of heaven;*
*When he reached the Ancient One*
*and was presented before him,*

*He received dominion, glory,*
*and kingship. . . .*
*His dominion is . . . everlasting . . . ,*
*his kingdom shall not be destroyed.*
Daniel 7:13–14 (NAB)

Jesus cited this vision of Daniel
and applied it to himself, saying:

*"You will all see the Son of Man*
*seated at the right side of the Almighty*
*and coming with the clouds of heaven!"*
Mark 14:62

The title "Son of Man" (used of Jesus
seventy times in the New Testament)
refers to Jesus' unique identity
as both "Son of God" and "Son of Man."

*D*aniel had the power to explain
dreams and writing. One day
writing appeared on a palace wall.
The king called Daniel, promising him gifts
if he would explain its meaning. Daniel said,
"Keep your gifts. . . . I will . . . tell you
what it means."  Daniel 5:17

A boy spent days decorating a classroom.
When he refused payment,
the teacher asked the boy's father
what gift he might give his son.
The father replied, "Give him the honor
of having done something out of love."

Record and share:
a. What important point the father made.
b. Why the reaction of the father and Daniel
is not more typical today.
c. A time when you chose love over money.

2. Stories like those of Daniel inspired Jews
to live nobly and stay faithful to God.
Three other stories that did this were
Tobit, Judith, and Esther.

For example, the Book of Esther tells
about a lovely Jewish girl raised in exile.
A Persian king, unaware of her origin,
made her queen. Haman, an evil leader,
tried to get the king to eliminate Jews
in his empire. Esther risked her own life
to oppose Haman and save her people.

Record and share:
a. Why stories have such great power
to motivate people to act nobly.
b. Two TV shows or movies that
had/have that power. Explain.
c. Two shows/movies that do the opposite.

3. The visions in the Book of Daniel are
filled with colorful, mysterious imagery.
This kind of writing style
is called *apocalyptic* writing.
The message is that God's action
in the present is nothing compared
to what God will do in the future.

It assures us that God's hand
is on the steering wheel of the universe.
It is a "call to trust."

Akin to apocalyptic writing
is *prophetic* writing.
It is also filled with colorful imagery,
but its message goes a step beyond
the apocalyptic message.

It assures us, also, that God's hand
is on the steering wheel of the universe.
But it also warns us to do our part and
says we will be judged on what we do.
It is a "call to responsibility."

a. Read Amos 5:11–24 and Daniel 7:9–18.
List the colorful images in each passage.
b. Explain which passage is a "call to trust"
and which is a "call to responsibility."

*T*he Book of Daniel is
a "call to trust" in God,
even when God seems
a million miles away.

*All I have seen teaches*
*me to trust the Creator*
*for all I have not seen.*
Ralph Waldo Emerson

*Call*
*to*
*Trust*

*W*hat book addresses
the situation created by
Antiochus? List and
describe the two major
sections into which it
divides.

2. What is the point of
the story of Daniel in the
lions' den?

3. What vision in the
Book of Daniel did Jesus
apply to himself?

4. Explain the difference
between apocalyptic
writing and prophetic
writing.

# 50  Unfinished Story

The persecution of the Jews reached a turning point in 168 B.C. Three brothers (Judas, Simon, and Jonathan Maccabeus, called Maccabees) organized a revolt against the Syrians.

Operating out of caves and ravines, the revolutionaries resisted heroically. Eventually Judas and Jonathan were killed, but Simon brought the revolt to a successful conclusion in 142 B.C.

was used to gain political goals. Finally, the clock struck midnight for the Hasmoneans. Roman armies under Pompey occupied Jerusalem in 63 B.C.

Hasmonean rule ended in 37 B.C., when the Romans crowned "Herod the Great" king of Judah. Herod catered to the Romans and used violence against Jews who opposed him.

Operating out of ravines and caves, like the one shown here, the young Jewish revolutionaries turned the tide against the Syrians.

When Simon died around 135 B.C., leadership passed to his son John. This began the Hasmonean Era. (Hasmonean is the name given to the descendants of the Maccabees.) Sadly, politics entered religion during this era: The office of high priest

*He murdered members of his own family—yet scrupulously observed Mosaic dietary laws and would eat no pork. This provoked his Roman master Augustus into jesting: "I would rather be Herod's pig than Herod's son."*

Howard LaFay, "The Years in Galilee"

Robert Coughlin
completes the portrait of Herod, saying:

*Herod was a brilliant, scheming,*
*ruthless, bloody man who reigned*
*from 40 to 4 B.C. . . . One of the few things*
*that recommended him to his subjects*
*was . . . that he began rebuilding the Temple*
*according to the grandiose plans of Solomon.*
*Who Was the Man Jesus?*

It was this man, with so many talents
and so many weaknesses,
who served as the bridge between
the Old Testament and the New Testament.

And so by their own admission,
the Hebrew Scriptures end "unfinished."
They end with faithful Jews,
especially "the poor,"
waiting and praying for the Messiah.

When the Old Testament period
came to a close, five groups
made up Judah: Pharisees,
Sadducees, Essenes, Zealots, and the poor.

*Pharisees* believed in the strict, external
observance of all religious laws, including
man-made traditions. They also believed
in angels, an afterlife, and a final judgment.

*Sadducees* were largely made up
of the wealthy class. Many chief priests
were of this group. They denied angels,
an afterlife, and a final judgment.   Acts 23:8

*Essenes* broke with conventional Judaism,
believing it was corrupt beyond repair
and that the end of the world was near.
They turned their backs on world problems,
and went into the desert
to prepare for the end.

*Zealots* were militant Jews.
They looked for a military messiah
who would make Judah a powerful nation.
They were more of a terrorist group
than a religious one.

*The poor* were the largest group.
They felt the Pharisees were too pious,
the Sadducees too political,
the Essenes too removed from life,
and the Zealots too militant.

They put all their hope in God and
God's promise of a messiah who
would rescue them from their plight.

Imagine you are a biblical talk show host.
Your guests are representatives
of the five groups that make up Judah.
a.  Have five volunteers prepare
for a discussion of their differences:
angels, afterlife, judgment, messiah.
b.  Have three volunteers pose
questions and evaluate how skillfully
the panelists represented each group.

2.  A fitting image of Judah at the end
of the Old Testament era is found
in *The Source* by James Michener.

*[Rabbi Asher saw an olive tree.]*
*Its interior was*
*rotted away, leaving an empty shell . . .*
*but somehow the remaining fragments*
*held contact with the roots,*
*and the old tree was still vital. . . .*
*Asher thought that it well summarized*
*the state of the Jewish people . . .*
*whose interior had rotted away,*
*but whose fragments still held their vital*
*connection with the roots of God. . . .*
*[Through these roots]*
*Jews could ascertain the will of God*
*and produce good fruit.*

Explain the link between the olive tree
and Judah.

After Julius Caesar was
assassinated in 44 B.C.,
his eighteen-year-old
adopted son, Octavian,
succeeded him.

He became Rome's first
emperor and took the
name Augustus Caesar.

During his reign, Jesus
would be born.   Luke 2:1

*Unfinished*
*Story*

Identify:
a.  Maccabees
b.  Hasmoneans
c.  Herod the Great
d.  Pharisees
e.  Sadducees
f.  Essenes
g.  Zealots
h.  The poor
i.  Julius Caesar
j.  Augustus Caesar

# IV
# World of Jesus

TIMELINE
*(Approximate Traditional Dates)*
*A.D. = After Christ*

| | |
|---|---|
| 1 | Jesus' birth |
| 30 | Jesus' preaching |
| 33 | Jesus' resurrection |

BIBLE *(Key Books)*

Matthew
Mark
Luke
John

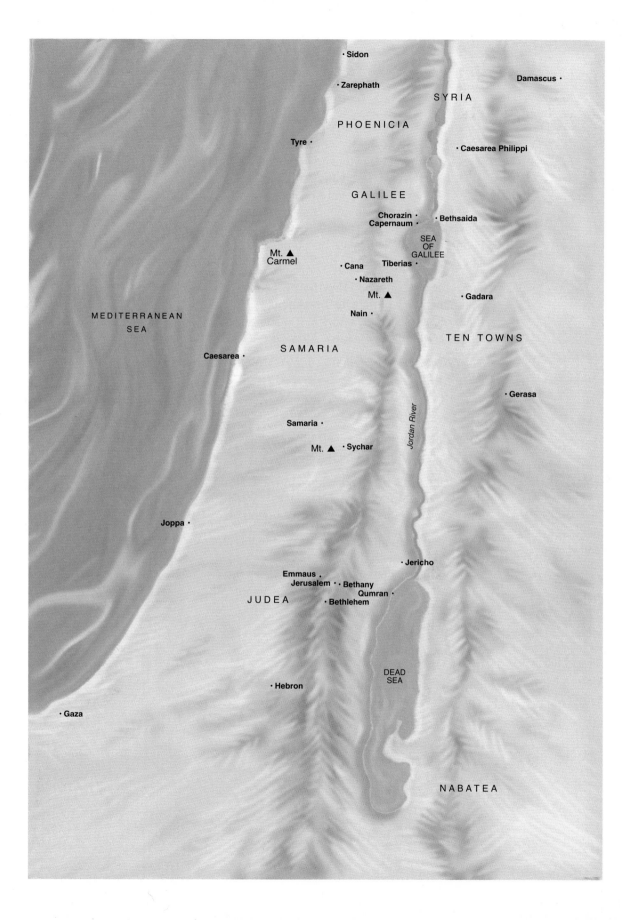

# CHAPTER TEN

# *Good News*

## *51 Gospels*

Nathaniel Hawthorne was dead. On his desk lay the outline of a story he never got a chance to write. It concerns an important person who is coming to a certain place. People excitedly anticipate his coming. They wait for him, but he never comes.

That story of Nathaniel Hawthorne is like the story of the Old Testament. It also centers around a person who is coming: the *promised Messiah.*

*The LORD says, "The time is coming when I will choose as king a . . . descendant of David . . . called 'The LORD Our Salvation.'"* Jeremiah 23:5–6

People plan for the promised Messiah. They wait for him, but he never comes.

It is against this biblical background that we put down the Old Testament and pick up a copy of the New Testament.

The Old Testament concerns the covenant that God made with the *Jewish people* through the mediation of *Moses.* The New Testament concerns the covenant that God made with *all people* through the mediation of *Jesus.*

The New Testament does not replace the Old Testament but fulfills it— much as adulthood fulfills childhood. The Old Testament is the foundation upon which the New Testament rests.

And just as the Old Testament divides into four categories of books (Torah, historical, prophetic, wisdom), so the New Testament divides similarly.

The four New Testament categories may be described as follows:

| | |
|---|---|
| Gospels | tell the "Good News" of the Messiah's coming; |
| Acts | tells how the "Good News" was preached to the world; |
| Letters | tell how the "Good News" was lived in the world; |
| Revelation | tells how the "Good News" is opposed by the world but will re-create it. |

This drawing of a stained-glass window shows Matthew riding piggyback on Isaiah.

The window is not the irreverent whim of a medieval artist. Rather, it dramatizes an important truth:

The New Testament does not replace the Old, but fulfills it, much as adulthood fulfills childhood.

Imagine a TV crew travels back into time to tape and computerize Jesus' life—minute by minute—from his birth to his ascension.

By keyboarding the name of the event, you can call it up on a screen.

Would you trade this "video version" for our "gospel version"?

he story "The Traveller" concerns a team of scientists who invent an energy screen for traveling backward into time.

Imagine such an screen exists and a TV crew travels back to gospel times, taping and computerizing Jesus' life from his birth to his ascension. By keyboarding the name of an event, you can call it up on a screen.

Imagine you could trade the old *gospel version* for this new *video version*. But there's a catch! If you make the trade, the world will lose the gospel version. In other words, future generations will no longer have it to read. Here is how two people responded:

LIZ　　*I'd keep the gospel version. The video would be 33 years long and in a language I wouldn't know.*

KEVIN　*I'd take the video version. You could see and hear everything that happened. Seeing is believing.*

a. What is your reaction to their replies?
b. Which version would you pick? Why?

2. The video version would be fantastic. But it would leave us with the same problem the disciples had. Many people observed what Jesus said and did, but they didn't understand it.

For example, a week before Jesus died, he rode into Jerusalem on a donkey. His disciples met him with palm branches and chants. But at the time they failed to understand they were fulfilling a prophecy.

*But when Jesus had been raised to glory, they remembered that the scripture said this about him and that they had done this for him.*　John 12:16

Similarly, if we had only a video version of Jesus' life, we might not understand it.

a. Why did the disciples understand later what they didn't understand at first?
b. Recall something from your life that you didn't understand at first and what helped you to understand it later.
c. How was your clarification different from the clarification that the disciples received?

*Gospels*

**E**xplain:
a. How Hawthorne's story is similar to the Old Testament story.
b. The relationship between the Old and the New Testaments.
c. Two ways the Old Testament covenant differs from the New.
d. The four categories of New Testament books.

# 52 Birth of Gospels

A TV commercial for a camera shows two students conversing. Someone snaps their picture and, instantly, a paper rolls from the camera. But it's totally blank; nothing is on it. Then the *light of the sun* floods it, and it turns into a beautiful picture.

Some events in Jesus' life were like that. At first they seemed blank, meaningless. But then the Holy Spirit came.

When the *light of the Holy Spirit*— who came on Pentecost—flooded them, they turned into beautiful pictures. Describing Pentecost, Luke says:

*All the believers
were gathered together in one place.*

*Suddenly . . . they saw what looked like
tongues of fire which spread out
and touched each person there.
They were all filled with the Holy Spirit.*
Acts 2:1–4

Jesus had foretold this event, saying:

*"I have much more to tell you, but now
it would be too much for you to bear.*

*"When, however, the Spirit comes,
who reveals the truth about God,
he will lead you into all the truth."*
John 16:12–13

And so the coming of the Holy Spirit clarifies the events of Jesus' life. Thus, in a real sense, the Gospel is born on Pentecost. The disciples' first reaction is not to sit down and *record* the Gospel. It is to go out and *preach* it.  Acts 2:5ff.

With a burning urgency, they carry the Good News of Jesus as far as Rome itself. The reason for their urgency is that they believe Jesus will return (Acts 1:11) after they have preached the Gospel to all nations (Matthew 24:14).

In their excitement, they think they can do this within their lifetime. When they see this is impossible, they arrange to have the Gospel recorded.

One reason for recording it before they died was to guard against having it distorted or changed by people. Peter writes:

*I shall soon put off this mortal body. . . .*
*I will do my best, then,*
*to provide a way for you*
*to remember these matters*
*at all times after my death.*    2 Peter 1:14–15

*A*rthur Butz, a university professor, wrote a book that denied that the Nazi holocaust actually happened. He said the claim that it did happen was "an orchestrated campaign" by Jewish special-interest groups.

Butz said Nazis who admitted taking part in it were "plea-bargaining" to get lighter sentences for war crimes. He blamed "high death rates" in Nazi camps on medical shortages.

a. Why could such a book be written, and why would people buy it and take it seriously?
b. How is this book related to TV shows that claim to have the inside story on just about everything that happens?

2. A situation similar to the one described above took place after Jesus' death and resurrection.

Read Jude 3–4 and 1 John 4:1–3. List *two ways* people began to distort the truth about Jesus and *one reason* the Letter from Jude gives for doing this.

3. Roger Price composed a book called *Droodles*. A droodle is a drawing that seems to be meaningless until it is given its proper title. Here is a droodle from Price's book.

a. Can you give the droodle a title that helps the drawing make good sense?
b. Explain how some of the events in Jesus' life were like droodles before the coming of the Holy Spirit.

4. Here is a droodle created by a Chicago high school student. Can you give it a meaningful title?

5. Draw two droodles and present them to the group to see if group members can give them a title that makes good sense.

A droodle is a drawing that seems meaningless until it is given its proper title.

Some events in Jesus' life were like droodles. They didn't make sense until the Spirit came and clarified them.

*Birth of Gospels*

**W**ho foretold Pentecost, and what did he say about it?

2. Why was the first reaction of the disciples to preach the Gospel, not to record it?

3. What was one reason why it was important for Peter to arrange to have the Gospel recorded before the apostles died?

# 53 Three Gospel Stages

*I*n the early days of space travel, rockets were boosted into orbit in three progressive stages. Each stage was vitally important.

We have something similar to this when it comes to the four Gospels.

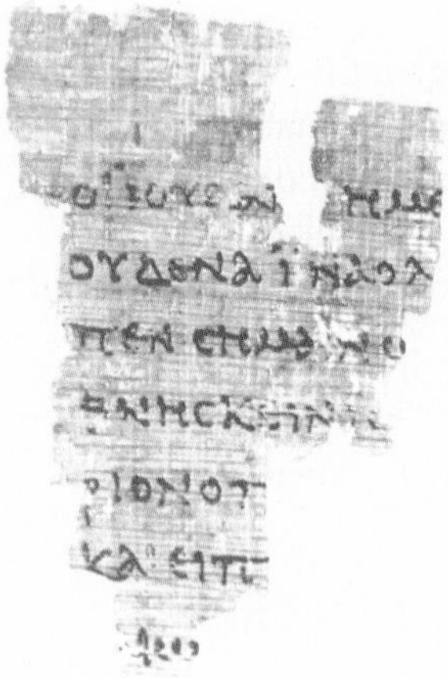

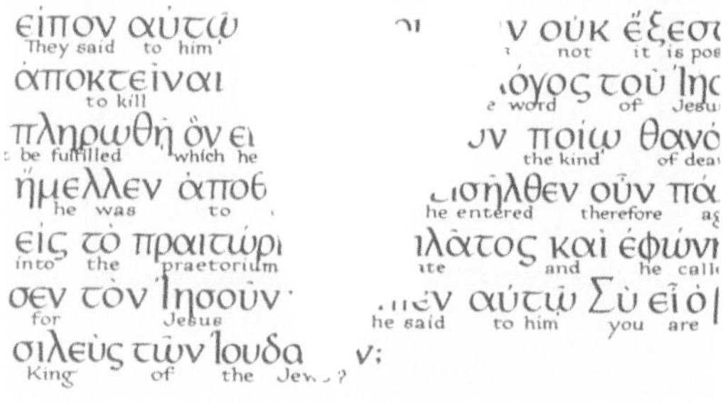

This fragment of John 18:31–33 dates from A.D. 130 and is the oldest-known copy of a Gospel manuscript.

The sketch shows how the fragment fitted into the original Greek manuscript.

The translation of the original Greek into English gives an idea of the flow and style of the Greek language.

ειπον αυτω
They said to him
αποκτειναι
to kill
πληρωθη ον ει
be fulfilled    which he
ημελλεν αποδ
he was    to
εις το πραιτωρι
into    the    praetorium
σεν τον Ιησουν·
for    Jesus
σιλευς των Ιουδα
King    of    the Jew   v:

ι        ν ουκ εξεστ
not    it is pos
ογος του Ιησ
e word    of Jesu
ον ποιω θανο
the kind    of dea
ιοηλθεν ουν πα
he entered    therefore    ag
ιλατος και εφωνι
ite    and    he call
ιεν αυτω Συ ει ο
he said    to him    you are

They also passed through three stages in reaching their final form: *life* stage, *oral* stage, and *written* stage.

The *life* stage began with Jesus' birth and ended with his ascension to heaven. Peter refers to it, saying, "With our own eyes we saw his greatness." 2 Peter 1:16

The *oral* stage began on Pentecost. Shortly after the Holy Spirit descended, Peter told a crowd, "This Jesus, whom you crucified, is the one that God has made Lord and Messiah!" Acts 2:36

The *written* stage began when the apostles realized they couldn't preach the "Good News" to every nation in their lifetime. Guided by the Spirit, they began to record it. Luke writes:

*Dear Theophilus:*
*Many people have done their best*
*to write a report of the things*
*that have taken place among us.*
*They wrote what we have been told*
*by those who saw these things*
*from the beginning*
*and who proclaimed the message.*

*And so, Your Excellency,*
*because I have carefully studied*
*all these matters . . . I thought it would*
*be good to write an orderly account*
*for you. I do this so that you will know*
*the full truth about everything*
*which you have been taught.* Luke 1:1–4

John alludes to all three gospel stages in his First Letter:

*What we have seen and heard* [life stage]
*we announce to you* [oral stage]. . . .
*We write this* [written stage] *in order*
*that our joy may be complete.* 1 John 1:3–4

And so the Gospels went through three stages in reaching their final form:

life        what the *disciples* experienced,
oral        what the *apostles* preached,
written     what the *evangelists* recorded.

The ocean floor is littered with thousands of sea shells. Some wash up onto the beach. One day an artist walks along the beach, picks up the best shells, and shapes them into a beautiful vase.

Explain how these three groups of shells (floor, beach, vase ) illustrate the stages by which the Gospels developed. In other words, which shells are like what stage and why?

2.  Imagine you are a yearbook editor. Your file contains many school photos. The question your staff asks is, How should we arrange the photos? You narrow the possible arrangements to the following three approaches: historical, biographical, invitational.

A *historical* approach means you arrange the photos in the same order in which they were taken. This makes the book a *history* of the year.

A *biographical* approach means you follow a typical student through the year. This makes the book a *biography* of what it was like to be a student that year.

Finally, an *invitational* approach means you pick out the important high points of the year and arrange them thematically. This makes the book an *invitation* to relive these "high point" events and experience what the students did.

Which of the three approaches would you choose and why?

3.  The four evangelists (gospel writers) faced a question similar to the one that the yearbook staff raised. What approach would you say they took, and what is your reason for saying so?

4.  The following passage from John holds the key to the approach that he and the other three evangelists followed in writing their Gospels. Identify and explain which one it was.

*Jesus performed many other miracles which are not written down in this book. But these have been written in order that you may believe that Jesus is the Messiah, the Son of God, and that through your faith in him you may have life.* John 20:30–31 ❧

The ocean floor is strewn with shells. Some wash up onto the beach, and an artist shapes them into a vase.

How are the three "shell" stages similar to the three gospel stages?

## Three Gospel Stages

List and explain:
a. The three stages by which the Gospels reached the form they now have.
b. The three approaches open to the evangelists when they sat down to record the Gospels.
c. The reason John gives for recording his Gospel.

This 800-year-old manuscript portrays John writing his Gospel.

Kim's dad describes her one way; her teacher, another; her best friend, a third way; and her volleyball coach, a fourth way.

There is only one Kim, but four different portraits of her.

# 54 Four Gospel Perspectives

A TV director was planning a series called *New York: A Tourist's View.* He decided to present the city through the eyes of four tourists who approach it in four different ways:

- by rail      train,
- by road     automobile,
- by water    boat,
- by air       airplane.

Thus television viewers would get not one but four different views of New York. As a result, their appreciation of the city would be greatly enriched.

We have something quite similar when it comes to Jesus' life and his teaching. Scripture approaches Jesus through the eyes of four evangelists, each writing

- at a different time,
- in a different place,
- for a different audience.

Experts don't agree totally on all times, places, and audiences, but they do agree that the following are probable:

|  | Time | Place | Primary Audience |
|---|---|---|---|
| Mark | –70 | Rome | Persecuted Romans |
| Matthew | 70+ | Syria | Converted Jews |
| Luke | 70+ | Greece | Lower-class Greeks |
| John | 90+ | Ephesus | All Christians |

We may extend our comparison between the TV producer's approach to New York and the evangelists' approach to Jesus.

Three approaches to New York City (rail, road, water) are quite similar, while the fourth (air) is quite different.

In a similar way, three gospel approaches to Jesus (Mark, Matthew, Luke) are quite similar, while the fourth (John) is quite different.

In fact, Mark, Matthew, and Luke are so similar that we refer to them as the *synoptic* Gospels. The word *synoptic*— *syn* ("together"), *optic* ("seen")— indicates that when "seen together," the similarities of these three Gospels are striking.

Kim's dad describes her one way; Kim's teacher, another way; Kim's best friend, a third way; and Kim's volleyball coach, a fourth way. We have one Kim, but four "portraits."

List three people who might describe you in totally different ways.

Take one example (like your readiness to help out when needed) and explain *how* and *why* these three people might describe you quite differently.

2. What is true of Kim is true of Jesus. We have four portraits of Jesus, not one. Mark, Matthew, and Luke are often called the *synoptic* Gospels. Sometimes the structure and wording of sizable sections of their Gospels are strikingly similar.

One explanation for the similarity might be that two of the evangelists simply adapted passages or stories of the evangelist who wrote first.

What might be two other explanations?

3. Experts say that by comparing the three synoptic versions of the same Gospel or passage, you can discover which evangelist wrote first and which adapted him. What are some clues that we might look for in deciding this question?

4. Study the three parallel accounts of the transfiguration of Jesus, printed side by side here. List their differences and try to decide who probably adapted whom.

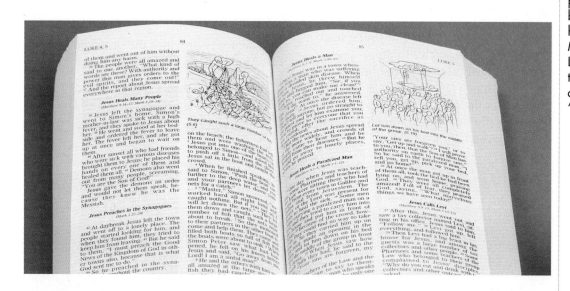

*The* three gospel passages reprinted below the photo show how some parts of Mark, Matthew, and Luke are so similar that these three Gospels are often referred to as the "Synoptic Gospels."

*Six days later
Jesus took with him
Peter, James, and John,
and led them up
a high mountain,
where they were alone.*

*As they looked on,
a change came over Jesus,
and his clothes became
shining white—whiter
than anyone in the world
could wash them.* Mark 9:2–3

*Six days later
Jesus took with him Peter
and the brothers James
and John and led them
up a high mountain
where they were alone.*

*As they looked on,
a change came over Jesus:
his face was shining
like the sun, and
his clothes were dazzling
white.* Matthew 17:1–2

*About a week after
he had said these things,
Jesus took Peter, John,
and James with him
and went up a hill
to pray.*

*While he was praying,
his face changed
its appearance,
and his clothes
became dazzling
white.* Luke 9:28–29

## Four Gospel Perspectives

*L*ist the probable time, place, and primary audience for which each of the four evangelists wrote his Gospel.

2. List the three synoptic Gospels, and explain why we give them this particular name.

# 55 Mark's Gospel

Fire swept through Rome in A.D. 64. Rumor spread as fast as the flames, claiming that Emperor Nero set the fire in order to rebuild the city and rename it for himself. To squelch the rumors, Nero blamed the fire on the Christians of Rome and began to persecute them brutally.

It was for these persecuted Christians, primarily, that Mark wrote his Gospel.

Tradition says Mark was the young man who guided the apostles to the upper room where Jesus celebrated the Last Supper. Mark 14:12–16 Some think the room belonged to Mark's mother and eventually became a meeting place for Christians. Acts 12:12

After the supper, young Mark may have followed the apostles and Jesus to the garden of Gethsemane, narrowly escaping arrest. Mark 14:51

Mark traveled with both Paul and Peter. 2 Timothy 4:11, 1 Peter 5:13 Tradition says he eventually ended up in Rome with Peter. There Mark wrote his Gospel, primarily, for Christians suffering persecution. Mark begins his Gospel, saying:

*This is the Good News
about Jesus Christ, the Son of God.*

This sentence provides the broad outline that Mark follows in his Gospel:

- Part One    Jesus is the Christ,
- Part Two    Jesus is the Son of God.

Part One focuses on Jesus as Christ ("the Messiah"). It ends with Peter saying to Jesus, "You are the Messiah." Mark 8:29

Christians met death while crowds cheered inside this arena.

It could be flooded for water spectacles and held 45,000 people.

Huge awnings protected spectators from the sun.

Part Two focuses on Jesus as "God's Son."
It ends with a Roman soldier
saying at Jesus' crucifixion, "This man
really was the Son of God."  Mark 15:39

And so Mark's portrait of Jesus stresses
the "suffering Messiah."
It reminds the Christians of Rome
that their Lord and God suffered,
and that they, too, can expect to suffer.
Mark 10:35–40

The Roman historian Tacitus
wrote about A.D. 110.
In his *Annals,* he describes
Nero's persecution of the Christians:

*They were put on crosses and,*
*at nighttime, burned as torches*
*to light up the darkness.*

Why treat the Christians so brutally?
Why not just execute them?

2.  Imagine you are an ancient Christian
scheduled to be burned in two hours.
Compose a prayer to Jesus
about what is going on inside
your mind and your heart at this time.

3.  A technique Mark uses in his Gospel
is to have one of the bystanders ask
a question and leave it unanswered.
For example, when Jesus casts out

an unclean spirit, bystanders ask,
"What is this?"  Mark 1:27  And when
Jesus calms the sea, his disciples ask,
"Who is this man?"  Mark 4:41

In light of the *invitational* approach,
which each evangelist uses,
why would this technique be effective?
How would you answer the two questions
posed by Mark above?
Briefly explain your answer.

4.  The Book of Revelation describes
God's throne as having around it
four creatures resembling a lion,
a bull, an eagle, and a man.  Revelation 4:2–7

From earliest Christian times,
artists have used the four creatures
as symbols of the four evangelists.
They based their conclusion
on a study of the way each evangelist
begins his Gospel.

Read Mark 1:1–3, Luke 1:5–9, Matthew 1:1–3,
and John 1:18, and try to figure out
why they associate

- the desert lion with Mark,
- the sacrificial bull with Luke,
- the man with Matthew, and
- the high-flying eagle with John.

(Be warned. Their reasoning is esoteric.
Some would even say it is far-fetched.)

Some artists linked the symbols circling Jesus to four great mysteries in his life rather than to the four evangelists:

incarnation (man), redemption (ox), resurrection (lion), ascension (eagle).

Folklore said the lion slept with its eyes open. Thus it symbolized the resurrection, when Jesus' divinity kept its eyes open while his humanity slept.

*Mark's Gospel*

What does tradition say concerning:
a. Who Mark was?
b. To whom the upper room belonged?
c. With whom Mark went to Rome?
d. For whom Mark wrote, primarily?

2. List and explain:
a. The two-part outline Mark followed in his Gospel.
b. The portrait of Jesus he stressed, and why.

Pat said,
"A ECNALG
at the prophecies
enabled me to say,
'stand
I.'"

Do you?

# 56  Matthew's Gospel

Tradition identifies Matthew as the tax collector whom Jesus called to be one of his apostles. Matthew 9:9

Some gospel readers suggest that Matthew's tax-collecting orderliness influenced the structure of his Gospel. It is beautifully structured, containing three main divisions:

- prologue    Jesus' early years,
- body    Jesus' kingdom teaching,
- epilogue    Jesus' death and rising.

Matthew's *prologue* and his *epilogue* are subtly matched.

For example, Matthew's quotation from Isaiah—"God is with us" (Matthew 1:23)— is matched by a quotation from Jesus— "I will be with you always" (Matthew 28:20).

Nowhere is Matthew's fondness for order more apparent than in the body of his Gospel, which he divides into "five instructions of Jesus."

These "five instructions of Jesus" act as a kind of symbolic parallel to the "five books of Moses" (Jewish Torah). Thus Matthew portrays them as a kind of *Christian Torah*.

Each instruction opens with a narrative that sets the stage for the instruction. All "five instructions" relate to the Kingdom of God:

- its demands,        5:1–7:28
- its proclamation,    10:5–11:1
- its development,    13:1–53
- its structure,        8:1–19:1
- its completion.    23:1–26:1

Each of the "five instructions" ends with a similarly worded formula: "When Jesus finished his teaching." Matthew 7:28, 11:1, 13:53, 19:1, 26:1

Writing mainly for Jewish Christians, Matthew is primarily concerned with showing how Jesus and his teaching fulfill Jewish prophecy and teaching.

Thus, Matthew takes pains to match Jesus' life with biblical prophecies. Matthew 1:23; 2:6, 15, 18, 23

And so Matthew's portrait of Jesus is that of the *teaching* Messiah. Jesus fulfills Jewish hopes and dreams.

This fifteenth-century wood carving portrays Matthew recording his Gospel.

The traditional title that has been given to Matthew's Gospel is The Gospel according to Matthew. The phrase "according to" is significant, because it leaves open the possibility that an associate of Matthew could have recorded it. (The same is true of the other Gospels.)

The important thing, however, is not who actually recorded it in writing. The important thing is that it is the *inspired record* of an oral tradition about Jesus, as preached by the apostle Matthew.

a. Why does the phrase "according to" leave open the possibility that Matthew need not have recorded his Gospel with his own hand?
b. Give an example to show that the media often use the phrase "according to" to document what the president said about something.

2. Luke traces Jesus' family tree all the way back to Adam.   Luke 3:38   Matthew traces it back only as far as Abraham.   Matthew 1:1

Keeping in mind the primary audience for which each wrote, why would Luke go back all the way to Adam and Matthew go back only to Abraham?

3. Matthew says of Mary's pregnancy, "[It was] to make come true what the Lord had said through the prophet, 'A virgin will become pregnant.'"
Matthew 1:22–23

And Matthew gives as the reason for Jesus' birth in Bethlehem, "This is what the prophet wrote."   Matthew 2:5

Finally, Matthew writes concerning Jesus' return from Egypt, "This was done to make come true what the Lord had said through the prophet, 'I called my Son out of Egypt.'"   Matthew 2:15

Explain how the above statements give us an important clue as to:
a. Who Matthew's *primary* audience was.
b. What point Matthew was trying to make regarding Jesus

**R**oman milestones, like this one, counted the miles along major ancient roads.

Roman law gave Roman soldiers the right to commandeer a Jew to carry baggage for him one mile.

Jesus said that if anyone presses us into service one mile, we should go two miles.   Matthew 5:38–42
What is Jesus' point?

## Matthew's Gospel

**L**ist and explain:
a. The three major parts into which Matthew divides his Gospel.
b. How Matthew portrays his Gospel as a kind of Christian Torah.
c. Why Matthew takes pains to match up Jesus' life with prophecies.
d. Why the expression "The Gospel *according to* Matthew" is significant.
e. Matthew's Jesus portrait.

119

# 57 Luke's Gospel

*I*t surprises some people to learn that Luke and Paul were travel companions on a number of occasions. Paul refers to this several times, saying:

- "Luke is with me." 2 Timothy 4:11
- "Luke sends you greetings." Philemon 24
- "Luke, our dear doctor, and Demas send you their greetings." Colossians 4:14

Likewise, Luke, who is also the author of the Acts of the Apostles Acts 1:1), alludes to Paul. He does this by shifting from "he" (Paul) to "we" (Luke and Paul). Acts 16:10–17, 20:5–21:18, 27:1–28:16

Luke structures his Gospel according to the following fivefold outline:

- ministry prologue, 1:5–4:13
- Galilean ministry, 4:14–9:50
- journey to Jerusalem, 9:51–19:27
- Jerusalem ministry, 19:28–21:38
- ministry epilogue. 22:1–24:53

Luke explains Jewish customs (Luke 22:1) and locates Jewish towns (Luke 4:31, 23:51). This helps orient his Greek readers, who were unfamiliar with Jewish practices and geography.

Luke stresses Jesus' special concern for society's oppressed citizens, especially the poor and the powerless:

*"Happy are you poor;*
*the Kingdom of God is yours!*
*Happy are you who are hungry now;*
*you will be filled!*
*Happy are you who weep now;*
*you will laugh!"* Luke 6:20–21

Luke's stress of Jesus' concern for the poor and the powerless inspired W. D. Davies to say that Luke might well have written the words of poet Emma Lazarus that are inscribed on the base of the Statue of Liberty in New York harbor:

*T*his 600-year-old copy of Luke's Gospel portrays the evangelist recording his Gospel. It begins: "Dear Theophilus."

Luke begins Acts with the same salutation. *Theophilus* means "beloved of God."

*Give me your tired, your poor,*
*your huddled masses*
*yearning to breathe free. . . .*
*Send these, the homeless,*
*the tempest-tost to me.*

And so Luke's portrait of Jesus is that of the *compassionate* Messiah, especially the "second-class" citizens of society. Jesus fulfills the dreams

- not only of Jews
- but also of Gentiles.

The words on the base of the Statue of Liberty are reflective of Luke's portrait of Jesus.

*Give me your tired, your poor. . . . Send these to me.*   Emma Lazarus

L uke is the only evangelist who notes that Jesus sweat blood in Gethsemane.   Luke 22:44
He also uses the correct Greek word for "convulsions" to describe how a demon threw a person down to the ground.   Luke 4:35

Explain how these two episodes support what Paul says about Luke (Colossians 4:14).

2.  Tradition says that Luke came from Antioch in Syria. Author G. B. Caird says of Luke:

*He was more interested in people*
*than in ideas.*
*He had a lively social conscience*
*and an inexhaustible sympathy*
*for other people's problems.*   Saint Luke

How does Caird's description of Luke fit the portrait of someone who would choose a medical profession? What is meant by a "lively social conscience," and how do we see it reflected in Luke's Gospel?

3.  Luke records four stories that no other evangelist refers to:

a.  the widow of Naim,          7:11–17
b.  Joanna and Susanna,        8:1–3
c.  the woman and the lost coin,  15:8–10
d.  the widow and the judge.    18:1–18

What common thread runs through them, and how does Luke's inclusion of them jibe with the portrait of Jesus that he wanted to stress?

4. Tax collectors were Jews who worked for Rome. They acquired the right to collect taxes by bidding for the job. It was up to them to get back their investment and a profit. This led to abuse, as William Barclay notes:

*If a man could not pay, sometimes*
*the tax collector would offer to lend him*
*money at an exorbitant rate of interest*
*and get him further into his clutches. . . .*

*A Roman writer tells that he saw*
*a monument to an honest tax collector.*
*An honest specimen of this renegade*
*profession was so rare that*
*he deserved a monument.*   The Gospel of Luke

a. How do Luke 18:9–14 and 19:1–9 give us an insight into Jesus' attitude toward tax collectors?
b. How does Luke's inclusion of these episodes jibe with the portrait of Jesus that he wanted to stress?

*Luke's Gospel*

List clues in Paul's letters and in Luke's Acts to show they traveled together at times.

2. List clues in Luke to show:
a. That he wrote, primarily, for people unfamiliar with Jewish customs and geography.
b. That he wanted to stress Jesus' special concern for society's "second-class" citizens.

# 58 John's Gospel

Tradition says that John was the son of Zebedee, the brother of James (Luke 5:10), and the disciple "whom Jesus loved" in a special way. We find him mentioned in a special way:

- at the Last Supper,      John 13:23
- under the cross,      John 19:26
- at the tomb,      John 20:2
- on the seashore.      John 21:7

John begins his Gospel somewhat as a musical composer begins a symphony: with a beautiful overture that previews and sets the tone for what is to follow. It tips us off that his approach to Jesus will differ dramatically from the other three evangelists. He writes:

*In the beginning*
*the Word already existed. . . .*
*The Word was the source of life,*

*and this life brought light to people.*
*The light shines in the darkness,*
*and the darkness has never put it out.*
      John 1:1, 4–5

One reason for John's different approach is that he writes at a later date and addresses maturer Christians.

Four ways that John's Gospel differs from the others are the following.

First, he rarely uses the story format. When he does, he is more interested in the story's symbolism:

- water      woman at well,      John 4:14
- bread      crowd feeding,      John 6:1–51
- blindness      sightless man.      John 9:39

Second, John has Jesus identify himself with God's sacred name "I am."      Exodus 3:14
Jesus says:

"I am the bread of life."      John 6:35
"I am the light of the world."      John 8:12
"I am the good shepherd."      John 10:11

Third, John identifies Jesus, almost immediately, as the Messiah.      John 1:41

Finally, John substitutes "eternal life" in place of the "Kingdom of God."

In brief, then, John's portrait of Jesus is that of the *life-giving* Messiah. Jesus himself sums up his purpose in coming in these words:

*"I have come*
*in order that you might have life—*
*life in all its fullness."*      John 10:10

This 800-year-old manuscript portrays John writing his Gospel.

Ancient manuscripts were copied by hand and sometimes elaborately illustrated.

A practical prayer with which to end each day is the "three-minute replay" prayer.

It helps focus thought and discern the general direction in which our lives are moving.

Scripture preserves for us four different portraits or perspectives of Jesus. We may list them as follows:

- Mark     *suffering* Messiah,
- Matthew  *teaching* Messiah,
- Luke     *compassionate* Messiah,
- John     *life-giving* Messiah.

By way of review, explain:
a. How the audiences for whom Mark and Matthew wrote, primarily, influenced their portrait of Jesus.
b. How Luke's Gospel reflects that the audience for whom he wrote, primarily, was unfamiliar with Jewish customs and Palestinian geography.
c. Four ways that John's Gospel differs from the three synoptic Gospels.

2. Some people think that one of the concerns of John's Gospel is to show a link between Jesus' miracles and the Church's sacraments.

For example, check the following gospel passages, and explain how some people see them linked to the Church's sacraments:

- Cana wine episode          2:1–11
- Nicodemus conversation     3:1–5
- Pool healing               5:1–14
- Hillside supper            6:1–52
- Festival words             7:37–39
- Cure of blind man          9:1–7
- Last Supper prayer         17:9–19

3. An excellent, practical night prayer is called the "three-minute replay." Directed to the Holy Trinity—Father, Son, and Holy Spirit—it goes like this.

FIRST MINUTE: Replay your day. Pick out a *high point:* something good that you did or that happened. Talk to the *Father* about it and *give thanks.*

SECOND MINUTE: Replay your day again. This time, pick out a *low point:* something unfortunate that you did or that happened to you. Talk to *Jesus* about it and *ask for forgiveness.*

THIRD MINUTE: Look ahead to tomorrow to a *critical point:* a situation you must deal with. Talk to the *Holy Spirit* about it and *ask for help.* Here is an example:

*Holy Spirit, I want to do the right thing, but I'm not always sure what it is. Help me know how to act toward my dad, who is under stress and is drinking heavily.*

Write out a "three-minute replay" of your day, using the above model.

*John's Gospel*

How does John begin his Gospel, and what does it tip us off to about his approach to Jesus?

2. What is one reason why John's Gospel differs so dramatically from the other three?

3. List four ways that John's Gospel differs from the synoptic Gospels.

# CHAPTER ELEVEN

# Preministry
## 59 Birth

*S*hepherds . . . were
*spending the night in the*
*fields, taking care of*
*their flocks.*   Luke 2:8

**D**arrel Doré was trapped
inside an oil rig that had just sunk
in the Gulf of Mexico.
As the platform filled with water,
a huge air bubble formed in one corner.
Darrel thrust his head inside it.

There he shivered and prayed for hours.
Just when he started to lose hope,
a tiny "star of light"
appeared in the watery darkness.
It was the light of a diver's helmet.

Doré's rescue from the sea
resembles humanity's rescue from sin.
Just when humanity was about to give up,
a tiny "star" of light appeared
in the darkness of the Bethlehem sky:

*Shepherds . . . were spending the night*
*in the fields, taking care of their flocks.*
*An angel of the Lord appeared . . .*
*[saying,] "This very day in David's town*
*your Savior was born—Christ the Lord! . . .*
*You will find a baby wrapped in cloths*
*and lying in a manger."*   Luke 2:8–12

The time and place where the angel
appears and the place where Jesus
is born point to:

- Jesus' *identity* and *mission,* and
- Jesus' future *lifestyle*.

First, the angel appears at night
when the shepherds are "in the fields,
taking care of their flocks."
Normally, shepherds crowded sheep
into pens for the night.
The one season they didn't do this
was lambing season
(lest new lambs be trampled to death).

Thus, Luke suggests Jesus was born
during lambing season in the spring.
Moreover, lambs born in Bethlehem
were destined for sacrifice
in the Temple in nearby Jerusalem.

And so Jesus' birth
during *lambing season* and *at Bethlehem*
acts as a poetic preview
of his *identity* and *mission:*
He is the "Lamb of God" whose mission
is to be "sacrificed" in Jerusalem.

Second, the place of Jesus' birth
points to his future *lifestyle*.
He is born in a stable and
his crib is a manger (animal feed box).

This suggests Jesus will live on earth,
not among the wealthy and powerful,
but among the poor and powerless.

An American tourist bought a nativity set in the Holy Land. It contained ten tiny figures. The airport security officer in Tel Aviv x-rayed each figure, saying, "We can't take chances. This set could contain an explosive."

What do you think is the *main* reason why Jesus was born in a dirty stable?

3. Create a Christmas card with a spiritual message different from the one you find on most cards— like this one composed by Jim Auer:

Most sheep were kept for wool. A shepherd was with his flock 365 days a year.

He got to know which sheep had tender hoofs, which got sick easily, and which were prone to stray. This explains Jesus' words:

*"I am the good shepherd. . . . I know my sheep and they know me. And I am willing to die for them."* John 10:14–15

As the tourist watched the x-raying, she thought to herself, "That set contains the most explosive power in the world, but there's only one way to detect it."

Briefly describe:
a. The explosive power the set contains.
b. The only way this power can be detected.

2. After meditating on the birth of Jesus, Morton Kelsey wrote:

*I am glad that the divine child was born in a stable, because my soul is much like a stable. . . . If the holy One could be born in such a place, the holy One can be born in me.*

A critic said of Kelsey's statement, "Besides lacking the Christmas spirit, it's too negative a view of yourself." What does Kelsey have in mind, and why do/don't you agree with the critic?

*Christmas is a good time to get a little crazy. After all, God did. He became a human being. That's pretty crazy.*

If you wish, use Auer's message and find a photo or drawing to illustrate it.

4. Explain the point of each of these quotes, and tell why you agree/disagree with it.

a. "Some business people are saying this could be the greatest Christmas. . . . I always thought the first was." Art Fettig

b. "A God too large to walk in human shoes has outgrown every hope of human use." Calvin Miller

c. "Child, dear child, help me to discover even in the most severe people the child asleep in their hearts." Dom Helder Camara

*Birth*

Explain how Luke's description of the angel's birth announcement points to:
a. Jesus' identity and mission.
b. Jesus' future lifestyle.

125

# 60 Presentation

*I*n *Roots,* Alex Haley describes the rites his African ancestors followed upon the birth of a child. Eight days after the birth, the father whispered the child's name in its ear. Africans believed the child should be the first to know its name.

The same night, under the night sky, the father completed the "naming" rite. Pointing to the star-filled sky,

*G*entle woman . . .
*peaceful dove, teach us*
*wisdom; teach us love.*
Carol Landry

the father said to the child, "Behold— the only thing greater than yourself."

Jewish parents also followed special rites for naming a child and introducing it to the world.   Luke 2:21–24

The rites took place in the Temple and included circumcision, presentation, and purification of the mother.
Genesis 17:10, Exodus 13, Leviticus 12

§ *Circumcision* initiated the child into the community of God's people.
§ *Presentation* consecrated the firstborn male to God in gratitude to God for saving Israel's firstborn from the final plague in Egypt.
§ *Purification* welcomed the mother back into full participation in the worshiping community.

When Joseph and Mary brought Jesus to the Temple for these rites, two elderly Jews, Simeon and Anna, happened to be there.

Both had prayed all their lives to see the promised Messiah before they died. Seeing Jesus, Simeon cradled him in his arms and thanked God, saying:

*"Lord, you have kept your promise. . . .*
*With my own eyes*
*I have seen your salvation . . . :*
*A light to reveal your will*
*to the Gentiles and*
*bring glory to your people Israel." . . .*

*[Simeon said to Mary,] "This child . . .*
*will be a sign from God which*
*many people will speak against. . . .*
*And sorrow, like a sharp sword,*
*will break your own heart."*

*[Similarly, Anna, a widow, devoted*
*her life to] fasting and praying. . . .*
*She . . . gave thanks to God and spoke*
*about the child to all who were*
*waiting for God to set Jerusalem free.*
Luke 2:29–30, 32, 34–35, 37–38

A college student came into the office of a retreat master and shared with him this poem, which he had written:

*The other day I saw a water lily
growing in a pond.
It had the purest yellow I'd ever seen.
The lily was a precious treasure,
unconcerned about whether
anyone noticed its astounding beauty.*

*As I sat there, watching it unfold
its petals noiselessly,
I thought of Mary pregnant with Jesus.
She, too, was a precious treasure,
unconcerned about whether
anyone noticed her astounding beauty.*

*But to those who did, she shared a secret.
Her beauty came not from herself,
but from the Jesus life within her,
unfolding its petals noiselessly.*

Record and share:
a. The point of the student's poem.
b. The difference between "inner beauty" and "outer beauty."
c. What God looked for most in the one who would mother Jesus. In the one who would father Jesus.

d. What children look for in parents.
e. The kind of relationship you hope to have with your children.

2. Jewish birth rites might be compared to the Christian baptism.
Interview your parents or sponsors about your baptism: Who baptized you?
Where? When?
Did anything unusual happen?
Why were you given the name you have?

3. Consult a book such as *Chronicles* or *On This Day in America* and list:
a. A celebrity whose birthday falls on the same day as yours.
b. An event that occurred on the exact day you were born.

4. *[Simeon said to Mary,]*
*"This child . . . will be a sign from God
which many people will speak against. . . .
And sorrow, like a sharp sword,
will break your own heart."*

a. List some questions that would go through your mother's mind if the minister baptizing you told her what Simeon told Mary.
b. Why would Simeon utter such a sad prophecy at such a happy time?

## Presentation

List and describe the three rites that took place when Mary and Joseph took Jesus to the Temple.

2. What prophecy does Simeon make concerning Jesus? Concerning Mary?

# 61 Magi

**S**ometime after Jesus' birth, magi from the East arrived in Jerusalem and made inquiries about the birth of the Jewish Messiah.

MAGI    *Where is the baby born to be the king of the Jews? We saw his star. . . .*

NARRATOR    *When King Herod heard about this . . . [he asked,] "Where will the Messiah be born?"*

ADVISORS    *In the town of Bethlehem. . . . The prophet wrote: "Bethlehem . . . from you will come a leader who will guide my people Israel." . . .*

NARRATOR    *And so [the visitors] left. . . . When they saw the child . . . they [presented him with] their gifts of gold, frankincense, and myrrh.*   Matthew 2:2–6, 9, 11

**H**erod was enraged when the magi left without telling him where Jesus was.

He ordered a massacre of all male babies. Jesus escaped when Joseph was warned in a dream to flee. Matthew 2:12–14

Herod was buried here (inside the Herodium). Located near Bethlehem, it was one of Herod's fortress-palaces.

This story may be compared to a tapestry of three threads, so artfully interwoven that it is almost impossible to say where one thread stops and the other starts. The three threads are:

- history    remembered events,
- prophecy    biblical prophecies,
- inspiration    divine guidance.

*History,* the first thread, says the magi were not kings but advisors to kings in religious and scientific matters. *Prophecy,* the second thread, says the promised Messiah will

- be born in Bethlehem,    Micah 5:1
- shine like a bright star,    Numbers 24:17
- receive royal gifts.    Psalm 72:10–11

*Inspiration,* the third thread, is the Holy Spirit's guidance of the evangelist. Matthew tells the magi story so that

*and when they have achieved fame,*
*most of those who knew them*
*as children are dead.*  Light on the Gospels

This was also true of Jesus. To solve the problem, Matthew and Luke consulted old people who remembered Jesus and Old Testament prophecies about Jesus.

Record and share:
a. How the problem Matthew and Luke faced was greater then than it is now.
b. How the stories of Jesus' childhood differ from stories of Jesus' adulthood, and how this affects the way we interpret them.

2. An ancient Jewish book, the Talmud, says of a Jewish boy:

*At five he must begin sacred studies;*
*at ten he must learn Jewish traditions;*
*at thirteen he must know the whole law*
*of Yahweh and live it faithfully.*

Today, the rite of Bar Mitzvah celebrates a boy's entry into adulthood. Although the rite did not exist in Jesus' time, the idea behind it explains Jesus' boyhood trip to Jerusalem.

Read Luke 2:41–51 and explain:
a. What happened when Mary and Joseph began their trip home.
b. What detail of the trip suggests that Jesus did not have brothers or sisters.
c. Jesus' response to Mary.

3. A Jewish boy told those gathered for his Bar Mitzvah: "It marks the occasion when I take on adult responsibilities toward the Jewish community."
Next, he read a letter he wrote to the Israeli prime minister protesting the war in Lebanon. He ended, saying:

*Instead of centerpieces and candy*
*and nuts for my Bar Mitzvah party,*
*I have asked my family to send money*
*to the Kiryat Sanz Laniado Hospital, where*
*Jews hurt in the war are being treated.*

a. Record and share your preparation for confirmation (Christian Bar Mitzvah).
b. Interview a Jewish boy about Bar Mitzvah: Where and when is it celebrated? What happens? Is there a rite for girls? 

it acts as a symbolic preview of two revelations about Jesus: who he is and how people will react to him.

From early times, Christians have interpreted the gifts of the magi as pointing to these facts about Jesus:

 *Gold* is the "king of metals" and points to his *kingship.*
 *Frankincense* is used in worship and points to his *divinity.*
 *Myrrh* is used in Jewish burial rites and points to Jesus' *humanity.*

Herod's hostile reaction to Jesus, opposed to the magi's positive reaction, previews how people will react to Jesus. Many *Jews will reject* him; many *Gentiles will accept* him.

**M**atthew and Luke decided to introduce their Gospels with a brief prologue about the birth and infancy of Jesus. This created a problem, as John L. McKenzie has pointed out:

*Details of the lives of famous men*
*become interesting*
*only after they have become famous;*

**T**his boy dons a skull cap (yarmulka), prayer shawl (tallith), and arm and head bands (tefillin) for prayer.

Tiny tefillin pouches contain Bible passages. One of these says of God's teachings:

*"Remember these commands. . . . Tie them on your arms and wear them on your foreheads as a reminder."*
Deuteronomy 11:18

*Magi*

**L**ist and explain the three threads of the magi tapestry, and give an example of each.

2. What did Herod do when the magi left Jerusalem, and how did Jesus escape his rage?

3. Explain how Christians have interpreted the gifts of the magi since early times.

4. How does the reaction of Herod and the magi preview future reaction to Jesus?

# 62 Baptism

Linda had one foot in the shower and one out. "This is a picture of my life," she thought. "I want to choose God, but I keep one foot in and one foot out." After a pause, she said, "I choose God!" Then she stepped into the shower. "That was a real baptism!" she said later.

John the Baptist invited people to make a similar decision and be baptized. One day John was shocked to see Jesus step into the water to be baptized. John hesitated, but Jesus said, " 'Let it be so for now. . . .' So John agreed." Matthew 3:15

*While [Jesus] was praying,*
*heaven was opened,*
*and the Holy Spirit came down upon him*
*in bodily form like a dove.*
*And a voice came from heaven,*
*"You are my own dear Son."* Luke 3:21–22

The key to understanding this passage is its three images: *heaven opening,* the *dove descending,* and the *voice speaking.*

Jews pictured the universe as three worlds stacked like pancakes.

God resided in the top world (heaven); people, in the middle world (earth); and the dead, in the bottom world (sheol).

After Adam's sin, the middle world grew more and more evil. Jews begged God to "tear the sky open," come down, and correct things. Psalm 144:5 The image of *heaven opening* signals that God is answering their prayers. A *new era* is dawning: God, in the person of Jesus, has come down from heaven to correct things.

The image of the *dove descending* recalls God's power descending upon the waters

This painting of the *Baptism of Jesus,* by the Italian painter Paolo Cagliari, was completed about 1570.

What are some things about it that you find surprising or different?

before the creation of the world.
Rabbis compared God's power to a dove.
The image of the dove descending signals
the dawn of a *new creation*.
God is fulfilling the promise to Isaiah:
"The LORD says, 'I am making a new earth.' "
Isaiah 65:17

Finally, the image of the *voice speaking*
from heaven identifies Jesus
as the *new Adam* of the *new creation*.
"The first Adam . . . came from the earth,
the second Adam came from heaven."
1 Corinthians 15:47

And so the baptismal images signal

  ⚶ a new era      heaven opening,
  ⚶ a new creation    dove descending,
  ⚶ a new Adam      voice speaking.

A holy water font stands inside
the door of each Catholic church
to remind us that we entered
the Church for the first time
through the waters of baptism.

Taking holy water and blessing ourselves
symbolizes the renewal of our original
baptismal commitment.

a. Ask three Catholic friends or family
members, "What is the purpose behind
blessing ourselves with holy water
as we enter a church?"
b. Record and share their responses.

2. John the Baptist said to the people,
"I baptize you with water,
but someone is coming who . . .
will baptize you with the Holy Spirit
and fire."    Luke 3:16
John's baptism involved *repentance—
rejecting* an *old* life.
Christian baptism involves *rebirth—
receiving* a *new* life.

What life is rejected? Received?

3. Organ transplants involve two steps:
removing the old and inserting the new.
How does this example illustrate
the connection between
John's baptism and Jesus' baptism?

4. New organs need special care
to prevent the body from rejecting them.
Explain how this is also true
of our new life in Christ.

5. Some people ask,
"Why did Jesus ask John to baptize him
if he was without sin?"
How would you respond?

6. Record and explain the point
of these quotes:

a. "The fall of the first Adam was
the end of the beginning;
the rise of the second Adam
was the beginning of the end."    S. W. Duffield

b. "A part of the act of baptism of the
Church of India is for the candidates
to place their own hand on their head
and say, 'Woe to me if I preach not
the Gospel.' "    E. Paul Hovey

c. "When a child is baptized, it involves
me also, for by baptism we become
closer than blood sisters or brothers."
Author unknown ⚶

This painting of the
*Baptism of Jesus* departs
dramatically from more
traditional religious art.

What are some things
about it that you find
surprising or different?

What do you think the
artist was trying to say
and why?

*Baptism*

List the three images of
Jesus' baptism, and
explain how they signal:
a. A new era.
b. A new creation.
c. A new Adam.

2. Explain:
a. How John's baptism
is both different from
and related to Jesus'
baptism.
b. The Catholic practice
of taking holy water and
blessing oneself upon
entering a church.

# 63 Temptations

The Holy Spirit led Jesus into the desert, where he fasted and prayed for forty days. At the end of the time, Jesus was hungry. Then the Devil appeared on the scene.

DEVIL   *If you are God's Son, order these stones to turn into bread.*

JESUS   *The scripture says, "Human beings cannot live on bread alone, but need every word that God speaks." . . .*

DEVIL   *If you are God's Son, throw yourself [from the Temple]. . . . Scripture says, ". . . [Angels] will hold you up with their hands. . . ."*

JESUS   *Scripture also says, "Do not put the Lord . . . to the test."*

NARRATOR   *Then the Devil . . . showed him all the kingdoms of the world in all their greatness.*

DEVIL   *All this I will give you if you kneel down and worship me.*

Jesus went into this desert to pray and do penance before starting his ministry.

JESUS   *Go away, Satan! The scripture says, "Worship the Lord . . . and serve only him!"*   Matthew 4:3–10

Jesus' clear-cut victory over Satan is a dramatic preview of his *identity.* He is not only *human* ("Son of Man"), but also *divine* ("Son of God").

The victory also previews Jesus' *mission.* He has come to right Adam's wrong. Satan tempted Adam to sin. That sin brought *death to all.*   Romans 5:12 Now Satan tempts Jesus, the *new* Adam. Jesus stands firm, and his victory restores *life to all.* Paul writes:

*As all people die because of their union with Adam, . . . all will be raised to life because of their union with Christ.*
1 Corinthians 15:22

Finally, Jesus' victory over Satan previews the future *lifestyle* of Jesus.

🔥 His refusal to *turn stone to bread* previews that his lifestyle will be to suffer, not to avoid suffering.   Luke 9:21–27
🔥 His refusal to *leap off the Temple* and *be rescued* previews that his style will be to serve, not to be served.   Mark 10:45
🔥 Finally, his refusal to *bow to Satan* previews that his style will be to destroy evil, not to barter with it.

And so Jesus' victory over Satan in the desert previews his

🔥 identity       human and divine,
🔥 mission      give life to all,
🔥 lifestyle     suffer, serve, destroy evil.

*D*oug Alderson left for a summer's hike down the Appalachian Trail. He said:

*I had just graduated from high school.*
*I had many questions. My goals in life?*
*My future? Was there a God? . . .*
*My hike was a search to find myself.*

Five months later Doug returned home a changed person. Even his dog eyed him suspiciously, as if to say, "Where've you been? You look different!" Doug was different. He'd found what he was searching for.

a. Did you ever do something akin to what Doug did? Explain.

b. What is your goal in life? Explain.

c. What about your future concerns you?

d. What do you believe/question about God?

2. Carlo Carretto became a monk and went into the Arabian desert to live a life of prayer.

In his book *Letters from the Desert,* Carretto tells how he experienced God's glory in the star-filled night skies above the desert.

*How dear they were to me, those stars. . . .*
*I had come to know them*
*by their names. . . .*
*Now I could distinguish their color,*
*their size, their position . . .*
*and I could calculate the time*
*without a watch.*

Carretto's words remind us of the words of George Washington Carver who wrote, "I love to think of nature as an unlimited broadcasting system through which God speaks to us . . . if we only tune in."

Record and share:

a. What aspect of nature speaks to you most about God.

b. A time when God seemed to speak to you through nature.

3. The Bible mentions fasting over seventy times. Often it is mentioned in connection with praying.

Record and share:

a. Why you think Jesus fasted during his time of prayer in the desert.

b. What fasting adds to praying.

c. A time you fasted or gave up something to show God the depth of your desire. ⸙

*T*radition locates Jesus' encounter with Satan on this mountain.

Carved into its side are scores of caves where hermits lived, praying and performing penance in imitation of Jesus.

An ancient monastery girdles the mountain.

## Temptations

*E*xplain how the desert encounter with Satan previews:

a. Jesus' identity.
b. Jesus' mission.
c. The threefold lifestyle that Jesus will follow.

# CHAPTER TWELVE

# Miracle Ministry

## 64 Inauguration

*W*hen Jesus left the desert,
"the power of the Holy Spirit
was with him."  Luke 4:14
He went to Galilee and began
preaching in towns and synagogues:

*"The Kingdom of God is near!*
*Turn away from your sins and*
*believe the Good News!"*  Mark 1:15

One day he came to Nazareth,
the town in which he grew up.

*He went as usual to the synagogue.*
*He stood up to read the Scriptures and*
*was handed the book of the prophet Isaiah.*
*He unrolled the scroll and*
*found the place where it is written,*
*"The Spirit of the Lord is upon me,*
*because he has chosen me. . . .*
*The time has come*
*when the Lord will save his people." . . .*

*[Then he added his amazing statement:]*
*"This passage of scripture*
*has come true today,*
*as you heard it being read."*  Luke 4:16–19, 21

Year after year, the people of Nazareth had
heard Isaiah's prophecy and had prayed
for the coming of God's kingdom.
Now Jesus, who grew up among them,
claims to be the promised Messiah.

Their reaction swings like a pendulum
from marveling at Jesus' eloquence
to being appalled at Jesus' claim.

When Jesus tries to reason with them,
the situation gets unbelievably ugly.

*They rose up,*
*dragged Jesus out of town,*
*and took him to the top of the hill*
*on which their town was built.*
*They meant to throw him over the cliff,*
*but he walked*
*through the middle of the crowd*
*and went his way.*  Luke 4:29–30

This episode shocks us.
It recalls Simeon's prophecy that Jesus
"will be a sign from God which many
people will speak against."  Luke 2:34
So, too, it reminds us of the magi story

*T*he synagogue had its
origin in Babylon, when
exiled Jews could no
longer frequent the
Temple.

When they were free
to return home, they
continued to meet in
synagogues, like this
one, to pray and study.

Israel's only Temple was
at Jerusalem, but almost
every town had a
synagogue.

and its revelation
that many Jews will reject Jesus.

The episode turns out to be
yet another straw in the wind
of what lies ahead for Jesus:
rejection by his own people
and even a violent death at their hands.

*If Jesus were to come today,
people would not crucify him.
They would ask him to dinner,
hear what he had to say,
and make fun of him.* Thomas Carlyle

Why haven't 2,000 years changed things?
A high school boy gave this answer:

*Why don't I take Jesus more seriously?
I guess it's because if I did,
I'm afraid my friends might reject me,
as Jesus' friends did him.
I couldn't take that right now in my life.*

On a scale of 1 (not at all) to 10
(almost fully), how fully do you identify
with the boy's response, and why?

2.  Imagine that you are Jesus walking away
from your hometown with the angry shouts
of your closest friends and neighbors
ringing in your ears.
Record and share your feelings.

3.  Imagine that you are the editor of the
*Nazareth Daily News* and that you witnessed
the episode described in Luke 4:29–30.
Write a brief editorial comment
on how you feel about this violent episode.

4.  A religious persecution hit the Sudan.
Young Paride Taban fled to Uganda,
where he became a priest.
When the Sudan persecution subsided,
Paride returned home. He says:

*People looked hard at me and asked,
"Do you mean to say, black man,
you're a priest? We can't believe it."*

To make matters worse, Father Taban
had to introduce his people to the changes
of Vatican II. They said, "He turns our altar
around and says Mass in our own language.
He cannot be a real priest."

If you were Paride, what would you do
to try to convince the people
that you were, indeed, a real priest,
like the white missionaries? Explain.

5.  Record and share how these quotes
apply not only to Jesus' friends
and neighbors in Nazareth but also
to all of us today.

a.  "A penny will hide the biggest star
in the universe if you hold it close enough
to the eye." Samuel Grafton
b.  "It takes wisdom to know whether
you're fighting for a principle or
defending a principle." Author unknown
c.  "O God, help us not to despise or oppose
what we do not understand." William Penn

*Every believer
in this world must
become a spark of light.*
Pope John XXIII

## Inauguration

With what was Jesus
filled as he left the
desert, and what
message did he begin
to preach?

2. Explain:
a. The prophecy Jesus
read and explained in
Nazareth.
b. How and why
the people reacted to
Jesus as they did.
c. Two earlier episodes
that the Nazareth
episode recalls.

3. When, where, and
why did the synagogue
begin and continue?

The map on the left shows:
MEDITERRANEAN SEA
· Dan
Hazor ·
Capernaum ·
· Cana    SEA OF GALILEE
· Nazareth

# 65 Signs

Jesus left Nazareth sick of heart.
He walked north
to the seaside city of Capernaum.
On the Sabbath he went to the synagogue
and preached to the people.

*They were all amazed at the way he taught,*
*because he spoke with authority.*
*In the synagogue was a man who had*
*the spirit of an evil demon in him. . . .*
*Jesus ordered the spirit, . . .*
*"Come out . . . !" The demon [left]. . . .*

*The people were all amazed. . . .*
*And the report about Jesus spread. . . .*
*All who had friends who were sick . . .*
*brought them to Jesus;*
*he . . . healed them all.*    Luke 4:32–33, 35–37, 40

The Gospels use three Greek words
to describe Jesus' miracles:
*teras, dynamis,* and *semion.*

◊ *Teras* means "marvel."
It stresses that Jesus' miracles
make people wonder.

◊ *Dynamis* means "power" (dynamite).
It stresses that Jesus' miracles reveal
a "godlike" power present in Jesus.
◊ *Semion* means "sign."
It stresses that Jesus' miracles make
people ask, "What does this mean?"

We might compare Jesus' miracles
to a flashing red light.
The key thing is not the flashing light,
but what it means.
It is the same way with Jesus' miracles.
The key thing is not the miracles.
Rather, it is their deeper meaning.

To put it in another way,
Jesus miracles operated at two levels:

◊ *sense* level    what Jesus does
(restores a man's sight), and
◊ *sign* level    what Jesus intends to say
to people by this action.

This leaves us with the key question:
What did Jesus intend
to say to people through his miracles?

This 1,700-year-old synagogue is located in Capernaum next to the Sea of Galilee.

Because of the Jewish custom of rebuilding on the same spot as the prior building, these ruins probably mark the exact spot of the synagogue in which Jesus taught and worshiped.

The wharfs of ancient Capernaum were filled with fishing boats like these.

Perhaps, at this very spot, Jesus said to the two fishermen brothers Peter and Andrew:

*"Come with me, and I will teach you to catch people."* Mark 1:17

The primary purpose of Jesus' miracles is twofold:

🔹 to *proclaim* Jesus is the Messiah, come to inaugurate God's kingdom, and
🔹 to *invite* people to open their hearts to him and his teaching.

We will see in the lessons ahead how Jesus' miracles accomplished this important twofold purpose.

J esus' miracles operated at two levels: the sense level and the sign level.
The *sense* level is what people saw (a blind man restored to sight), and the *sign* level is the deeper meaning of this miracle.

Someone said the difference between these levels is the difference between a photograph and an X ray.
Explain what the person had in mind.

2.  The miracles of Jesus were *invitations* to people to open their hearts to Jesus and his preaching.
What does it mean to "open your heart," and how do you go about doing it?

3.  One day a large crowd spent the whole day listening to Jesus.
The hour grew late and the crowd hungry.
Jesus said to his disciples:

*"Where can we buy enough food to feed all these people?" . . . Andrew . . . said, "There is a boy here who has five loaves of barley bread and two fish. . . ."*

*Jesus took the bread, gave thanks to God, and distributed it to the people. . . . He did the same with the fish, and they all had as much as they wanted. . . .*

*[The next day the crowd returned and Jesus said to them,] "You are looking for me because you ate the bread and had all you wanted, not because you understood my miracles."*
John 6:5, 8–9, 11, 26

Explain Jesus' point.

4.  Louis Evely writes in his book *The Gospels without Myth:*

*The true miracle of the loaves and fishes is this: Jesus persuaded one man to risk sharing what he had, and that man's example led others to put into a common pot the food they had been hiding for their own use. And thus the crowd gained a blessing greater than that which a full stomach could confer.*

Record and share:
a.  What blessing Evely is referring to.
b.  What you think of Evely's interpretation.

5.  Some years ago, Joseph Lewis said over a Miami radio station:

*If I had the power . . . Jesus had, I would not cure one person of blindness; I would make blindness impossible. I would not cure one person of leprosy; I would abolish leprosy.*

How would you respond to Lewis? 🔹

## Signs

List and explain the three Greek words that the Gospels use to refer to the miracles of Jesus.

2. List and explain the twofold purpose of Jesus' miracles.

3. In what sense might we compare:
a. Jesus' miracles to a flashing red light?
b. The two levels of Jesus' miracles to a photograph and an X ray?

# 66 Proclamations

The movie *The Exorcist* is based on an actual case of a fourteen-year-old boy who, in 1949, lived in Mount Rainier, Maryland.

*The boy's bed would suddenly move about.*
*At night, he could hardly sleep.*
*After he was admitted*
*to Georgetown University Hospital, . . .*
*while strapped helplessly to his bed,*
*long red scratches appeared on his body.*
*[The boy underwent an exorcism and*
*is now completely normal.]*    Newsweek

Jesus performed a similar exorcism in the synagogue at Capernaum.

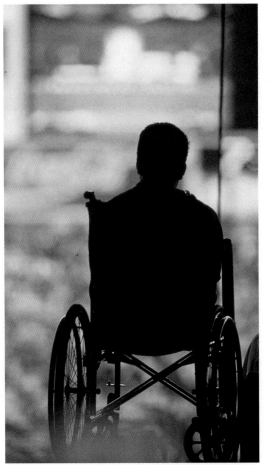

Sin, sickness, and death entered the world through Adam's sin.

Jesus' power over these three evils signals the demise of Satan's kingdom and the rise of God's kingdom.

"The people were all so amazed that they started saying to one another, 'What is this?' "    Mark 1:27

Jesus answered the question himself, saying, "[It] proves that the Kingdom of God has . . . come to you."    Luke 11:20

Jesus proclaimed the coming of God's kingdom in yet another way:

- by forgiving sinners,    Luke 5:17–26
- curing the sick, and    Mark 1:29–31
- raising the dead.    Luke 7:12–16

These evils—sin, sickness, and death—entered the world with Adam's sin. They were signs of Satan's kingdom on earth.
Jesus' power over these three evils is a dramatic sign pointing to the demise of Satan's kingdom and the rise of God's kingdom.

Finally, miracles proclaim Jesus to be the promised Messiah. The prophet Isaiah had foretold that the following signs would proclaim the Messiah's arrival:

*The blind will [see] . . .*
*the deaf will hear.*
*The lame will leap.*    Isaiah 35:5–6

When some disciples of John the Baptist ask Jesus if he is the promised one, Jesus cites his miracles as fulfilling Isaiah's prophecy.    Luke 7:18–23

And so Jesus' miracles act as a twofold *proclamation*. They proclaim the coming of

- the Kingdom of God and
- the promised Messiah.

*If I could translate . . .*
*harmony through*
*a piano, why could I not*
*translate it directly . . . ?*

*Then I took the boy's*
*head in my hands. . . .*
*I prayed. . . .*
*His sobs quieted . . .*
*and he fell asleep.*
Marta Korwin-Rhodes

Pianist Marta Korwin-Rhodes was in Warsaw when Nazis invaded it. She stayed on to help in hospitals. One night she stopped at the bed of a sobbing soldier. Placing her hands on his head, she prayed with all her heart. He stopped crying and fell asleep.

*The American Journal of Nursing* says that studies at New York University show that "the patient's power to recover improves when nurses lay on hands."

In *The Power to Heal,* Francis McNutt says that "loving people" seem to have a natural power or energy.

*[It] is communicated in a special way*
*through the power of touch,*
*and the patient absorbs [it] . . .*
*in such a way that the sick body*
*can build up its own life-giving forces.*

Read Luke 4:40 and 8:41–48 and explain:
a. How these passages tend to support NcNutt's thesis.
b. Why it was/wasn't necessary to touch or to be touched by Jesus to be healed.

2. A fourteen-year-old girl reported seeing visions of Mary at Lourdes, France, in 1858. The sick visited the site and were healed. Today the Medical Bureau of Lourdes has on file over 1,200 cures, confirmed by a commission of twenty physicians of all faiths and nations.

Nobel prize winner and nonbeliever Dr. Alexis Carrel went to Lourdes to study firsthand what happened there. While en route by train, he was called several times to attend to a sick girl who was also going to Lourdes. He told a friend, "If a case such as hers were cured, I would never doubt again."

Carrel accompanied the girl to Lourdes and witnessed her cure with his own eyes.

Record and share your thoughts about:
a. Lourdes and its 1,200 cures.
b. The fact that there are fewer cures at Lourdes today than formerly.

3. Someone said, "The greatest miracles of Lourdes are those involving people who go there seeking to be healed physically, but are healed in a spiritual way instead."

Record and share:
a. The person's point and to what extent you agree/disagree with it.
b. What cure you would you ask for if Jesus offered you a miracle.
c. A prayer asking Jesus for that cure. ❧

## Proclamations

List and explain:
a. Two ways miracles proclaim the coming of God's kingdom.
b. One way miracles proclaim Jesus to be the promised Messiah.

2. Identify:
a. Lourdes
b. Dr. Alexis Carrel

# 67 Invitations

**B**ruce Marshall wrote a novel called *Father Malachy's Miracle.* It centers around a priest in Scotland, who gets the idea of praying for a miracle so obvious that no one can deny it. He prays that the town's sinful nightclub be lifted up and transported to an island off the town's coast.

**T**his blind beggar in modern Jerusalem recalls Jesus' healing of the man born blind. Jesus says:

*"I came . . . so that the blind should see and those who see should become blind."*
John 9:39

Explain Jesus' words.

The miracle happens, but it backfires. The nightclub owners and their patrons turn it into a profitable publicity stunt. The story ends with Malachy realizing you can't *compel* belief, only *invite* it.

Besides serving as *proclamations* of God's kingdom and the Messiah, Jesus' miracles also served as *invitations* to people. How so?

Jesus' healing of the blind man, his restoration of hearing to the deaf, and his raising of the dead— these were not permanent changes. The eyes of the blind would dim again; the ears of the deaf would close again; those raised to life would die again.

What, then, is their deeper meaning? What is their long-term significance?

🔸 The healing of the blind is an invitation to *open our eyes* to what Jesus does.
🔸 The healing of the deaf is an invitation to *open our ears* to what Jesus says.
🔸 The raising of the dead is an invitation to *open our hearts* to Jesus' teaching and to God's kingdom (let God reign as king over our hearts).

Those who opened their hearts are traditionally divided into three groups: the unnumbered crowd, the 72 disciples, "the Twelve."

The unnumbered crowd are those who accepted Jesus' teaching and put all their trust in him.

The disciples are the "seventy-two" whom Jesus sent out

*two by two, to go ahead of him to every town . . . where he himself was about to go. He said to them, "There is a large harvest, but few workers to gather it in."* Luke 10:1–2

Finally, there are apostles under the leadership of Peter. Luke 6:13, Matthew 16–18 Jesus entrusted to them God's kingdom. They are the tiny mustard seed from which grew the great tree we now call the Church.

**W**illiam Barclay theorizes about the miracle in which Jesus raises a widow's son back from death to life, saying:

*It may well be that Jesus
with those keen eyes of his saw
that the lad was in a cataleptic trance
and saved him from being buried alive. . . .
It does not matter; the fact remains
that Jesus claimed for life a lad who
had been marked for death.*   The Gospel of Luke

Record and share:
a.  Why you like/dislike Barclay's theory.
b.  How well it agrees with Luke 7:11–17.

b.  When Jesus grew up, would he live with
(1) fisherman on the Gulf of Mexico,
(2) street people in Washington, D.C.,
(3) ordinary people anywhere?

c.  Would Jesus do most of his preaching
(1) around shopping malls, (2) in churches,
(3) on college campuses, (4) on radio
and TV?

d.  From what three groups would Jesus
pick four apostles each:

Create an ad that would appeal to young people today and challenge them to consider doing ministry full-time as their life's work.

2.  Imagine a dead parent or relative
returned from the dead and said to you,
"Life on the other side is exactly
as the Bible and Jesus say it is."
How would their words affect your faith
and the way you are living it out? Explain.

3.  *As Jesus walked along the shore . . .
he saw . . . Simon and his brother Andrew,
catching fish with a net. Jesus said . . .
"Come with me, and I will teach you
to catch people." At once they left their
nets and went with him.*   Mark 1:16–18

Imagine Jesus came today in America
rather than in Palestine years ago.

a.  Would his parents likely live in
(1) a small town, (2) the inner city,
(3) a typical suburb, (4) a trailer park?

(1) athletes, (2) college students,
(3) homeless people, (4) business people,
(5) minority blue-collar workers,
(6) used-car sellers, (7) rock musicians?

4. Imagine you run an ad agency.
You are hired to design an ad challenging
young people to enter ministry full-time
as their life's work. The full-page ad
(8½" × 11") is to include a photo and
have fewer than twenty words of copy.
Team up with a friend and design the ad.

5.  Read Matthew 19:16–30 ("RSVP").
Record and share:
a.  What struck you most about the reading.
b.  One question it raised in your mind.

*Invitations*

List and explain:
a.  The twofold way miracles serve as signs.
b.  How the following miracles act as invitations to people:
(1) healing the blind,
(2) healing the deaf,
(3) raising the dead.

2. List and describe the three groups into which tradition divides Jesus' followers.

> *When we
> do
> what we can,
> God will
> do
> what we can't.*
>
> E. C. McKenzie

# 68 Responses

People replied to Jesus' invitation in different ways.
Some accepted and believed.   John 4:53
Some refused and didn't believe.   John 9:18
Some were impressed by Jesus but said Satan gave him his power.   Luke 11:15

Today, people still respond differently to Jesus' miracles and teaching.
Some say he cured people of epilepsy, which ancients interpreted as a demon.
Still others say Jesus raised people from comas, but not from the dead.

Jesus told this parable to dramatize the four typical ways people respond to his miracles and teaching.
A farmer sowed seed in his field.
(Ancient farmers sowed seed atop the soil and then plowed it under.)

🌸 Some seed fell on a path by the field. Birds stole it and ate it instantly.

🌸 Some fell on the soil beneath which were rocks. It sprouted quickly but died when the sun baked the soil.

🌸 Some blew into thornbushes that formed a fence around the field to keep out animals. It sprouted but got choked to death by the thick thorns.

🌸 Finally, some seed fell on good soil and bore abundant fruit.

*[Jesus said,] "The seeds that fell along the path stand for those who hear; but the Devil comes and takes the message. . . .*

*"The seeds that fell on rocky ground stand for those who hear the message and receive it gladly. . . . But when the time of testing comes, they fall away.*

*"The seeds that fell among thorn bushes stand for those who hear; but the worries and riches and pleasures of this life . . . choke them, and their fruit never ripens.*

*"The seeds that fell in good soil stand for those who hear the message and . . . bear fruit."*   Luke 8:12–15

The following shows how we may sum up

🌸 the "beds" into which the seeds fell,
🌸 the "fate" of the seeds, and
🌸 the "meaning" for our lives.

| Beds | Fate | Meaning |
|---|---|---|
| Path | Stolen | We heed not |
| Rock | Withered | We heed and fall |
| Thorns | Choked | We heed and forget |
| Soil | Grew | We heed and follow |

> *"A man . . . went out to sow grain. . . . Some of it fell along the path, where it was stepped on, and the birds ate it up.*
>
> *"Some of it fell on rocky ground, and . . . dried up because the soil had no moisture."*   Luke 8:5–6

He ended by surrendering his life to God. After he did, he thought that God would make his future hard—even painful. Just the opposite happened. He said later, "Since I gave my life over to God, I've been blessed in a thousand ways."

d. Clarence and Robert Jordan committed themselves to Jesus in their youth. Clarence became a civil rights activist; Robert, a lawyer with political dreams. One day Clarence asked Robert for help. But Robert refused, saying it could hurt his political future.

2. A teacher read to her students Jesus' parable about the farmer whose seeds fell into four "seedbeds." Then she asked them three questions:

What seedbed are you in?
Why are you there?
What might you do to get out of it?

A girl wrote:

*What seedbed? I am being choked by thorns.*
*Why? Because my dad is emotionally sick.*
*I try to act right toward him*
*but get frustrated and give up.*
*What? I should return to church again*
*to grow stronger and fight the thorns,*
*but that's easier said than done.*

a. What advice would you give the girl?
b. Record your own answers to the above three questions.

3. Interview two adults, asking them:
a. Do you think it's harder or easier for young people to follow Jesus today? Why?
b. What was your biggest obstacle to following Jesus when you were my age? ✍

*E*xplain how these four stories illustrate the four "seedbeds" in Jesus' parable.

a. British TV celebrity Kenneth Clark had a "spiritual experience" so intense that he considered making major changes in his life. But he ended up doing nothing, saying, "I think I was right. I was too deeply embedded in the world to change course. But that I had 'felt the finger of God' I was quite sure."

b. A high school girl confessed, "Jesus' seed parable hit home for me. Last year my counselor helped me see a lot of things I should work at, and I made several resolutions. Then it hit me: I got so involved this year that I haven't followed up on any of them."

c. *Finding God* by Louis Savary and Thomas O'Connor has a story about a man who got into trouble. Although he hadn't prayed in years, now he prayed mightily.

*A*ncient farmers sowed seed atop the soil and then plowed it under.

*Responses*

*L*ist:
a. Three ways people in Jesus' day responded to his invitation to believe.
b. Two ways some people try to explain away Jesus' miracles.

2. Concerning Jesus' parable of the farmer, list:
a. The four seedbeds into which the seeds fell.
b. The fate of the seeds.
c. The parable's fourfold meaning for your life.

143

PRACTICE
RANDOM KINDNESS
AND
SENSELESS ACTS
OF BEAUTY.

*Anne Herbert*

The ancient road from Jerusalem to Jericho was a favorite haunt for outlaws.

Historical records document that travelers often had to pay protection money to local thugs for safe passage along it.

It was this dangerous road that provided Jesus with the setting for his parable of the Good Samaritan.

# CHAPTER THIRTEEN

# Teaching Ministry
## 69 Love As I Love

Pro star Reggie Williams said in a Super Bowl interview that he was born partially deaf. Unsuspecting teachers called him "slow." When he got to the third grade, a Miss Chapman took an interest in him and discovered his problem. Result? He became an outstanding student.

Miss Chapman's love for Reggie dramatizes Jesus' *first* great teaching: "Love one another, just as I love you."   John 15:12 Jesus made this love the *sign* of God's kingdom, and the *power* that spreads it.

First of all, love is the *sign* of God's kingdom: "If you have love for one another," Jesus said, "then everyone will know that you are my disciples."   John 13:35 In other words, when people see this love, they know God's kingdom is present.

Second, Jesus made love the *power* by which God's kingdom spreads on earth. A true story will illustrate.

A man was about to board a bus when someone jumped ahead of him, almost knocking him to the pavement. He said to the person in *mock* sincerity, "I'm sorry! I didn't mean to block your way!" The other person apologized and said with *true* sincerity, "Forgive me! That was really rude of me."

The offending person had responded to the man's mock display of love as if it were real, and was changed by it. The man said later, "This incident taught me why love is so powerful and how it spreads God's kingdom on earth. It destroys the 'chain reaction of evil' unleashed by Adam's sin and replaces it with a 'chain reaction of good.'"

A final point. Jesus said our love must extend even to our enemies.   Luke 6:27 Gerald Lipke is an example of what Jesus had in mind. Jerry's parents were killed when their plane exploded over Colorado. The students in Jerry's class asked their pastor for a prayer service.

When the pastor asked Jerry
if it would be okay, he said, "Yes."
Then Jerry added,
"Could we also say a prayer for the man
who killed my father and mother?"

It is this kind of witness to love
that makes it the

🔖 *sign* of God's kingdom and the
🔖 *power* by which it spreads on earth.

A New York woman was stabbed
to death while her own neighbors
watched from their houses, making
no effort to help her. A disgusted columnist
said, "We ought to tear the parable of the
Good Samaritan out of our Bibles.
No one lives it anymore."

A college professor got fed up with all
the "random acts of senseless violence"
reported on TV.
He stunned his class, saying, "This week's
assignment is to perform one 'random act
of senseless kindness' and report on its
impact on you and on the recipient."

It was the most effective assignment
he gave all year. Commenting on the
concept, *Glamour* magazine wrote:

*Like all revolutions,
guerrilla goodness begins slowly,
with a single act. Let it be yours.*

Perform one act of "senseless kindness."
Record and share the impact it had
(a) on you, personally, (b) on the recipient.

2. Someone said, "Just as tragic as our lack
of kindness toward our neighbors is
our lack of kindness toward our family."
Evaluate your kindness toward your family,
using this scale: 1 = rarely, 2 = sometimes,
3 = usually, 4 = always.

___ a. Am usually kind and considerate.
___ b. Show respect to those over me.
___ c. Communicate well with everyone.
___ d. Accept correction well.
___ e. Help out voluntarily.
___ f. Keep calm during disputes.
___ g. Apologize when appropriate.
___ h. Keep a neat room.
___ i. Pray for family members.
___ j. Share what I have.

Evaluation: 40–30 I'm a joy! (I hope.)
           29–24 I'm okay! (I think.)
           23–19 I'm not so hot! (Ouch!)
           18–10 I'm a drag! (Help!)

Have at least one family member evaluate
you, using the above criteria.
a. How do you explain the differences?
b. How revealing was this exercise?

3. Imagine you subscribe to the *Cana News*.
Four items catch your attention.
🔖 For sale: Coffin. Used only one night.
Boy's size. See widow of Nain.   Luke 7:11–15
🔖 Rent-a-Donkey: Scrubbed, fed, and ready
to trot. Come in and see why we're #1.
Zeb's Stables.   Mark 11:1–3
🔖 Overheard: "Wasn't that little kid
from Nazareth fantastic today?"
"Terrific for a twelve-year-old!"   Luke 2:46
🔖 Open House. Celebrate our daughter's
cure. Monday 6–8 P.M. Jairus.   Luke 8:50

Identify each item. Team up with a friend
and create one or two items of your own. 🔖

*I slept and dreamed
that life was a joy.*

*I woke and saw
that life was service.*

*I served and understood
that service was joy.*
      Rabindranath Tagore

*Love
As I
Love*

Explain in what sense
Jesus made love the *sign*
of God's kingdom and
the *power* that spreads it.

2. Explain how the
physical setting and
the characters Jesus
selected for his parable
of the Good Samaritan
were in perfect accord
with the historical
facts of the time.

# 70 Forgive As I Forgive

One day Jewish religious leaders grew angry when they saw how Jesus was welcoming sinners. Jesus responded by telling a parable.

*"A man . . . had two sons.*
*The younger one [took his inheritance,*
*left home, spent it, and returned broke.]*
*He was still a long way from home*
*when his father saw him; his heart*
*was filled with pity, and he ran,*
*threw his arms around his son,*
*and kissed him. . . .*

*"The father called to his servants. . . .*
*'Put a ring on his finger*
*and shoes on his feet . . .*
*and let us celebrate.' "*  Luke 15:11–12, 20, 22–23

This touching parable brings us to Jesus' *second* great teaching: *forgive as I forgive.*  Matthew 18:22, Luke 23:34

🍃 Hugging his son shows that the father *welcomes* him back fully.
🍃 Putting shoes on his feet shows that the father *forgives* him fully.

(Shoes were the sign of a free person; bare feet, the sign of a slave.)
🍃 Giving his son a (signet) ring shows that the father *restores* the boy to full family membership.

The end of Jesus' parable focuses on the older son, who gets mad because his father is so forgiving. This son won't even come inside and celebrate his brother's return— even when his father begs him, saying:

*"But we had to celebrate . . .*
*because your brother was dead,*
*but now he is alive; he was lost,*
*but now he has been found."*  Luke 15:32

Jesus doesn't tells us if the older son changed his mind. This is because the older son stands for the religious leaders, who get mad because Jesus welcomes sinners.

In other words, Jesus constructs his parable so that the religious leaders must write their own ending to it.

A measure of the prodigal son's plight was that he hired himself out to take care of pigs (a repulsive job for Jews, who detested this unclean animal).

Worse yet, he got so hungry that "he wished he could fill himself with the bean pods [shown here] the pigs ate."  Luke 16:16

They must decide whether
they will go inside and celebrate
or sit outside and sulk.

And so Jesus' parable is both
a *revelation* and an *invitation:*

☙ it *reveals* how forgiving God is, and
☙ it *invites* us to forgive as God does.

The film *The Heart Is a Lonely Hunter* has a scene in which a girl tries to explain to a deaf man what music sounds like. She stands in front of him so he can read her lips and watch her body move. But her idea doesn't work, and they both end up laughing.

Jesus faced a similar problem.
Trying to explain to people
how merciful and forgiving God is
was like trying to explain sound
to a deaf person.
This explains why Jesus told parables.
He used them as *word windows*
through which people could look
and glimpse God and God's kingdom.

a. How does the parable of the two sons act as a *word window?*
b. Pick a song and try to communicate its name to the group without speaking.

2. Besides composing parables
to act as *word windows,* Jesus used
parables to act as *word mirrors.*
He composed them so that they mirrored
persons in his listening audience.
Sometimes he composed them
so that the same parable acted as both
a word window and a word mirror.

a. Explain how Jesus' parable of the two
sons acts as a window and as a mirror.
In other words, how does it help people
glimpse God or God's kingdom,
and how does it help them see their own
forgiving or unforgiving attitude?
b. Why were mirror parables ideal for
confronting people, like Jewish leaders?

3. How do you understand these quotes about forgiveness?
a. "Forgiveness is the fragrance a violet sheds on the heel that crushes it."
Mark Twain
b. Jesus told Peter he must forgive "not seven times, but seventy times seven, because the Kingdom of heaven is like this." Matthew 18:22–23

4. A little girl asked her grandmother about a picture on her bedroom wall. It showed three mirrors. One reflected a beast; the second, a fool; and the third, Jesus. The grandmother said:

"It reminds me that
when I hurt people's feelings,
I am like that beast;
when I judge people's motives,
I am like that fool;
when I forgive people, I am like Jesus."

Record and share
which of these three reflections poses
the biggest challenge to you and why. ☙

*Forgive
As I
Forgive*

**E**xplain the meaning
of these images:
a. Hugging the son.
b. Giving the son shoes.
c. Giving him a ring.

2. How does the
parable of the Prodigal
Son act as both a *revelation* and an *invitation?*

3. Why didn't Jesus say
what the older son did?

4. Explain:
a. How window
parables differ from
mirror parables.
b. The purpose of each.

MUCH PRAYER
**MUCH**
POWER,
LITTLE PRAYER
**LITTLE**
POWER,
NO PRAYER
**NO**
POWER.

# 71 Pray As I Pray

One night Dr. Martin Luther King Jr. was about to doze off when his phone rang. He picked it up. An angry voice said, "Listen up, nigger. We've taken all we want from you. Before next week, you'll be sorry you ever came to Montgomery."

Suddenly, all King's fears came crashing down on him. He didn't know what to do. In this state of confusion and panic, he bowed his head and prayed. Instantly, he felt the presence of God as he had never felt it before.

Dr. King's prayer introduces us to Jesus' *third* great teaching. Besides teaching us to *love* and to *forgive,* he teaches us to *pray* as he did. And how did Jesus pray?

First of all, Jesus prayed *often.* Luke tells us, "He would go away to lonely places, where he prayed." Luke 5:16 And again, "Jesus went up a hill to pray and spent the whole night there praying to God." Luke 6:12

Second, he prayed in *different settings.* Besides praying alone, Jesus prayed in two other settings: in small groups with friends (Luke 9:28) and with the larger community (Luke 4:16).

Finally, Jesus prayed *with freedom;* that is, he used different prayer postures and prayer styles.

First, he used different prayer postures. He knelt (Luke 22:41), raised his eyes to heaven (John 17:1), and prayed out loud (Matthew 26:42).

Second, he used different prayer styles. He used *free* prayers that he made up on the spot. John 17:1 He also used *fixed* prayers that had been a part of the Jewish faith for centuries. For example, on the cross, Jesus prayed Psalm 22. Mark 15:34

And so Jesus' third great teaching is pray as I pray:

- *often;*
- *in different settings:*
  alone,
  in small groups, and
  with the community;
- *with freedom:*
  using different postures and
  using different prayers: free and fixed.

"**B**e still and know that I am God." Psalm 46:10 (Grail)

**T**he LORD said, "I was ready
to answer my people's prayers,
but they did not pray.
I was ready for them to find me,
but they did not even try."   Isaiah 65:1

Record and share:
a.  How many days a week
do you usually pray?
b.  How many minutes daily
(–1 = less than a minute,
1+ = more than a minute)
do you usually pray, when you pray?
c.  How many times a week do you
pray to God in a small-group setting,
for example, with your family?
d.  How many times a month
do you find yourself praying with
the Christian community on Sunday?
e.  On a scale of 1 (minimally) to
10 (maximally), how interested are you,
at this time in your life, in learning
how to pray better?
f.  Explain your answer to *e*.

2.  Prayer can take place in one of four
forms, sometimes referred to
by the word *ACTS* (*A*doration, *C*ontrition,
*T*hanksgiving, and *S*upplication).

🖎 *Adoration* acknowledges God as God.
For example, the apostle Thomas
fell on his knees and prayed to Jesus,
"My Lord and my God!"   John 20:28

🖎 *Contrition* acknowledges that
we are sinners in need of God's mercy.
For example, the blind beggar cried out,
"Jesus! Son of David!
Have mercy on me!"   Luke 18:38

🖎 *Thanksgiving* acknowledges God's
many gifts to us. Jesus himself prayed,
"Father, Lord of heaven and earth!
I thank you . . ."   Luke 10:21

🖎 *Supplication* acknowledges our need
for God's help. For example, Jesus taught
his disciples, "Ask, and you will receive;
seek, and you will find."   Luke 11:9

a.  Which of these forms does your prayer
usually take? Explain.
b.  Write out a prayer that contains all
four forms. Label them in your prayer.

3.  The Lord's Prayer may be divided
into two groups of petitions: three *your*
petitions and three *our* petitions.
a.  List the three *your* petitions.
b.  List the three *our* petitions.

4.  Some people ask, "Why do we pray
in the Lord's Prayer for the *coming*
of God's kingdom? Didn't Jesus establish it?
If so, why pray for it to come?"
How would you answer them? 🖎

*Pray
AS I
Pray*

**L**ist and explain:
a.  The three settings
in which Jesus prayed.
b.  The way Jesus
exercised freedom
in the way he prayed.
c.  The four forms
that prayer can take.
d.  The two groups
of petitions into which
the Lord's Prayer divides.

# 72  Be Ready Always

Ancient weddings lasted for days.
A high point was the arrival
of the groom at the bride's home.
Young women carrying lighted oil lamps
waited there to greet him.

It is against this background that
Jesus told the parable of the young women.
Its purpose was to answer the question:
When will God's kingdom be complete
and the Son of Man return?

The parable describes ten young women.
Five are wise
and have a full supply of oil.
Five are foolish
and have only a small supply of oil.

When the bridegroom delays in coming,
the young women fall asleep.
At midnight, they are awakened
by the shout, "Here is the bridegroom!"

The foolish ones discover,
to their dismay, that their oil is used up.
Since the supply of the wise women
is low, the foolish women
are forced to go off to get more oil.
While they are gone, the groom arrives.

*"The five who were ready
went in with him to the wedding feast,
and the door was closed."*  Matthew 25:10

This parable introduces us to Jesus'
*fourth* great teaching. It is this:

*"The Son of Man
will come at an hour when you
are not expecting him."*  Matthew 24:44

The point of Jesus parable
of the young women is
that God has not seen fit to tell us
when God's kingdom will be complete
and the Son of Man will return.
Therefore, we must be ready always!
For only those who are ready
will enter the wedding feast.
To these, Jesus will say, joyfully:

*"Come and possess the kingdom
which has been prepared for you
ever since the creation of the world.
I was hungry and you fed me . . .
naked and you clothed me. . . .
Whenever you did this for the least
important of these followers of mine,
you did it for me!"*  Matthew 25:34–36, 40

Sheep and goats graze
together, but at night
they are separated.
The goats are herded
into a warm place.

Jesus used this image
to teach that during life
good and bad people
live side by side.

At death they will be
separated and dealt
with appropriately.
Matthew 25:31–46

To those who are not ready,
Jesus will say just the opposite.

And so Jesus' fourth great teaching
is this: "Be ready always! The end will
come at a time when we least expect it."

A farmer planted wheat in a field.
One night an enemy oversowed
the field with weeds. When they
appeared, the workers asked the farmer
if they should pull them up.

*"'No,' he answered . . . 'you might pull up*
*some of the wheat along with them. . . .*
*Let [them] grow together until harvest.*
*Then I will tell the harvest workers*
*to pull up the weeds . . . and burn them,*
*and then to gather in the wheat*
*and put it in my barn.' "* Matthew 13:29–30

What point about God's kingdom does
Jesus make in this parable, and what do
the following images stand for in life?
(Check Jesus' explanation.)   Matthew 13:36–43

a.  Sower        f.  Harvest
b.  Field        g.  Harvest workers
c.  Good seed    h.  Destroying weeds
d.  Weeds        i.  Saving wheat
e.  Enemy

2.  A missionary nurse who spent a lifetime
in China returned on the same plane
as a singer who spent a week there.
A crowd welcomed the singer home;
no one welcomed the missionary.
"Lord," she said, "why does a crowd
welcome the singer, and no one me?"
The Lord replied, "You're not home yet."
What is the Lord's point, and how does it
relate to the parable of the weeds?

3.  American poet Edwin Markham wrote:
"The few little years we spend on earth
are only the first scene in a Divine Drama
that extends into eternity."

a.  What is Markham's point, and how
does it apply to your life?
b.  What is one way you could bring your
life more in tune with Markham's point?

4.  Imagine you learned that you will die
tomorrow. Record and share:

a.  Your greatest regret. Greatest fear.
b.  How you would spend your last hours.

Here is the response of a college girl:

*I would . . . contact all the people*
*I had ever really loved, and I'd make sure*
*they knew I had really loved them.*
*Then I would play all the records*
*that meant the most to me, and*
*I would sing all my favorites songs. . . .*
*I would look at my blue skies*
*and feel my warm sunshine.*
*I would tell the moon and the stars*
*how lovely and beautiful they are.*
*I would say "good-bye"*
*to all the little things I own—*
*my clothes, my books, and my "stuff."*
*Then I would thank God for*
*the great gift of life, and die in his arms.*
John Powell, *The Secret of Staying in Love*

*I would . . .*
*contact all the people*
*I had ever really loved,*
*and I'd make sure*
*they knew I had really*
*loved them.*

*Then I would play*
*all the records*
*that meant the most*
*to me, and . . .*

## Be Ready Always

**H**ow long did
ancient weddings last,
and what was a high
point of them?

2. Retell Jesus' parable
of the young women,
and explain how it
illustrates Jesus' fourth
great teaching.

# Last Supper

## 73 Storm Clouds

Dr. Martin Luther King Jr. gave this warning to his followers toward the end of his life:
"We've got some difficult days ahead. But it doesn't matter with me now. . . . I just want to do God's will."

Dr. King's words echo a similar warning that Jesus gave his followers toward the end of his life, when he said:

*"The Son of Man will be handed over to those who will kill him."*   Mark 9:31

Jesus was referring to the escalating hostility between himself and the Jewish leaders of the time. The leaders saw Jesus as a threat to the way they interpreted Jewish faith.

The hostility of the Jewish leaders began when Jesus started his ministry. One day, after healing a man, Jesus said to the man, "Your sins are forgiven." When the leaders heard this, they erupted:

*"Who is this man who speaks such blasphemy! God is the only one who can forgive sins!"*   Luke 5:21

Some time after this, Jesus heals a man on the Sabbath. The leaders are furious that he did this on the Sabbath.   Luke 6:11

And so the gap between Jesus and the leaders widens with each passing week. Finally, the breaking point comes when Jesus raises Lazarus from the dead. News of the miracle spreads everywhere.

The Jewish leaders begin to worry. Where will all this end?

LEADERS   *If we let him go on . . . the Roman authorities will take action and destroy our Temple and our nation! . . .*

CAIAPHAS   *It is better . . . to have one man die . . . instead of . . . the whole nation. . . .*

NARRATOR   *He did not say this of his own accord; . . . he was prophesying that Jesus was going to die for the Jewish people, and not only for them, but also to bring together into one body all the scattered people of God.*
John 11:48, 50–52

From that day on, the Jewish leaders plotted to kill Jesus.   John 11:53

**W**hen the disciples all came together . . . Jesus said to them,

*"The Son of Man is about to be handed over to those who will kill him. . . ."*

The disciples became very sad.
Matthew 17:22–23

The raising of Lazarus recalls a parable about another Lazarus. He was a poor invalid who begged at the door of a fabulously rich man. The beggar hoped for "scraps" from the the rich man's table. But it seems the rich man's dogs were kinder to Lazarus than the rich man was. At least the dogs licked his sores.

Both men died suddenly and their fates reversed. The rich man asked Abraham to send Lazarus back from the dead to warn his rich brothers, lest they end up as he did. Abraham refused, saying:

*"If they will not listen to Moses and the prophets, they will not be convinced even if someone [Lazarus] were to rise from death."* Luke 16:31

Record and share:
a. How Jesus' raising of Lazarus adds meaning to Jesus' parable of Lazarus.
b. How you might react if a friend returned from the dead and warned you to change. Explain.

2. Some Jewish leaders were watching to see if Jesus would heal the crippled hand of a poor person on the Sabbath.

*[Jesus] looked around at them all; then he said to the man, "Stretch out your hand." He did so, and . . . became well. . . . [The leaders] were filled with rage.* Luke 6:10–11

Isn't Jesus partly to blame for provoking this ugly confrontation? Why did Jesus aggravate the situation by waiting until the Sabbath to heal the person?

3. Jesus' disciples ate without washing their hands according to a religious ritual prescribed by Jewish religious leaders. The leaders confronted Jesus, who said:

*"How right Isaiah was when he prophesied about you! . . . 'These people . . . honor me with their words, but their heart is really far away from me. . . . They teach human rules as though they were my laws!' "* Mark 7:6–7

Why didn't Jesus soften the harshness of Isaiah's words? As it was, Jesus alienated the leaders even more.

4. Read Matthew 23:1–27 ("Stormy North Side of Jesus"). Record and share:
a. What struck you most.
b. What questions the reading raised. ❧

Jesus compared leaders of his day to "white-washed tombs, which look fine on the outside but are full of bones and decaying corpses on the inside." Matthew 23:27

Above-ground tombs are still part of the Jerusalem landscape.

Leaving a stone on a tomb is a ritualistic sharing in the burial of someone.

*Storm Clouds*

Explain the reason for:
a. The escalating hostility between Jesus and the Jewish religious leaders.
b. The decision of the leaders to eliminate Jesus.

2. Explain in what sense Caiaphas' words were a prophecy in disguise.

> *He cut through all the phony ideas and told them the truth. And he still does. Jesus really knows the truth about God.*
>
> — Norman Habel

# 74  Moment of Truth

The Passover Festival was near. People wondered if Jesus would dare go to Jerusalem for it, because authorities had issued an order for his arrest.   John 11:55–57
The answer was not long in coming.
Suddenly, all of Jerusalem buzzed
with the news that Jesus was on his way.

Jesus entered the city on a donkey.
The crowds cut palm branches
and waved them excitedly, shouting,
"God bless him who comes
in the name of the Lord!"   Matthew 21:9

When Jesus arrived at the Temple,
he was shocked.
Its outer court looked like a carnival.
Sellers hawked animals for sacrifice.

"Hosannas" echo from Jerusalem walls as modern pilgrims celebrate Jesus' entry into the great city.

When Jesus began kicking over tables
on which money was stacked,
the Temple officials became incensed
and demanded an explanation.

The crowd sensed a showdown
and grew deathly silent.
Jesus surprised everyone by holding up
to the officials a *word mirror.*

It concerned
a landowner who planted a vineyard.
He rented it out to tenants for a share
of the crops. When harvesttime came,
he sent slaves to collect his share;
but the tenants killed them.
Again the owner sent other slaves,
but the tenants did the same thing.

*"Last of all he sent his son to them. . . .
But when the tenants saw the son,
they said, . . . 'Come on, let's kill him,
and we will get his property!'
So they grabbed him . . .
and killed him."*   Matthew 21:37–39

*[Jesus ended his parable, asking,]
"When the owner of the vineyard comes,
what will he do to those tenants?"* . . .

*[The officials answered,]
"He will certainly kill those evil men . . .
and rent the vineyard out
to other tenants, who will give him
his share of the harvest."*   Matthew 21:40–41

Suddenly, it dawned on the officials
what Jesus had done. The account ends,
"The chief priests and the Pharisees . . .
knew that [Jesus]
was talking about them."   Matthew 21:45

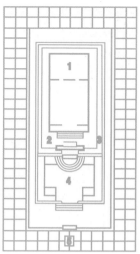

Schematic of the Temple's main areas:

1 Holy of Holies
2 Court of Priests
3 Court of Men
4 Court of Women
5 Court of Gentiles

Jesus' parable of the tenants has been called a "mini-Bible." This is because it sums up the entire Scripture story. Its "cast of characters" is as follows:

a. Landowner     _____
b. Vineyard     _____
c. First renting     _____
d. First tenants     _____
e. Slaves     _____
f. Other slaves     _____
g. Owner's son     _____
h. Second renting _____
i. Other tenants     _____

Read Matthew 21:33–46 and match up the events and characters in the parable with their real-life counterparts, explaining your choice:
(1) apostles, (2) Jesus, (3) early prophets, (4) God, (5) Israel, (6) old covenant, (7) new covenant, (8) later prophets, (9) Jewish leaders.

2. A scene in *Hamlet* has the young prince confront his mother, the queen:

HAMLET   *Sit down. . . . You go not*
*till I set you up a glass*
*Where you may see*
*the inmost part of you.*

QUEEN   *O Hamlet, speak no more.*
*Thou turns't mine eyes*
*into my very soul.*
*And there I see such black*
*and grained spots*
*As will not leave their tinct.*

Hamlet set before his mother a *word* mirror, not a *glass* mirror; and she saw reflected in it her own ugly part in his father's tragic murder.

Some of Jesus' parables acted like this. Jesus constructed them in such a way that they mirrored the situation of his listening audience.

a. How does the parable of the tenants act as a "mirror parable"?
b. How does a "mirror parable" differ from a "window parable"?
c. Read the parables listed below. After reading each parable, explain:

(1) The point Jesus is making in each.
(2) How the point applies to your life.
(3) Whether you think the parable should be classified as a *mirror* parable, a *window* parable, or a *combination of both*.

🔖 House builders   Luke 6:46–49
🔖 Mustard seed   Luke 13:18–19
🔖 Lost coin   Luke 15:8–10 🔖

*Moment of Truth*

Why were people wondering if Jesus would show up in Jerusalem for the Passover, and what shocked Jesus when he got to the Temple?

2. Explain how the parable of the tenants "mirrors" the following:
a. God
b. Israel
c. old covenant
d. leaders
e. early prophets
f. later prophets
g. Jesus
h. new covenant
i. apostles

# 75 Passover Supper

Medieval folklore held that the pelican fed its young with its blood. This explains how it came to symbolize Jesus and the Eucharist.

E lie Wiesel's novel *Town Beyond the Wall* illustrates a powerful friendship. It comes not from the friend directly but from the memory of the friend. Michael lives through torture because his friend Pedro lives in his memory.

Wiesel touches upon a deep truth here. Memory not only links us to the past but also keeps us alive in the present. This truth is deeply rooted in the Bible.

*To remember*
*is not simply to look back at past events;*
*more importantly, it is to bring*
*these events into the present and*
*celebrate them here and now. For Israel,*
*remembrance meant participation.*
Henri Nouwen, *The Living Reminder*

It is with this understanding that Jesus gathers with his apostles to celebrate the Passover supper.

It is to do something far more than "remember" the event that freed Israel from Egyptian slavery. It is to bring this event, *by faith,* into the present, to relive it, and to share in its original power and blessing.

Leonardo da Vinci's *Last Supper*.

Acting as the father, Jesus begins the Passover in a surprising way.

He pours water into a basin and begins by washing the feet of each apostle.

For Jews, washing feet was humiliating. Only slaves performed this task. Jesus' action created a deep impression on the apostles. When he ended, he said:

*"I, your Lord and Teacher,*
*have just washed your feet.*
*You, then, should wash one another's feet.*
*I have set an example for you."* John 13:14–15

*[Then Jesus prepared a cup of wine,*
*saying to all,] "Take this and share it. . . .*
*I tell you that from now on*
*I will not drink this wine*
*until the Kingdom of God comes."*
Luke 22:17–18

The wine was probably red and would have recalled

❧ the Passover *blood* smeared on Israelite houses the night the Israelites fled Egypt. Exodus 12:22
❧ the covenant *blood* sprinkled on the Israelite people to seal their pact with God at Mount Sinai. Exodus 24:8

When all had drunk from the cup, Jesus began the Passover meal.

Each panel of this tabernacle door refers to a gospel event that relates to the Last Supper. Identify each event and explain its relationship.

The door's horizontal wording is
*Caro mea vere cibus.*
*Sanguis meus vere potus.*
("My body is the real food. My blood is the real drink.")   John 6:55

The vertical wording is
*His est panis qui de caelo descendit.*
("This . . . is the bread that came down from heaven.")   John 6:58

A criminal turned his life around. When a woman asked how he did it, he took from his wallet the photo of his caseworker, saying, "When I'm tempted to return to crime, I look at this photo and remember what this person did for me."

a.  How is the way that the criminal remembered the caseworker similar to, but also different from, the way Israel remembered God's freeing them from Egypt and making them God's Chosen People?
b.  How does the Israelite idea of memory give greater meaning to Jesus' words, "Do this in memory of me"?
c.  Open your wallet, select something, and tell what memory it holds for you.

2.  Early Christians had no trouble with Jesus' miracle at Cana (John 2:1–12), which foreshadowed (pointed to) what Jesus did at the Last Supper. Each summer their grape vines drew water out from the soil and, with the sun's help, changed it into wine.

Explain in what sense the miracle at Cana pointed to the Last Supper.

3.  Early Christians also had no trouble with the miracle of the multiplication of the loaves (John 6:10–13), which foreshadowed what Jesus did at the Last Supper. They planted five bushels of grain; and by the end of summer, it multiplied into five hundred bushels.

a.  To what event during Israel's sojourn in the desert did Jesus compare the multiplication of the loaves?   John 6:31
b.  What remarkable promise did Jesus make in connection with this miracle that linked it to what he would do at the Last Supper?   John 6:50–51

4. Interview two Catholics who attend Mass regularly and asked them:

a.  Why do you continue to attend Mass when many other people no longer do so?
b.  How would you explain to someone who no longer attends Mass why they ought to rethink their decision to say no to Jesus' invitation: "Do this in memory of me"?

*Passover Supper*

Explain:
a.  The Jewish understanding of "remembering."
b. What was "remembered" in the celebration of the Passover meal.
c.  The surprising way Jesus began the meal.
d.  What Jesus was teaching his disciples through it.
e.  Two events the drinking of red wine would recall.

*Jesus of Nazareth
requests the honor
of your presence
at a dinner
to be given
in his honor
tomorrow morning.'
Attire is informal.
RSVP*

# 76 Invitation to Remember

The Passover meal began with Jesus preparing the ceremonial food: bitter herbs, unleavened bread, sauce for the herbs, and a roasted lamb.

The bread that Jesus took into his hands at the Last Supper may have resembled this bread being carried through Jerusalem streets to be sold in a bakery.

🍃 *Bitter herbs* recall Israel's years of bitter slavery in Egypt.
🍃 Clay-colored *sauce* recalls Israel's years of making bricks under the hot sun.
🍃 *Unleavened bread* recalls Israel's haste in fleeing Egypt, not waiting for the next day's bread dough to rise.
🍃 The *lamb* recalls its sacrificial *blood* that the Israelites smeared on their doorposts, saving them from the "angel of death," and its sacrificial *body* that they ate to nourish them for their journey.

When the Passover meal was prepared, Jesus took the bread, gave thanks, broke it, and gave it to the apostles, saying:

*"This is my body, which is given for you. Do this in memory of me."* Luke 22:19

Identifying the bread as his body recalls the day Jesus told the people:

*"I am the living bread that came down from heaven. . . . The bread that I will give you is my flesh."* John 6:51

The rest of the meal follows routinely. When it is over, Jesus prepares a last cup of wine. Silence falls over the apostles as they watch him take the cup, raise his eyes to heaven, and pray:

*"This cup is God's new covenant sealed with my blood, which is poured out for you."* Luke 22:20

The phrase "God's new covenant" recalls God's promise: "I will make a new covenant with the people of Israel." Jeremiah 31:31

The phrase "sealed with my blood" recalls the words of the old covenant, "This is the blood that seals the covenant, which the LORD made wth you." Exodus 24:8

As the apostles drink from the cup, their minds are filled with questions: Is this the "new covenant"? What does Jesus mean when he says "sealed with my blood"?

Mark ends his Last Supper account, saying, "Then they sang a hymn and went out to the Mount of Olives." Mark 14:26

The apostles were happy as they walked from the Last Supper room to the Mount of Olives. But it was a bittersweet happiness. Jesus said too many sorrow-shadowed things to allow for unrestrained joy. List and explain two of these things.

2. Jesus said to the people seated on the hillside outside Capernaum:

*"The bread that I will give you is my flesh, which I give so that the world may live."* This started an angry argument

among them. *"How can this man give us his flesh to eat?" they asked. . . . "This teaching is too hard."* John 6:51–52, 60

How does this passage make clear that Jesus meant exactly what he said at the Last Supper, when he took bread and said, "This is my body"?

3. Paul wrote to the Corinthians concerning the Eucharist, "Every time you eat this bread and drink from this cup you proclaim the Lord's death until he comes." 1 Corinthians 11:26 A modern writer adds:

*Therefore, every time ministers call their people around the table, they call them to experience*

*not only the Lord's presence but his absence as well; they call them . . . to sadness as well as to joy.*
Henri Nouwen, *The Living Reminder*

Explain the writer's point and how it applies, in a practical way, to your life.

4. "Before Communion the sacred bread does not look as if Christ is present in it. After Communion, Christians don't always look as if Christ is in them." Frank Sheed
a. Explain why you agree/disagree.
b. If you agree, what suggestion would you give for remedying this situation?

5. The movie *E.T.* contains two scenes that deal with food. In one, the boy leaves candy to show E.T. that he is his friend. In the other E.T. raids the refrigerator.

Someone noted that behind the warmth and humor of these scenes is a basic message: Without food we die, whether human or extraterrestrial. The person adds, "What is true of bodily life is true also of spiritual life."

Compose two brief prayers that you can memorize—or put in your wallet—
a. To prepare yourself for Communion.
b. To give thanks after receiving it. ✦

The eucharistic minister says, "The body of Christ." We say, "Amen." The eucharistic minister says, "The blood of Christ." We say, "Amen."

This solemn exchange recalls Paul's words:

*When we drink from [the cup], we are sharing in the blood of Christ. . . . When we eat [the bread], we are sharing in the body of Christ.*
1 Corinthians 10:16

## Invitation to Remember

List and explain the four foods that Jesus prepared at the Last Supper and what each recalled.

2. Explain what these words of Jesus recalled:
a. "This is my body."
b. "God's new covenant."
c. "Sealed with my blood."

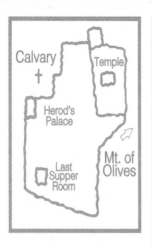

Calvary †  Temple

Herod's Palace

Last Supper Room

Mt. of Olives

# CHAPTER FIFTEEN

# Death & Rising

## 77 Agony & Arrest

The Mount of Olives lies across the valley from Jerusalem. On its slope is a tiny grove of ancient olive trees. Experts think it marks the very spot where Jesus and his disciples went after the Last Supper.

*[Arriving at the Mount of Olives,]*
*Jesus said to his disciples,*
*"Sit here while I pray."*
*He took Peter, James, and John with him.*

*Distress and anguish came over him,*
*and he said to them,*
*"The sorrow in my heart . . . almost*
*crushes me. Stay here and keep watch."*

El Greco's *Agony in the Garden of Gethsemane.*

*He went a little farther on, threw himself on the ground, and prayed. . . .*

*"Father! All things are possible for you. Take this cup of suffering away. . . . Yet not what I want, but what you want."*
                                            Mark 14:32–36

Jesus returns to find the disciples asleep. He wakes them, saying:

*"Keep watch, and pray*
*that you will not fall into temptation. . . ."*
*He went away once more and prayed. . . .*

*[Returning a final time, he said,]*
*"The hour has come! . . ."*
*Jesus was still speaking when Judas, one of the twelve disciples, arrived. With him was a crowd armed with swords and clubs.*   Mark 14:38–39, 41, 43

Judas greets Jesus with a kiss. Jesus says, "Judas, is it with a kiss that you betray the Son of Man?"   Luke 22:48 The disciples scuffle with the soldiers briefly, think the better of it, and flee.

Totally alone, Jesus is taken to the residence of the high priest. Peter follows at a distance and then slips unnoticed into the courtyard.

Minutes later, Peter is recognized and accused three times of being a disciple. But each time he denies it, vehemently. Then a rooster crows, and Peter recalls what Jesus had said to him earlier.

*"Before the rooster crows two times, you will say three times that you do not know me." . . .*
*[Peter] broke down and cried.*   Mark 14:72

A musician said of Frederic Chopin's nocturne in C sharp minor: "In this piece all is trouble . . . until he begins to talk with God . . . ; then it is all right." William Barclay notes:

*That is the way it was with Jesus.*
*He went into Gethsemane in the dark;*
*he came out in the light—*

Imagine you are a guard who fell to the ground. Write a brief report for your commanding officer, telling how you felt in the presence of Jesus and how his presence has affected you since then.

3. Mark ends his account of Jesus' arrest with this unusual comment:

On the Mount of Olives, Peter, James, and John saw Jesus in a "moment of agony" — when his *humanity* shone through dramatically.

Earlier, on Mount Tabor, the same three disciples saw Jesus in a "moment of ecstasy" — when his *divinity* shone through dramatically.

*because he talked with God.*
*He went into Gethsemane in agony;*
*he came out with peace in his soul—*
*because he talked with God.*     The Gospel of Luke

a. Record and share a time when you were in deep trouble and talked with God.
b. What trouble? What did you say? With what result?

2. Daniel says of one of his visions: "Gabriel . . . stood beside me, and I was so terrified that I fell to the ground." Daniel 8:17 John describes the same thing happening in the garden when Jesus identified himself to the guards. "They moved back and fell to the ground." John 18:6 One writer suggests:

*It may very well be that in this instance,*
*the guards suddenly felt the full force*
*of Jesus' personality and were utterly*
*dismayed. . . . In any case . . . John intends*
*to picture it as miraculous, . . .*
*emphasizing the perfect freedom*
*with which Jesus accepted arrest.*
Guiseppe Ricciotti, *The Life of Christ*

*A certain young man, dressed only*
*in a linen cloth, was following Jesus.*
*They tried to arrest him, but he ran away*
*naked, leaving the cloth behind.*    Mark 14:51

Why would only Mark include this detail?

4. Tradition says that Mark was a youth at the time of the Last Supper. Test your detective powers and see if you can explain how Mark 14:12–16 and Acts 12:12 point to (a) the home in which the Last Supper was eaten and (b) why young Mark happened to be in Gethsemane.

5. What difference do these words suggest between Jesus and other leaders: "The penalty of sin is not to have to face the anger of Jesus, but the heartbreak in his eyes"?    William Barclay

## Agony & Arrest

Explain:
a. How the "Mount" events (Olives and Tabor) are totally different but closely related.
b. How the guards reacted when Jesus said, "I am he." John 18:5

2. What prophecy is fulfilled in the courtyard of the high priest?

3. Why do many think that the young man who fled naked from Gethsemane was Mark?

# 78 Trial & Suffering

The next morning, guards took Jesus before the Sanhedrin, a council of chief priests and Jewish leaders. They asked Jesus, "Are you the Messiah?"

*[Jesus answered,] "If I tell you,*
*you will not believe me; and if I ask you*
*a question, you will not answer.*
*But from now on the Son of Man*
*will be seated at the right side*
*of Almighty God." They all said,*
*"Are you, then, the Son of God?"*
*He answered them, "You say that I am."*
Luke 22:67–70

*The High Priest tore his clothes*
*and said, "Blasphemy! . . ."*
*They answered, "He . . . must die."*
Matthew 26:65–66

*The whole group rose up and*
*took Jesus before Pilate, . . . [saying,]*
*"We caught this man misleading our people,*
*telling them not to pay taxes to the Emperor*
*and claiming that he himself is the Messiah,*
*a king."* Luke 23:1–2

The leaders know that religious charges will never fly with Pilate, so they shift to political charges. After all, Jesus had discussed taxes (but didn't oppose them). Matthew 22:15–22 He was also called a king (but refused the title in a political sense). John 6:15

Pilate is not fooled by their strategy and tries to keep from executing Jesus.

*[But the leaders] started shouting*
*at the top of their voices: "Crucify him!"*
*When Pilate saw . . . that a riot might*
*break out, he . . . washed his hands . . .*
*and said, "I am not responsible*
*for the death of this man! . . ."*

*After he had Jesus whipped,*
*he handed him over to be crucified.*
Matthew 27:23–24, 26

*Pilate . . . sat down on the judge's seat in the place called "The Stone Pavement." (In Hebrew the name is "Gabbatha.")* John 19:13

The stone shown here is part of the pavement. Some think its markings refer to the game of "King" and inspired the soldiers to make sport of Jesus.

The game was popular with off-duty soldiers. It derives from a pagan sport in which a man is crowned king before a festival, honored during it, and killed after it.

*The soldiers took Jesus inside . . . [and]*
*made a crown out of thorny branches,*
*and put it on his head.*
*Then they began to salute him:*
*"Long live the King of the Jews!"*
*They beat him over the head . . . ,*
*spat on  him, . . . and bowed down to him.*

*When they had finished making fun*
*of him, . . . they led him out.*   Mark 15:16–20

When the soldiers reach Golgotha
(Calvary), they crucify Jesus
between two thieves.   Mark 15:24–28

*U*SA Today carried a story about
Jesus' crucifixion. It concluded
that we romanticize Jesus' death.
Actually, it was brutal beyond all belief.

Psalm 22 hints at how brutal it was.
Written six hundred years before the
Romans devised crucifixion, it describes
Jesus' situation with incredible accuracy:

*My strength is gone, gone like water*
*spilled on the ground.*
*All my bones are out of joint;*
*my heart is like melted wax.*
*My throat is as dry as dust, and my tongue*
*sticks to the roof of my mouth. . . .*
*They tear at my hands and feet.*
*All my bones can be seen.*
*My enemies look at me and stare.*
*They gamble for my clothes*
*and divide them among themselves.*
                    Psalm 22:14–18

Team up with another. Compare Psalm 22
with Mark 15:22–39. List parallels.

|                    | Mark 15 | Psalm 22 |
| ------------------ | ------- | -------- |
| Stripped           |         |          |
| Divided clothes    |         |          |
| Diced for robe     |         |          |
| Crucified (nails)  |         |          |
| Jeered             |         |          |
| Thirsted           |         |          |
| Forsaken           |         |          |

2.  Jesus suffered four ways: emotionally,
mentally, physically, and spiritually. He:

- agonized over what was at hand,
- felt crushed and sweat blood,

- was accused falsely,
- experienced betrayal and denial,
- was crowned with thorns and whipped,
- felt abandoned by God.

a.  Identify and explain the above pains.
b.  Which would you find worse and why?

3.  Flannery O'Connor's "Parker's Back"
concerns Parker and his wife, Sarah Ruth.
They live in the rural South and are poor.

Sarah prides herself on being religious
and nags Parker continually for his lack
of religion. She also despises the tattoos
that cover his body. One day Parker
decides to try to please Sarah Ruth
by having Jesus' face tattooed on his back.

When Sarah Ruth sees it,
she shouts, "Idolatry," grabs a club,
and beats Parker savagely across the back.
He stands in stunned silence.
Meanwhile, welts and cuts appear
on the tattooed face of Jesus.

a.  List some points O'Connor makes
in her story. What is the main one?
b.  Record and share a time you tried
to please someone and were rejected

**A**rchaeologists found
this dedication stone in
1961 while excavating
an ancient amphitheater
at Caesarea. It reads:

TIBERIEUM,
[PON]TIUS PILATUS,
[PRAEF]ECTUS
IUDA[EAE]

The stone is part of
a larger one in which
Pontius Pilate, Prefect of
Judah, dedicated the
amphitheater to Tiberius
Caesar.

*Trial*
*&*
*Suffering*

**I**dentify:
a.  Sanhedrin
b.  Gabbatha
c.  game of "King"
d.  Pilate stone

2.  Explain:
a.  Why Jesus was sent
to Pilate.
b.  How charges against
Jesus were shifted
once Jesus was there.
c.  Why Pilate agreed
to crucify Jesus.
d.  How the soldiers
made fun of Jesus.

World Youth Day
"Way of the Cross."

# 79 Crucifixion

*A*t noon the whole country
*was covered with darkness,*
*which lasted for three hours.*
*At three o'clock Jesus cried out . . .*
*"My God, why did you abandon me?" . . .*
*With a loud cry Jesus died.*

*The curtain hanging in the Temple*
*was torn in two, from top to bottom.*
*The army officer who was standing*
*there in front of the cross*
*saw how Jesus had died [and said,]*
*"This man was really the Son of God!"*
Mark 15:33–34, 37–39

Two points stand out in Mark's dramatic
description of Jesus' crucifixion:

- the tearing of the Temple curtain and
- the officer's act of faith.

Early Christians interpreted the tearing
of the curtain as a sign pointing to the end
of the Old Testament *Temple* and
of the Old Testament *sacrifice.*    Hebrews 10:9
The new Temple and the new sacrifice
have just been "born" on the cross:

- Temple    Jesus' body,    Ephesians 2:21
- sacrifice    Jesus' death.    Hebrews 10:9

The second point that stands out is
the officer's act of faith.
The Roman officer becomes the first person
in an endless parade of people
who look at Jesus on the cross,
believe in him, and win eternal life.
Jesus foretold this would happen, saying:

*"The Son of Man must be lifted up,*
*so that everyone who believes in him*
*may have eternal life."* John 3:14–15

The events of Calvary (*Golgotha* in
Hebrew) end with the body of Jesus being
taken down from the cross and buried.

*Pilate gave orders for the body*
*to be given to Joseph [of Arimathea].*

*So Joseph took it, wrapped it in a new*
*linen sheet, and  placed it in his own tomb,*
*which he had just recently dug*
*out of solid rock.*

*Then he rolled a large stone across the*
*entrance to the tomb and went away.*
Matthew 27:58–60

*T*he crude simplicity of
this student's portrayal
of Jesus' death
captures the violence
and the pathos
of one of history's
darkest hours.

Identify the seven
figures and what
they are doing.
Luke 23:33–43, Mark 15:39

In his novel *Legion*, William Blatty portrays a Jewish detective all alone in a church. A priest has been killed while hearing confessions. The detective shakes his head and sits. Lifting his eyes to the crucifix, he says:

*Who are you? God's son?*
*No, you know I don't believe that.*
*I just asked to be polite. . . .*
*I don't know who you are,*
*but you are Someone. . . .*
*Do you know how I know?*
*From what you said.*
*When I read, "Love your enemy,"*
*I tingle. . . . No one on earth*
*could ever say what you said.*
*No one could even make it up. . . .*
*The words knock you down. . . .*
*Who are you?*
*What is it that you want from us?*

a. What is your answer to the detective's very last question?
b. Using the detective's monologue as a model, compose a similar monologue to Jesus on the cross.

2. A retreatant showed a retreat master a card that his wife had given him and that he had carried for years. It read:

*I carry a cross in my pocket. . . .*
*It's not for . . . all the world to see.*
*It's simply an understanding*
*Between my Savior and me. . . .*
*It reminds me to be thankful*
*For my blessings day by day*
*And strive to serve Him better*
*In all that I do and say. . . .*
*Reminding no one but me*
*That Jesus Christ is Lord of my life*
*If only I'll let him be.*  Author unknown

Record and share:
a. Two things that tend to keep you from making Jesus the "Lord" of your life.
b. How do you try to overcome them?
c. What is one religious card or object you carry in your pocket? Explain.

Goya's *Dead Jesus*.

3. An old Polish Jew who survived the Nazi holocaust said of Jesus:

*As I looked at the man upon the cross . . .*
*I knew I must make up my mind . . .*
*and either take my stand beside him and*
*share in his undefeated faith in God . . .*
*or else fall finally*
*into a bottomless pit of bitterness,*
*hatred, and . . . despair.*
S. Paul Shilling, *God in an Age of Atheism*

Record and share:
a. The old Polish Jew's point.
b. What comes to your mind when you look at the man on the cross and decide what you must do with your life.

*Crucifixion*

Explain:
a. The two points Mark stresses in his crucifixion account.
b. The meaning of what happened in the Temple when Jesus died.
c. The New Testament Temple and sacrifice.
d. What specific prophecy the soldier's act of faith in Jesus fulfills.

# *80  Resurrection*

The day following the death and burial of Jesus was the Sabbath. So the disciples remained indoors, praying together and mourning deeply.

NARRATOR *As Sunday morning was dawning, Mary Magdalene and the other Mary went to look at the tomb. Suddenly there was a violent earthquake; an angel of the Lord . . . spoke to the women.*

ANGEL *You must not be afraid. . . . I know you are looking for Jesus, who was crucified. He is not here; he has been raised, just as he said. Come here and see the place where he was lying. Go quickly now, and tell his disciples, "He has been raised from death. . . ."*

NARRATOR *So they left the tomb in a hurry, afraid and yet filled with joy, and ran to tell his disciples. Suddenly Jesus met them.*

JESUS *Peace be with you. . . . Do not be afraid. . . . Tell my brothers to go to Galilee, and there they will see me.*   Matthew 28:1–2, 5–10

The disciples' reaction to this report is one of disbelief.   Luke 24:11 The response of the two disciples returning to Emmaus is typical.

Suddenly a "stranger" approaches and walks along with the two disciples. They tell him about Jesus' terrible death.

JESUS *How foolish you are. . . . Was it not necessary for the Messiah to suffer . . . and then to enter his glory?*

NARRATOR *And Jesus explained to them what was said about himself in all the Scriptures, beginning with the books of Moses and . . . the prophets. As they came near the village . . . , Jesus acted as if he were going farther. . . .*

The two then explained to them what had happened on the road, and how they recognized the Lord when he broke the bread. Luke 24:35

DISCIPLES *Stay with us; . . .*
*it is getting dark.*
NARRATOR *So he went in to stay. . . .*
*He sat down to eat with them,*
*took the bread, and*
*said the blessing;*
*then he broke the bread*
*and gave it to them.*
*Then their eyes were opened*
*and they recognized him,*
*but he disappeared. . . .*
*They got up at once*
*and went back to Jerusalem.*

Luke 24:25–31, 33

A man sat in a canoe reading.
Suddenly a water beetle crawled
up the side of the canoe.
It hooked its talons to the wood and died.
The man continued reading.

Three hours later, he glanced down again.
The beetle had dried in the sun, and its
back was cracking open. As he watched,
something emerged from the opening:
first a moist head, and then wings.
It was a lovely dragonfly.

The man nudged the dried-up shell of
the beetle with his finger. It was like an
empty tomb. The man watched with awe
as the dragonfly fluttered above
the other water beetles in the water.
They saw it but didn't recognize it.

List similarities between this episode and
Jesus' death and resurrection.

2. Explain how Jesus' words on the road
to Emmaus and his action around the table
in Emmaus resemble (a) the Liturgy of the
Word and (b) the Liturgy of the Eucharist.

3. After meditating on the story
of the two discouraged disciples returning
to Emmaus, a student wrote:

*Lord Jesus, look kindly on us*
*who still find it hard to believe.*
*Come to us, again,*
*as you did to the disciples at Emmaus.*
*Explain anew to us the Scriptures,*
*as you did to them.*

*Lord,*
*look kindly on us*
*who still find*
*it hard to believe.*

*Set afire within us the embers of faith*
*still smoldering in our hearts.*
*Sit down with us at table again,*
*and show yourself anew to us*
*in the breaking of the bread.*

Write a similar prayer to Jesus.
Make it come from the heart.

4. Explain the important point
that each of the following makes:

a. "The Gospels don't explain Easter.
Easter explains the Gospels."   Author unknown
b. Resurrection is not a restoration
to a former life, but a quantum leap
into an infinitely higher life.

c. Calvin Miller's *The Song*
contains a story of an atheistic woman.
She married and had three sons.
One by one the sons died. At the funeral
of the first, she remained a nonbeliever.
At the funeral of the second,
she became a seeker.
At the funeral of the third,
she wept and became a believer. 🍂

*Resurrection*

**W**hat is the disciples'
reaction to the news
that Jesus is risen?

2. Describe what
happens:
a. On the road to
Emmaus.
b. In the house in
Emmaus.

167

# 81 Two Commissions

Two postresurrection appearances of Jesus are of special significance and result in two profoundly important commissions.

The first took place on Easter night when the disciples of Jesus were gathered together in a room. Suddenly, Jesus appeared in their midst.

the power to forgive people's sins?" Answer? It is the perfect Easter gift. It is why Jesus died and rose, that we might be "put right with God."   Romans 5:9

Jesus not only forgives his disciples but also commissions and empowers them to communicate his forgiveness to those yet unborn.

This spot marks the vicinity where tradition says Jesus cooked breakfast for his disciples.

Peter's triple testimony of love erases his triple denial of Jesus.

Jesus' triple response commissions Peter to succeed Jesus as shepherd of the flock.

NARRATOR   *The disciples*
                    *were filled with joy. . . .*
JESUS          *Peace be with you.*
                    *As the Father sent me,*
                    *so I send you. . . .*
                    *Receive the Holy Spirit.*
                    *If you forgive people's sins,*
                    *they are forgiven;*
                    *if you do not forgive them,*
                    *they are not forgiven.*   John 20:20–23

Some ask, "Why did Jesus pick Easter night to give his disciples

The second commission takes place one morning some time later when some disciples return empty-handed from a fishing trip. As they approach the shore, they see a stranger there preparing breakfast. At first, they ignore him.

Then the stranger calls to them, "Throw your net out on the right side." They do, and it fills up with fish. John stares at the stranger and gasps, "It is the Lord!"   John 21:6–7

After the disciples pull ashore
and take care of their catch of fish,
they sit down and eat with Jesus.

Then Jesus does something beautiful.
He asks Peter three times,
"Do you love me?"

Three times Peter says, "Yes, Lord!"
Three times Jesus says, "Feed my sheep!"

Peter's three affirmations of love
erase his three denials of Jesus.
Jesus' three responses "Feed my sheep!"
commission Peter to be the shepherd
of the flock of Jesus' followers.    John 21:15–17

The disciples didn't recognize
Jesus on the beach. This is typical
of Jesus' resurrection appearances.
When he appeared to Mary Magdalene,
she did not know him.    John 20:14
When Jesus appeared to the disciples,
they thought he was a ghost.    Luke 24:37

a.  How do you explain the inability of the
disciples to recognize the risen Jesus?
b.  How is the risen Jesus dramatically
different from the earthly Jesus?
The resuscitated body of Lazarus?
John 11:40–43

2.  Writing to the Corinthians,
Paul says the resurrection of Jesus
is a pledge of our own resurrection.

*Someone will ask,
"How can the dead be raised to life?
What kind of body will they have?"
You fool! When you plant a seed
in the ground,
it does not sprout to life unless it dies.*

*And what you plant is a bare seed . . .
not the full-bodied plant. . . .
God provides that seed with the body
he wishes; he gives each seed
its own proper body.*    1 Corinthians 15:35–38

Explain Paul's point.

3.  Paul continues discussing the
resurrection of our body, saying:

*When the body is buried, it is mortal;
when raised, it will be immortal.
When buried, it is ugly and weak;
when raised, it will be beautiful and strong.
When buried, it is a physical body;
when raised it will be a spiritual body.*
1 Corinthians 15:42–44

How does Paul's description accord
with the inability of the disciples
to recognize the resurrected Jesus?

4.  *Tulip flowers are lovely.
But they grow old, get ugly, and die.
When spring comes, however, the tulip
bulb produces a lovely new blossom.
I think the tulip makes a good image
of our own resurrection.*    Anonymous

Explain and evaluate this observation.

5.  Pick one of the following passages.
After reading it:
a.  Summarize its main point.
b.  Tell how it relates to this chapter.
c.  List one or two thoughts
that occurred to you as you read it.

* Over 500 saw him    1 Corinthians 15:1–12
* Seeds and stars    1 Corinthians 15:35–58
* Whose wife is she?    Mark 12:18–27

*Jesus said to them,
"Come and eat." . . .*

*Jesus went over,
took the bread,
and gave it to them;
he did the same
with the fish.*
John 21:12-13

## Two Commissions

**E**xplain Jesus' Easter
gift to his disciples
and why it was perfect.

2. Describe and explain:
a. The Easter night
commission Jesus gave
to his disciples.
b. The breakfast
morning commission
Jesus gave to Peter.

# V
# World of Paul

## TIMELINE
*(APPROXIMATE TRADITIONAL DATES)*
*A.D. = AFTER CHRIST*

| | |
|---|---|
| 33 | Pentecost |
| 34 | Paul's conversion |
| 45–49 | First missionary trip |
| 49–52 | Second missionary trip |
| 53–58 | Third missionary trip |
| 58 | Paul's arrest |
| 67 | Paul's execution |

## BIBLE *(KEY BOOKS)*

| | |
|---|---|
| Acts | 1–2 Timothy |
| 1–2 Thessalonians | Titus |
| 1–2 Corinthians | James |
| Galatians | 1–2 Peter |
| Romans | 1–3 John |
| Philippians | Jude |
| Colossians | Hebrews |
| Philemon | Revelation |
| Ephesians | |

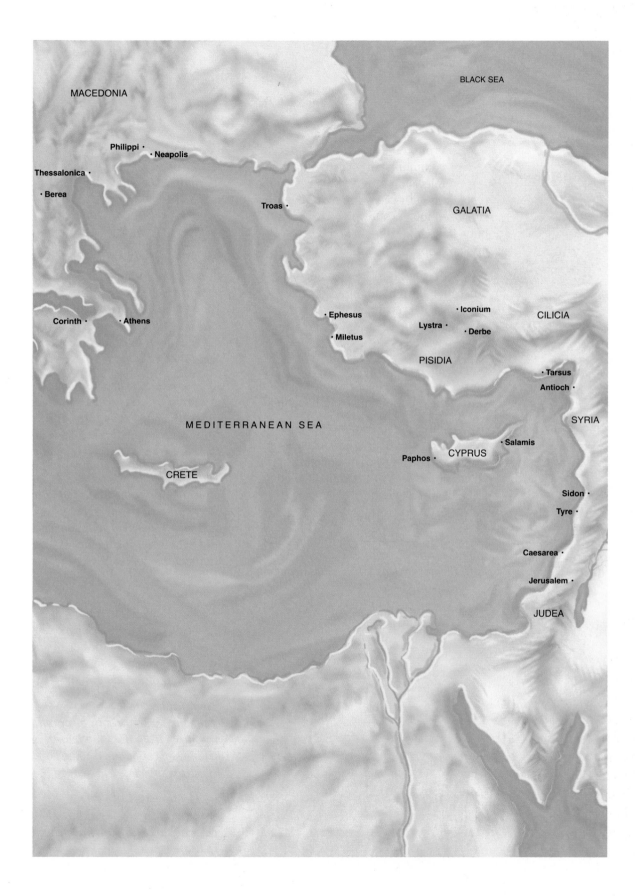

# CHAPTER SIXTEEN

# Spirit's Coming
## 82 Ascension

The Ascension doesn't remove Jesus from earth. It frees him from space and time and makes him present everywhere on earth.

*D*uring the Cold War, East Berlin communist officials built a giant television tower with a revolving restaurant at the very top of it. It was supposed to be a showpiece to the West, but a fluke in design turned it into an embarrassment.

When the sun hit it at a certain angle, it became a bright shimmering cross. Officials tried repainting the tower to "blot out" the cross, but to no avail.

Something similar happened after Jesus' crucifixion on Calvary. Jesus' opponents hoped his terrible death would "blot out" Christianity, but the opposite happened.

Christianity spread so rapidly that by A.D. 64 it was flourishing as far away as Rome. The story of its amazing spread is told in the Acts of the Apostles. Luke begins, saying:

*In my first book [Gospel] I wrote about
all the things that Jesus did and taught
from the time he began his work
until the day he was taken up to heaven. . . .*

This stairway leads to an upper room on the exact site where tradition says Jesus and his disciples ate the Last Supper.

Tradition also says that it was the room where they gathered to prepare for the coming of the Holy Spirit.

The structure shown here, however, dates only from about A.D. 1350.

*For forty days . . . he appeared
to [the apostles] many times in ways
that proved beyond doubt that he
was alive. . . . He gave them this order:*

*"Do not leave Jerusalem,
but wait for the gift I told you about,
the gift my Father promised. . . .
In a few days you will be baptized
with the Holy Spirit. . . .
You will be filled with power,
and you will be witnesses for me
in Jerusalem, in all of Judea and Samaria,
and to the ends of the earth."*

*After saying this, he was taken up
to heaven. . . . Two men dressed in white
suddenly stood beside them and said, . . .
"This Jesus . . . will come back in the
same way that you saw him go to heaven."*

*Then the apostles went back to
Jerusalem from the Mount of Olives. . . .
They gathered frequently to pray
as a group, together with the women
and with Mary the mother of Jesus
and with his brothers.*   Acts 1:1–5, 8–12, 14

*O*ne day while the disciples were at prayer, Peter proposed that they restore the number of apostles to twelve by picking a successor to Judas. Peter said of the successor:

*"He must be one
of the men who were in our group . . .
beginning from the time John preached
his message of baptism until the day
Jesus was taken . . . to heaven."*

*So they proposed two men. . . .
Then they prayed, "Lord, . . . show us
which of these two you have chosen. . . ."
They drew lots . . . and the one chosen
was Matthias.*   Acts 1:21–24, 26

a. Before drawing lots, what two important things did the disciples do?
b. Why was it important to do both?
c. Explain why you do/don't think the procedure used to pick a successor to Judas could be applied to picking a college or a career.
d. How can you be reasonably sure that the choice you make is God's will?

2. Henry Ward Beecher said, "The strength of a person consists in finding out the way God is going, and going that way."

a. What is meant by the expression "finding out the way God is going"?
b. How do you go about finding out which way "God is going" in your life—that is, the direction God seems to be pointing you? Give some examples.

3. Saint Ignatius of Loyola placed the highest priority on seeking and doing God's will. His favorite prayer was:

*Lord, teach me to be generous.*
*Teach me to serve you as you deserve;*
*to give and not to count the cost;*
*to fight and not to heed the wounds;*
*to toil and not to seek for rest;*
*to labor and not to ask for reward,*
*except to know*
*that I am doing your will.*

a. Explain how the spirit of Saint Ignatius' favorite prayer is similar to the prayer Jesus taught us.
b. Take a few minutes to copy Saint Ignatius' prayer. Put it in your wallet and pray it daily for the next week. Then do a brief report of the experiment. ✍

The passing of the baton is a high point in a relay race. More races are won or lost at that moment than at any other moment during the race.

Pentecost might be compared to this key moment. The baton of God's kingdom has been passed to us.

It is now up to us to complete the work that Jesus began.

## Ascension

What order did Jesus give his disciples before ascending to heaven?

2. What message did the "men dressed in white" give the disciples?

3. Where did the disciples go, and what did they do to prepare for the Spirit's coming?

# 83 Pentecost

*P*entecost ("fiftieth") occurred fifty days after Passover. Pentecost was a time for thanking God for the year's harvest and for the Sinai covenant with Israel.

The main celebration of the feast took place in the Jerusalem Temple. People living far from Jerusalem tried to get to the city at least once in a lifetime to celebrate Pentecost. Thus, on Pentecost, people from many countries (speaking many languages) came to the city.

On the first Pentecost after Jesus ascended into heaven, his disciples were gathered in the upper room in Jerusalem.

*Suddenly there was a noise . . .*
*like a strong wind blowing. . . .*
*Then they saw what looked like*
*tongues of fire which spread out*
*and touched each person there.*
*They were all filled with the Holy Spirit*
*and began to talk in other languages,*
*as the Spirit enabled them to speak.*
Acts 2:2–4

The "noise" of the "strong wind" attracted a huge crowd of people. They came running to see what occurred. Peter and the disciples went outside to explain.

As Peter spoke, the crowd was amazed, because all heard him speak in their own foreign tongue. They said:

*"Some of us are from Rome. . . .*
*Some of us are from Crete and Arabia—*
*yet all of us hear them*
*speaking in our own languages. . . .*
*What does this mean?"* Acts 2:10–12

*T*he crowd that gathered outside the upper room on Pentecost said:

*"Some of us are from Crete and Arabia — yet all of us hear them speaking in our own languages."* Acts 2:11

Arabia included the city of Petra, with its royal tombs carved out of solid rock cliffs.

Shown here is the tomb known as the "Treasury."

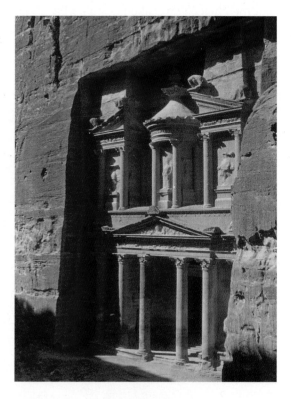

The answer to their question is found in the Tower of Babel event in the Book of Genesis. Before Babel (and people's sin of pride), all the people spoke the same language. After it, God mixed their language and scattered them everywhere. Genesis 11:19

The Spirit's coming on Pentecost reverses the Babel event. What sin *disunited* and *de-created,* the Holy Spirit *reunites* and *re-creates.*

And so Pentecost is immensely significant and important, not just for Jews, but for all people. With the coming of the Holy Spirit, God's plan for *re-creating* the world takes a giant leap forward.

A little boy got a toy sailboat for his birthday. He was so excited that he ran to the window, looked up to the sky, and shouted, "O God! Have you seen my boat?" Then, turning to his mother, he asked, "What is God like?"

Before she could give an answer, the boy began jumping up and down, saying, "I know! God is like the wind!"

Ancient Jews would have applauded the boy's answer, for they too saw a link between God and the wind.

a. List similarities between God and wind.
b. List similarities between God and fire.
c. List three times in Israel's history when fire pointed to God's presence.

2. A famous old hymn reads: "Teach us, good Lord, to serve the needs of others; Help us to give and not to count the cost; Unite us all, for we are born as brothers; Defeat our Babel with your Pentecost."

a. Explain how the hymn's final line sums up what Pentecost is all about.
b. If the coming of the Holy Spirit was such a giant leap forward in God's plan to unite and re-create the world, why is it still so disunited and de-created?

3. God said of Pentecost, "I will pour out my Spirit on everyone." Acts 2:17
God added that when this happens, young people will "see visions."

a. List three "visions" you have regarding (1) our world, (2) your family, (3) yourself as we move into the new millennium.

b. Pick one of your "visions" and explain what you conceive to be the biggest obstacle to the realization of that "vision" and what you, personally, might do about it.

4. *Alone we are only a spark,*
*but in the Spirit we are a fire.*
*Alone we are only a string,*
*but in the Spirit we are a lyre.*
*Alone we only an ant hill,*
*but in the Spirit we are a mountain.*
*Alone we are only a drop,*
*but in the Spirit we are a fountain.*
Inspired by a poem by Amado Nervo

a. Explain the point and message contained in this poem.
b. What is the key to implementing both?
c. Compose a poem similar to this one, using your images.

Lord's Supper, World Youth Day in Denver.

*Alone,*
*we are only a spark,*
*but in the Spirit*
*we are a fire.*

## Pentecost

When did Pentecost occur, and what was its twofold purpose?

2. What image portrayed:
a. The Spirit's coming?
b. The Spirit's descent upon the disciples?

3. Explain the link between Pentecost and the Babel event.

**W**alk through
the Scriptures
until the
Scriptures walk
*through you.*

# 84 Day of the Lord

**T**he coming of the Holy Spirit impacted the disciples powerfully. Suddenly everything became clear, just as Jesus had foretold, saying:

*"[The Spirit] will teach you everything
and make you remember
all that I have told you."* John 14:25–26

**J**esus said to the Samaritan woman,

*"If you only knew . . .
who it is that is asking
you for a drink, you
would ask him, and he
would give you life-
giving water." . . .*

*Jesus said this about the
Spirit, which those who
believed in him were
going to receive.*
John 4:10, 7:39

It is against this backdrop that we read Peter's explanation of Pentecost to the crowd gathered outside the upper room:

*"Let me tell you what this means. . . .
This is what the prophet Joel spoke about: . . .
'In the last days, God says:*

*"'I will pour out my Spirit on everyone.
Your sons and daughters will proclaim
my message; your young men will
see visions, and your old men will
have dreams. . . . I will perform miracles
in the sky above and wonders
on the earth below . . . before the great
and glorious Day of the Lord comes.*

*"'And then, whoever calls out to the Lord
for help will be saved.'"* Acts 2:14, 16–17, 19–21

The title "Day of the Lord" refers to that moment in history when Jews believed God would intervene in history and that God's glory would be manifested in a spectacular way to all the world.

Much as Christians think of history as divided into *before* and *after Christ,* Jews thought of it as divided into *before* and *after* the *Day of the Lord.*

Peter interprets the "Day of the Lord" to be that extended period *beginning* with the Holy Spirit's coming on Pentecost and *ending* with Jesus' second coming.

Peter's words move the people and they ask, "What shall we do?" Peter responds:

*"You must turn away
from your sins and be baptized
in the name of Jesus Christ,
so that your sins will be forgiven;
and you will receive . . . the Holy Spirit." . . .*

*About three thousand people
were added to the group that day.* Acts 2:38, 41

An image of how we should dedicate ourselves to completing the work Jesus gave us is the rock climber:

*Never glancing down, he sometimes stops to shake out his hand, then climbs on.*
James Salter

We frequently hear people say that Jesus came to bring about the "salvation" of the world. But what does this mean? Albert Palmer answers this way:

*Salvation is not something that is done for you but something that happens within you. It is not the clearing of a court record but the transformation of a life attitude.*

a. Explain Palmer's point.
b. Explain how the salvation of the world is a collaborative effort in which you and Jesus both play an important role.

2. No tape recorder was running when Peter spoke on Pentecost. Nor was anyone taking notes.

How did Luke reconstruct the text of what Peter said that day and what others, like Paul, said later on? (About a third of Acts is made up of sermons or direct address.)

3. The "we" sections in Acts indicate the times when Luke and Paul traveled together.   Acts 16:10–17, 20:6–15 At these times, Luke may have kept notes of what Paul said. At other times, Luke had to rely on the reports of others.

The ancient historian Thucydides, who lived centuries before Luke, writes:

*I found it hard to recall the precise words I heard spoken at an event. The same is true of those who gave me reports of an event.*

*So I put in the mouths of the speakers what I thought to be most opportune for them to say in the given situation. At the same time, I have kept as closely as possible to the general sense of what was actually said by them.*
History of the Peloponnesian War

a. Why do/don't you think Luke did this?
b. What immense advantage did Luke have over Thucydides, if he did this?

4. Recall an episode in your life when you can't remember the exact words that were spoken, but when you can remember the idea or spirit of what was said.

Write out the episode and explain how it could relate to Luke and Acts.

## Day of the Lord

Explain:
a. The impact that the Spirit's coming had on the disciples.
b. How Peter explained the coming of the Spirit.
c. What Jews believed would happen on the "Day of the Lord."
d. How Peter interpreted the "Day of the Lord."
e. The effect of Peter's sermon on the people and what he told the people they must do.

# Local Witness

## 85 Peter & John

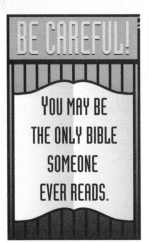

Peter Matthiessen and a friend were hiking in a third-world nation. They came upon a crippled girl dragging herself along a gravel road. Her mouth actually scraped the stones.

Peter's friend told him that sometimes, for business purposes, beggars break the knees of their own children to achieve this pathetic effect.

Poverty and begging were widespread in biblical times. One day Peter and John were just about to enter the Temple. A crippled man asked them for money.

PETER      *I have no money at all,
           but I give you what I have:
           in the name of Jesus Christ
           of Nazareth I order you
           to get up and walk! . . .*
NARRATOR   *At once the man's feet and
           ankles became strong;
           he jumped up . . . and started
           walking around. . . . The people . . .
           were all surprised and amazed.*
                                    Acts 3:6–10

News of the miracle spreads rapidly. The apostles now have the same power to heal that Jesus did. The news sets off a firestorm of activity.

*Crowds of people came in from the towns around Jerusalem, bringing those who were sick or who had evil spirits in them; and they were all healed.*   Acts 5:16

Jewish authorities arrest the apostles and forbid them to preach or heal.

PETER      *We must obey God,
           not men. . . .*
NARRATOR   *When the members
           of the Council heard this,
           they were . . . furious. . . .*
GAMALIEL   *Fellow Israelites, be careful
           what you do to these men. . . .
           Leave them alone!
           If what they have planned
           and done is of human origin,
           it will disappear,
           but if it comes from God,
           you cannot . . . defeat them.
           You could find yourselves
           fighting against God!*
NARRATOR   *The Council followed
           Gamaliel's advice.*
                            Acts 5:29, 33, 35, 38–39

This artist's reconstruction of the Temple follows the general plan of the Avi-Yonah model. A schematic of the plan is found on page 155.

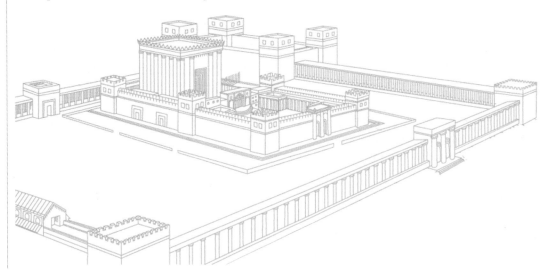

*P*eter Matthiessen was told by his friend that beggars in the country they were visiting sometimes break the knees of their children for business purposes. His observation recalls these words of the famous Greek dramatist Euripides: "Poverty possesses this sickness: it teaches people to do what is evil."

a.  Make a list of the evils that poverty teaches people. Explain your choices.
b.  Make a list of the reasons why many people today ignore beggars. Evaluate the validity of the reasons.
c.  Explain why you do/don't think that Jesus would want us to do what Peter and John did for the beggar.
d.  Why are miracles so rare these days?

2.  Saint Augustine (ca. 400 B.C.) said, "People ask why miracles that happened in the past don't happen today. I might reply that they were necessary before the world believed, to bring it to belief."

a.  Why do/don't you think miracles would promote belief among people today?
b.  Make a list of things that you think might foster belief among people today.
c.  Which of these are within your power and, therefore, "miracles" you can do?

3.  Gamaliel's advice about taking action against the apostles was this:

*"If what they have planned and done is of human origin, it will disappear, but if it comes from God, you cannot possibly defeat them."*

Why do/don't you think history has judged Christianity and proven that it comes from God?

4.  Pick a reading from the list below.
a.  Read it and sum up its main point.

El Greco's rendering of Saint Martin dividing his cloak with the beggar.

b.  Explain how it relates to this chapter.
c.  List one or two thoughts or questions that entered your mind as you read it.

☙ The warning      Acts 4:1–21
☙ The lie          Acts 5:1–11
☙ Miracles and wonders   Acts 5:12–16 ☙

*Peter & John*

*B*riefly describe the responses of:
a.  Peter and John to the Temple beggar.
b.  The Council to the apostles' activity.
c.  Peter to the Council.
d.  Gamaliel's advice to the Council.

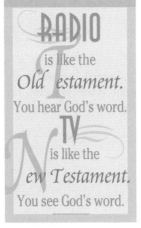

# 86 Stephen

The young Church grew rapidly, creating a need for organization. Seven "deacons" were chosen to manage the Church's *material* needs. This freed the apostles to give full time to its *spiritual* needs.   Acts 6:1–7

One of the seven "deacons" chosen was a young man by the name of Stephen.

F rench archaeologists found this cornerstone. A part of it reads:

*Theodotus, son of Vettenus . . . built this synagogue.*

The lettering and the place where it was found lead some experts to trace it to the Freedmen's Synagogue, whose members martyred Stephen.

"Richly blessed by God and full of power," he worked "great miracles and wonders among the people."   Acts 6:8

*Some men who were members of the synagogue of the Freedmen . . . started arguing with Stephen. . . . When he spoke, they could not refute him. So they bribed some men to say, "We heard him speaking against Moses and against God!". . . The High Priest asked Stephen, "Is this true?"*   Acts 6:9–11, 7:1

Stephen begins his defense by tracing the history of God's dealings with Israel. He shows how the Israelites' ancestors "resisted the Holy Spirit."   Acts 7:51

For example, God's servant Joseph was sold into slavery by his brothers. God's servant Moses was opposed by the Israelites in the desert. God's servants the prophets were persecuted by the people. Stephen concludes, saying, "Now you have betrayed and murdered [God's Son]." Acts 7:52

The members of the synagogue explode. They drag Stephen out of the city.

*Then they all rushed at him at once . . . and stoned him. The witnesses left their cloaks in the care of a young man named Saul [Paul]. They kept on stoning Stephen as he called out . . . , "Lord Jesus, receive my spirit! . . . Do not remember this sin against them!" He said this and died.*
Acts 7:57–60

And so, even in death, Stephen tries to imitate his Master, who also forgave his executioners.   Luke 23:34

The death of Stephen, the first martyr of the Church, sparks more persecutions, threatening the Church's very existence.

*All the believers, except the apostles, were scattered throughout the provinces of Judea and Samaria. . . . The believers who were scattered went everywhere, preaching the message.*
Acts 8:1, 4

The story of Stephen's martyrdom has generated two famous remarks. The first was made by Saint Augustine, who said, "The Church owes Paul to the prayer of Stephen." The second was by the early Christian Tertullian, who said, "The blood of martyrs is the seed of the Church."

a. Why would "the prayer of Stephen" have impacted Paul so powerfully?

b. Why does "the blood of martyrs" impact the Church in a positive way?

2. Westerns were once popular on TV. They projected an image of a savior-hero who made viewers feel good. He rode into town, saved innocent people from bad guys, and rode off again unhurt into the purple sunset.

In time, new savior-heroes replaced the guys in the white hat: doctors, social workers, police, detectives. They too saved people and walked away with only a dent or smudge on their suits of shining armor. They too gave the false impression that we can defeat evil without great personal price or sacrifice.

By way of contrast, history shows that real-life savior-heroes often pay a high price in their war against evil.

a. List some real-life savior-heroes.

b. Record and share some encounter with evil that cost you a price.

3. *Cowardice asks . . . "Is it safe?"*
*Expedience asks . . . "Is it politic?"*
*Vanity asks . . . "Is it popular?" . . .*
*There comes a time when one must take a position that is neither safe, politic, nor popular, but one must take it because it is right.*
Dr. Martin Luther King Jr.

List some positions that are neither safe, politic, nor popular:

a. That Christians today must take.

b. That young people, especially, must take in schools and part-time jobs.

4. Imagine that you are Saul. The night after Stephen's murder, you go back to the site were it occurred. You look at the blood on the ground. You see a button from his clothes.

Record and share your thoughts as you sit down under the starless sky, meditating on what happened there that afternoon. &

## Stephen

**W**ho was Christianity's first martyr, and what position did he hold in the young Church?

2. Why, by whom, and how was he martyred?

3. What chain reaction followed his martyrdom, and how did it further the preaching of the Gospel?

# 87 Samaritan Pentecost

**M**odern Samaritans accept only the Pentateuch, or Torah (first five books of the Old Testament), and they have their own priesthood.

The priests shown here hold the manuscript of the Pentateuch that modern Samaritans (small in number) follow. Scholars date it to about A.D. 1200.

**D**r. Charles Townes was awarded a Nobel prize for his work in developing the laser beam. A major breakthrough in his work came accidentally, while he was sitting on a park bench studying some flowers.

History shows that other discoveries and advances in history owe their origin to accidents rather than to human design.

The Church's first major missionary outreach is an example. Had Christians not been persecuted in Jerusalem, they would not have gone out— at least as early as they actually did— to preach in Samaria and Judea.

A young deacon by the name of Philip spearheaded the outreach in Samaria.

*Philip went to the principal city in Samaria and preached the Messiah to the people there. The crowds paid close attention . . . to him and saw the miracles that he performed. Evil spirits came out from many people. . . . Many paralyzed and lame people were healed. So there was great joy in that city. . . .*

*The apostles in Jerusalem heard that the people of Samaria had received the word of God, so they sent Peter and John to them.*

*When they arrived, they prayed for the believers that they might receive the Holy Spirit. For the Holy Spirit had not yet come down on any of them; they had only been baptized in the name of the Lord Jesus.*

*Then Peter and John placed their hands on them, and they received the Holy Spirit.*
Acts 8:5–8, 14–17

And so Peter and John "confirm" the Samaritan Christians, sharing with them the gift of the same Holy Spirit that they received on Pentecost.

*Peter and John went back to Jerusalem. On their way they preached the Good News in many villages of Samaria.* Act 8:25

**T**ake two small paper cups and a cigarette lighter. Hold the lighter under one cup so that the flame touches it. Result? Now fill the other cup with water and hold the lighter under it in the same way. What happens?

Imagine that you teach ten-year-olds. How might you use the second cup

Americans who were held hostage in Iran.

to teach the children what effect
the coming of the Spirit in confirmation
has upon our lives?

2.   Robert Tuzik writes in *Liturgy 80:*

*People tell candidates for confirmation that
at baptism their parents made the decision
to initiate them into the church,
and now at confirmation they restate
this baptismal commitment.*

If confirmation is a restatement
of our baptismal commitment,
at what age should it be done? Explain.

3.   Iranians held 52 Americans hostage
for 444 days in the early 1980s.
One night one hostage, Kathryn Koob,
awoke with a start. She had the feeling
that someone was in the room. She says:

*But no one was there. Instantly
I was reminded of the Holy Spirit
the Comforter.
And with the sense of this presence
came a very real knowledge
that I had a source of strength.*

Kathryn said that before the experience
she was terrified. After it she was not,
and she stayed peaceful until her release.

a.   Record and share a time
when you experienced something
similar to what Kathryn did.
b.   What suggests that Kathryn's experience
of a "presence" in the room was real
and not a figment of her imagination?

4.   Pick one of the following passages.
After reading it:
a.   Summarize its main point.
b.   Explain how it relates to this lesson.
c.   List one or two thoughts that entered
your mind as you read it.

- Spirit's gifts    1 Corinthians 12:1–11
- Spirit's fruits   Galatians 5:16–26
- Spirit life       Romans 8:1–17

## Samaritan Pentecost

In what sense did the Church's first major missionary outreach take place more by accident than by design?

2. Who was Philip, and what major missionary outreach did he spearhead?

3. Why did Peter and John pray over the Samaritans who had been baptized, and what happened when they did?

183

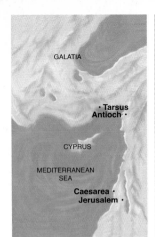

GALATIA

Tarsus
Antioch

CYPRUS

MEDITERRANEAN
SEA

Caesarea
Jerusalem

# *88 Philip in Judea*

Pagan gods and goddesses
and religious superstition
were widespread in Philip's day.
Spiritually sensitive Gentiles
grew increasingly dissatisfied
with the trends of popular religions.

As a result, many looked to Judaism,
with its one God and noble moral code.
And so "searching" Gentiles
began to frequent Jewish synagogues.

Some of these "searchers" converted
and were called *proselytes.*   Act 13:43
Others simply attended the synagogue
and were called *God-fearers.*   Acts 10:2

One God-fearer was an Ethiopian official.
Philip chanced upon him one day,
just as the official was preparing to
return to Egypt after visiting Jerusalem.

He was seated in his carriage reading
this passage in the Book of Isaiah:

*"He was like a sheep
that is taken to be slaughtered. . . .
He was humiliated,
and justice was denied him. . . ."*

*The official asked Philip, "Tell me,
of whom is the prophet saying this?
Of himself or of someone else?"
Then Philip began to speak;
starting from this passage of scripture,
he told him the Good News about Jesus.*

*As they traveled down the road,
they came to a place
where there was some water. . . .
The official ordered the carriage to stop,
and both Philip and the official
went down into the water,
and Philip baptized him.*   Acts 8:32–38

This memorial stone
preserves the memory
of a Roman soldier,
like Cornelius.

*Sacred to the Memory
L. Magnius Felix
10th Legion, Fretensis,
orderly to a tribune
18 years service;
died age 39.*

Centurions, like
Cornelius, commanded
a century (nominally
100 soldiers).
Sixty centuries
made up a legion,
commanded by a legate
and six tribunes.

Another "God-fearer"
was a Roman centurion named Cornelius,
who was stationed at Caesarea.    Acts 10:1
One day while Cornelius was praying,
an angel appeared and told him
to send for Peter, who was preaching
in the nearby town of Joppa.

Cornelius was overjoyed.
He located Peter and sent for him.
Cornelius could hardly wait.
He sensed something momentous
was about to happen.

Cornelius was right.
His meeting with Peter
would be a dramatic "turning point"
not only in his own life
but also in the life of the young Church.

*J*ohn Newton ran a slave ship
between Africa and America.
One night a great storm
engulfed his ship and its human cargo.
He promised God that if they all survived,
he would quit the slave business
and become God's "slave" forever.
All did survive and he kept his promise.

Newton became a pastor of a small church
in England and wrote this famous hymn
to celebrate his conversion:

*Amazing grace! how sweet the sound*
*That saved a wretch like me. . . .*
*How precious did the grace appear*
*The hour I first believed. . . .*
*'Tis grace that brought me safe thus far,*
*And grace will lead me home.*

a.   Record and share a time
when you felt grace acting in your life
in a more-than-ordinary way.
b.   Compose a prayer
celebrating that moment,
just as Newton composed a hymn to do this.
If you have never felt such a moment,
compose a prayer
asking for such an experience.

2.   Explain the point of each saying
and how it applies to conversion.

a.   "Lord, I confess I am not
what I ought to be, but I thank you, Lord,
that I'm not what I used to be."    Maxie Dunnam
b.   "When you're through changing,
you're through."    Bruce Barton
c.   "The only person I can think of
who welcomes change is a wet baby."
Author unknown

d.   "Everyone thinks of changing humanity,
but nobody thinks of changing themselves."
Leo Tolstoy
e.   "It is easier to put on slippers
than to try to carpet the world."
Anthony de Mello (adapted)
f.   " 'How does one become a butterfly?'
she asked.
'You must want to fly so much
that you are willing
to give up being a caterpillar.' "
Trina Paulson, *Hope for the Flowers*
g.   "Before God can do God's thing,
you must do your thing."    Augustine (adapted)

3.   Select one of the above sayings and
design a poster (photograph or drawing)
to illustrate it. (You may work in pairs.) ✑

*Philip*
*in*
*Judea*

**W**hy did some Gentiles
in Philip's time turn
to Judaism to satisfy
their spiritual hunger?

2. Identify:
a. proselyte
b. God-fearer

3. List two prominent
God-fearers, and
explain how they
happened to end up
as Christians.

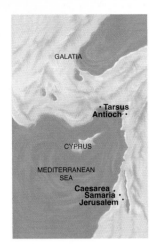

GALATIA

• Tarsus
Antioch •

CYPRUS

MEDITERRANEAN
SEA

Caesarea •
Samaria •
Jerusalem •

These excavated, partially restored remains of Caesarea date to Herod the Great.

Herod built the city and named it in honor of the Roman emperor.

It was here that the Roman army was stationed. One of its officers was Cornelius.

# *89 Gentile Pentecost*

Three delegates sent by Cornelius reached Peter's house the next day about noon. They explained their mission, saying:

*"Cornelius sent us. . . . He is a good man who worships God and is highly respected by all the Jewish people.
An angel of God told him to invite you to his house, so that he could hear what you have to say."* Acts 10:22

And so Peter and the delegation set out for Cornelius's house. What happens when they reach it becomes a turning point in Christianity.

Peter begins to proclaim the "Good News" when, suddenly, the Holy Spirit descends upon all the Gentiles present. They begin to speak in strange tongues, and Peter says to the Jews present:

*"These people have received the Holy Spirit, just as we also did. Can anyone, then, stop them from being baptized with water?"* So he ordered them to be baptized in the name of Jesus Christ.* Acts 10:47–48

And so, by way of review, the Spirit descends upon the early believers in three progressive stages:

- on *Jews* in Jerusalem,         Acts 2:4
- on *half-Jews* in Samaria,      Acts 8:17
- on *Gentiles* in Caesarea.      Acts 10:44

Significantly, it is Peter who presides over each of the three "Pentecosts."

The Spirit's descent upon the Gentiles eventually leads to a big problem. Conservative Jewish Christians insist that Gentile converts to Christianity be circumcised before being baptized. That is, they insist that the Gentiles become Jews as a preliminary step to becoming Christians.     Acts 15:1–35

To settle this matter, the apostles call the first Church council in history. After prayerful deliberation, the council decides against the requirement, saying:

*"The Holy Spirit and we have agreed not to put any other burden on you."* Acts 15:28

This sentence in its official response is a beautiful expression of faith that the Holy Spirit guides the Church, especially when it gathers in council.

At a point in the Civil War,
the morale of the Northern troops
dropped dangerously low.
President Lincoln studied his generals
and concluded there was only one man
who could rally them: McClellan.

McClellan saddled his great black horse
and rode off to Virginia.

*He cantered down the dusty roads and
met the heads of the retreating columns,
and he cried words of encouragement
and swung his little cap, and he gave
the beaten men what no other man alive
could have given them—
enthusiasm, hope, confidence. . . .*

*The stumbling columns came alive, and
threw caps and knapsacks into the air,
and yelled . . . because they saw this
dapper little rider outlined against
the purple starlight. And this, in a way,
was the turning point of the war. . . .
And American history would be different
forever after.*   Bruce Caton, *This Hallowed Ground*

Peter gave this kind of "turning-point"
leadership to the early Church.

Record and share:
a.  A "turning-point" event in your life.
b.  What caused it? Who helped you make it?
c.  How did it impact your life or thinking?

2.  *Cornelius* is a book of cartoon strips
based on the biblical soldier Cornelius.
In one strip, Cornelius says,
"A lot of folks don't believe
in organized religion.
But that only leaves one alternative:
disorganized religion."

a.  What did Cornelius have in mind?
b.  List advantages and disadvantages of an
organized community of Jesus' followers.
c.  How does Matthew 16:13–19 give us
an insight into Jesus' mind on the question?

3.  Pick one of the following passages.
a.  Read the passage and sum it up briefly.
b.  Tell how it relates to the matter at hand.

🖋 The magician      Acts 8:4–25
🖋 The vision        Acts 10:1–8
🖋 The decision      Acts 11:1–18

4.  Why do you think it is significant
that Peter presided over
each of the three "Pentecosts"? 🖋

## Gentile Pentecost

**W**hat "turning point"
in Christianity's history
took place at Cornelius's
house in Caesarea?

2. List the three stages
by which the Spirit
descended upon the
early Church. In what
sense were the stages
"progressive"?

3. When was the first
Church council called?
What problem did it
address, and what
"act of faith" did its
official response reflect?

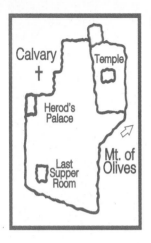

This street in the old city of modern Jerusalem still reflects what the city was like in Peter's time.

It was through streets like this that Peter ran the night of his miraculous prison escape.

# 90 Peter's Departure

An ancient Roman coin portrayed an ox facing an altar and a plow. The inscription on the coin read, "Ready for either."

In other words, the ox must be ready for swift sacrifice on an altar or for the long, hard life of pulling a plow.

The ox's fate dramatizes the fate that faced early Christians in a pagan society: swift death by the executioner's sword or a long life of hardship and hostility.

One Christian who died a swift death was James. Acts says:

*King Herod . . . had James, the brother of John, put to death by the sword. When he saw that this pleased the Jews, he went ahead and had Peter arrested.*
Acts 12:1–3

Peter's imprisonment was short lived. One night a strange light lit his cell.

*An angel of the Lord stood there. . . . At once the chains fell off Peter's hands. . . . He went to the home of Mary, the mother of John Mark, where many people had gathered and were praying. . . . He explained to them how the Lord had brought him out of prison. "Tell this to James and the rest of the believers," he said; then he left and went somewhere else.*
Acts 12:7, 12, 17

Two points stand out in this account.

First, the statement "he left and went somewhere else" marks Peter's departure in Acts. Except for a brief mention in connection with the first Church council, Peter disappears from public sight.

Presumably, a price was on his head, and he judged his public presence in Jerusalem too great a danger to the rest of the Christian community.

A fourth-century historian, Eusebius, says Peter eventually went to Rome, where he was martyred years later.

The second point that stands out is Peter's instruction to tell "James" (not John's brother). It introduces us to the person who will assume leadership of the Jerusalem church after Peter leaves.

A Chicago teacher asked a group of students when they made the transition from a childhood faith to an adult faith. One wrote:

*Something has happened to me here in college. . . . I've become preoccupied with Jesus Christ, who I feel is working within me. I can't explain this feeling.*

*It came about mainly these past months, when I began reading about the early Christians. I was so amazed and in awe of these people that I found it impossible to question Jesus or to doubt who he is— the Son of God. . . . I began to believe thoughtfully and firmly what I was taught since I was a child. . . .*

*I still have occasional doubts, but there remains that unexplainable something inside me. . . . Call it crazy, psychotic, whatever . . . I can't explain it, nor does it go away, nor did I induce it to come on. It just happened.*

a. Explain what is meant by a "transition from a childhood faith to an adult faith."
b. How does the student's explanation reflect such a transition?
c. To what extent have you made such a transition? Explain.
d. How does John 4:39–41 relate to a transition from a cultural faith to a personal faith?

2. Explain the following and illustrate each with an example, if possible:
a. "Saints . . . make it easier for the rest of us to believe in God."  Nathan Soderblum
b. "Holy men and women serve this world by reflecting in it the light of another." John W. Donohue
c. "A candle loses nothing by lighting another candle."  James Keller

3. English leader Oliver Cromwell hired an artist to do his portrait. When he saw that the artist had omitted some warts on his face, he told him to correct the omission, saying, "Paint me, warts and all."

The Acts of the Apostles is like a painted portrait of the early Church. It also has a few "warts." Read Acts 6:1–4 and Acts 15:36–41.

a. How are these two episodes "warts"?
b. Why would Luke include them?
c. What are some "warts" on the face of today's Church, and why do/don't they affect your faith in Jesus and the Church he founded on Peter?  Matthew 16:18

## Peter's Departure

How did Peter end up in prison, and how did he get out?

2. Apart from trying to avoid authorities, why did Peter probably disappear from sight?

3. Where did Peter eventually go, and what probably happened to him?

4. Who assumed leadership of the Jerusalem church after Peter's departure?

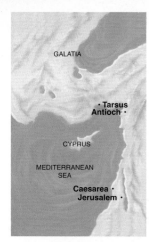

GALATIA

Tarsus
Antioch •

CYPRUS

MEDITERRANEAN
SEA

Caesarea •
Jerusalem •

# CHAPTER EIGHTEEN

# Global Witness

## 91 Paul's Conversion

**B**ritish journalist Douglas Hyde
detested the Catholic Church.
One day he was reading *The Catholic
Church against the Twentieth Century*
by Avro Manhattan.

He was searching
for dirt with which to smear the Church.
But just the opposite happened. He says:

*Instead of acquiring ammunition to damage
the Church, I learned . . . of the Church's
social teaching. Manhattan's book
was written to make me anti-Catholic.
It helped to make me "pro."*

Paul (Saul) had a similar experience.
He also began as an enemy of the Church,
actively persecuting its members.

One day he was going to Damascus.
Suddenly a light flashed from the sky.
Paul fell to the ground, and a voice said:

*"Saul! Why do you persecute me?"*
*"Who are you, Lord?" he asked.*
*"I am Jesus, whom you persecute. . . .*
*Go into the city, where you will be told
what you must do."*   Acts 9:4–6

Totally blinded by the light from the sky,
Paul has to be led to the city.
There a Christian named Ananias
lays hands on him and his sight returns.
Paul believes in Jesus and is baptized.

To everyone's amazement, Paul begins
preaching the Gospel everywhere.
His witness is so powerful
that his old allies plot to kill him.

Paul flees to Tarsus, his birthplace,
where he stays for a prolonged period.
He resumes preaching when some
Christians bring the "Good News"
to nearby Antioch. Acts says:

*The Lord's power was with them,
and a great number of people believed
and turned to the Lord.
The news about this reached the church
in Jerusalem, so they sent Barnabas
to Antioch.*   Acts 11:21–22

Recalling that Paul had fled to Tarsus,
Barnabas goes there to enlist Paul's help.

*He took him to Antioch, and for a whole year
the two met with the people of the church
and taught a large group.
It was at Antioch that the believers
were first called Christians.*   Acts 11:26

**T**his ancient archway
leads to Paul's birthplace,
the city of Tarsus.
It was once a center
of culture and learning
that surpassed even
Athens.

Citizens of Tarsus
were granted full
Roman citizenship.
Having this citizenship
helped Paul more than
once in his ministry.
Acts 22:25–29

*I*magine that television existed in Paul's time. Station SUN-TV Damascus sends you to interview Paul as he enters the city totally blind. Team up with a friend and do the interview. Among the questions, ask:

a. What did the voice sound like?
b. What message did the voice give you?
c. What do you think the message means?
d. Do you think you imagined all of this because of guilt feelings you have about what you've been doing?
e. Is your blindness God's punishment?
f. What are your plans now?

End by having your group do "phone-in" questions to Station SUN-TV.

2. Chris says, "I don't need the Church. I have my own way of relating to Christ." Kim says, "That's like the hand saying, 'I don't need the rest of the body. I have my own way of relating to the head.' "

a. How fully do you find yourself in agreement with Chris? With Kim?
b. Read 1 Corinthians 12:12–27 to see what Paul says about this very point.

3. Antioch, located near the Mediterranean, was popular with tourists and sailors. But its popularity brought problems. The city became so wild that a Roman general ruled it "off limits" to his troops. Surprisingly, it was in this wild city that Christians preached the Good News with such success.

a. Why do you think the people of Antioch were so ready for Jesus' message?
b. How might this be saying something to us today? Explain.

4. "To preach to people who *are not* ready is a waste of time. But *not* to preach to people who *are* ready is a waste of human beings."   Confucius

a. How ready are people today? What group might be especially ready?
b. What makes people ready?
c. List some reasons why you think young people today are/aren't ready for the message of Jesus.

5. Explain each of the following, and try to give an example to illustrate your point.
a. "We must evangelize the poor with our hands before we evangelize them with our lips."  Saint Peter Claver
b. "Be careful. . . . You may be the only Bible some people ever read."  W. J. Toms
c. "It's not enough for me to love God if my neighbor doesn't love God."
Saint Vincent de Paul 🖎

*W*hat makes people ready to hear the message of Jesus?

## Paul's Conversion

*R*ecount the story of Paul's conversion and how it gave him a totally different view of Jesus' followers.

2. Why did Paul have to flee for his life?

3. When, why, and in what place did Paul resume preaching?

4. In what city were believers first called Christians, and what kind of city was it from a spiritual viewpoint?

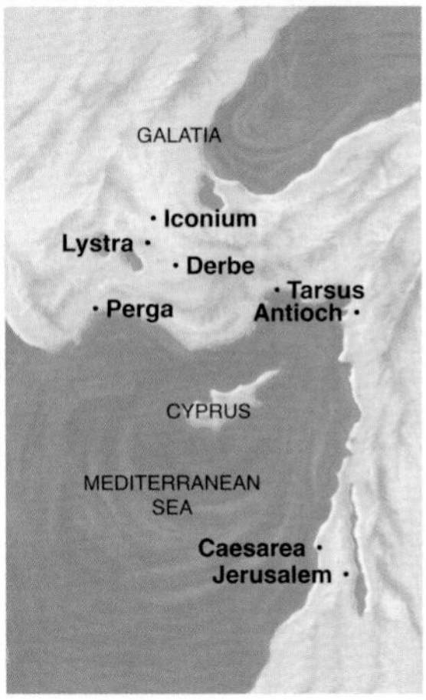

GALATIA

· Iconium
Lystra ·
· Derbe
· Tarsus
· Perga    Antioch ·

CYPRUS

MEDITERRANEAN
SEA
Caesarea ·
Jerusalem ·

# 92  First Missionary Trip

*I n the church of Antioch . . .
were some prophets and teachers. . . .
The Holy Spirit said to them,
"Set apart for me Barnabas and Saul
[Paul], to do the work to which I have
called them." They fasted and prayed,
placed their hands on them,
and sent them off.*   Acts 13:1–3

The two begin by going to Cyprus,
where Barnabas was born.

There they preach in synagogues and
even before the governor of the island.

Next they go to Asia Minor (Turkey)
and preach in such cities
as Perga, Iconium, and Lystra.
At Lystra, Paul heals a crippled man.
When the crowds see this, they exclaim:

*"The gods have become like men
and have come down to us!"
They gave Barnabas the name Zeus,
and Paul the name Hermes,
because he was the chief speaker.*
Acts 14:11–12

Why this surprising reaction?
A clue might be the writings of Ovid.
This poet describes a legendary visit
of Zeus and Hermes to Lystra.
The two gods come in disguise
and are badly treated by everyone
except one elderly couple.
Before leaving Lystra, the gods
punish the hostile townspeople
and reward the elderly couple.

Perhaps the citizens of Lystra
remembered this legend and did not
want to make the same mistake again.

The preaching of Paul and Barnabas
is cut short by the arrival
of influential Jews who oppose
their Christian message.
Violence erupts and Paul is stoned.
After Paul recovers,
he and Barnabas go to Derbe.
There they continue their preaching.

Eventually the time comes
for Paul and Barnabas to return home.
They have been on the road for four years
and are badly in need of a rest.
The date is A.D. 49.

The people of Lystra
mistook Paul for the
Greek god Hermes,
pictured on this pillar
from the temple
of Artemis in Ephesus.

*and for this reason he would call for him often and talk with him.* Acts 24:26

When Paul refuses to play Felix's game, he pays dearly for it. He is warehoused in prison for the next two years.

Felix's life reads like a movie script. Born a slave, he was freed and married the lovely granddaughter of Cleopatra and Mark Antony. He went on to become the first slave in Roman history to occupy the seat of a Roman governor.

But Roman historians tell us that Felix had a dark side. Tacitus says, "He took bribes wherever and whenever he could get them." Why do you think God lets scoundrels like Felix keep saints like Paul from doing God's work?

2. A woman said of Paul's refusal to play Felix's game (bribery): "Given the kind of person Felix was, why shouldn't Paul play his game? Why let someone like Felix lock him up for the next two years?" Why do you agree/disagree with her?

3. How do the following quotes touch on the woman's question: "Why shouldn't Paul play Felix's game?"

a. "People may doubt what you say, but they will believe what you do." Lewis Cass
b. "What a person believes might be ascertained, not from his creed, but from the assumption on which he habitually acts." G. B. Shaw
c. "The worst danger that confronts the younger generation is the example set by the older generation." E. C. McKenzie

4. Some political prisoners in Russia were standing before a firing squad. Seconds before the order "Fire!" a messenger rode up with a letter commuting their sentences to hard labor. One of those prisoner was Dostoevski, who went on to write some of the world's greatest literature.

Paul, who wrote some of Christianity's greatest literature, had a similar brush with death in Jerusalem. Concerning Paul's and Dostoevski's brushes with death, someone asked, "Do you think God ever intervenes to protect or to rescue someone who has been given a special mission or job?"

a. What do you think about this?
b. To what extent might you agree with Heidi Quade, who said, "A coincidence is a small miracle in which God chooses to remain anonymous"?

5. Imagine you are a Jerusalem reporter covering the explosive near riot described in Acts 21:27–23:11. Team up with a friend and prepare a TV or radio report on it. Present your report to the group. ✍

A walled barrier encircled the Temple. Stone signs warned:

*Whoever is caught taking a foreigner beyond this barrier will have only themselves to blame for their death which will follow.*

Paul was accused of taking Trophimus, a Gentile, beyond this barrier. Acts 21:28

The fragment of the warning sign shown here was found in 1936.

*Paul in Custody*

Why was Paul:
a. Attacked outside the Temple?
b. Moved to Caesarea?
c. Kept in prison by Felix?

2. List three facts about Felix's life.

3. What was Paul given to understand while being held in prison under Roman custody in Jerusalem?

# 97 Paul to Rome

**D**ietrich Bonhoeffer, a Lutheran pastor, openly opposed the Nazis and their movement in Germany. He was arrested, imprisoned, and put to death by the Nazis.

Paul endured similar agonizing nights during his imprisonment at Caesarea.

Then one day his hopes soared briefly when Festus replaced Felix as governor.

But Paul's hopes crashed back to earth just as quickly as they soared to the sky. Paul's enemies got to Festus first and persuaded him to return Paul to Jerusalem for trial.

Fearing he'd never get a fair trial locally, Paul asked to be tried in Rome. Roman citizens, like Paul, had this right.

Luke and Aristarchus accompanied Paul to Rome, probably signing on as his personal servants.    Acts 27:2

An ancient letter of Pliny testifies that Roman citizens had a right to maintain servants, even in custody.

Before the voyage reached midpoint, a great storm blew up. It became so violent that the captain ordered cargo thrown overboard. Luke writes:

*For many days we could not see the sun or the stars, and the wind kept on blowing.*    Acts 27:20

One night the ship blew into dangerous waters. The situation became desperate.

*Before dawn . . . Paul took some bread, gave thanks to God before them all, broke it, and began to eat. They took courage, and every one of them also ate some food. . . .*

*After everyone had eaten enough, they lightened the ship by throwing all the wheat [cargo] into the sea.*
Acts 27:33, 35–36, 38

**W**hile a prisoner, Paul probably drank water that flowed down this aqueduct to the city of Caesarea.

The water's origin was Mount Carmel, 20 miles to the north.

Aqueducts sloped an average of 12 inches every 200 feet. They were the lifelines of cities and had to be carefully protected.

Like Paul, Bonhoeffer used his prison hours to write. His "Night Voices in Tegel" takes us inside his mind and his heart prior to his execution on April 9, 1945.

Bonhoeffer lies wide awake on a prison cot, shut off from the sounds and stars of the sweet summer night.

He stares unseeing into prison darkness— listening to sleepless men sighing, listening to his own body breathing. He wonders what tomorrow will bring.

F ive British explorers froze to death during a polar expedition.

An excerpt from the journal of one of the explorers, Edward Wilson, sounds like something Paul might have written as he set out for Rome. It reads:

*I am in God's hands, to be used to bring others to him . . . or to die tomorrow if he so wills. . . . We must do what we can and leave the rest to him. . . . My trust is in God so that it matters not what I do or where I go.*

Some people say that Wilson's words are too fatalistic. What do you say, and why?

2. Just as Wilson kept a journal of the British expedition, so Luke kept a journal of Paul's trip to Rome.

Listen to a reading of Acts 27:13–44 ("The Storm"), prepared by three people. (Before the reading, draw or point out on a map the route that the voyage took.)

3. The fear created by the storm caused some passengers to quit eating and shows how fear can traumatize people. A recent survey asked young people, "What is a fear you have, right now?" Here are some of their responses:

____ Not fitting in or being put down
____ Being unhappy or failing in life
____ Losing faith in almost everything
____ Increasing crime and violence
____ Growing greed and materialism
____ Being abused, hurt, or killed

a. Number the responses (1–6) in the order in which you share these same fears.
b. Briefly explain the reason for your "number one" fear.
c. Add one fear not listed, and explain why it is a fear for you.
d. List something that gives you hope in the midst of your fears.

4. Along with the above survey on fear, young people were asked, "What advice would you give parents today?" Here are some of their responses:

____ Set clearer rules and be firmer
____ Show me you approve of me
____ Don't put down my friends
____ Don't nag me about my music
____ Compliment me when I do well
____ Treat me with more respect

a. Using A, B, C, D, and F, grade how well your parents do on the above points.
b. List one other suggestion for parents.

## Paul to Rome

**W**hat made Paul's hopes soar briefly during his imprisonment, and why was he tried in Rome?

2. Who accompanied Paul to Rome? Why were they permitted to do this? Why do we have such an excellent description of the trip?

3. What architectural structure still visible in Caesarea was there in Paul's time?

MACEDONIA
• Rome
• Three Inns
• Market of Appius
• Puteoli
ITALY
Phillippi •
Thessalonica •
ACHAIA
• Rhegium
SICILY
• Syracuse
Athens • Corinth
MEDITERRANEAN
SEA
MALTA
CRETE
LIBYA

# 98 Shipwrecked

The final night of the storm at sea the ship's crew and passengers hardly slept. When dawn came, no one was sure where they were.

*They noticed a bay with a beach and decided that, if possible, they would run the ship aground there. . . .*

*But the ship hit a sandbank . . . ; the back part was being broken to pieces by the violence of the waves. . . .*

There were other shores where they would not have been welcome.

The survivors stay on the island until suitable sailing weather returns. Then they resume their voyage on a ship called *The Twin Gods.*

Eventually they reach Puteoli (below) on the Italian coast. From there, Paul and the other prisoners are marched on foot to Rome.

*The next day a wind began to blow from the south, and in two days we came to the town of Puteoli.* Acts 28:13

*[An officer] ordered everyone who could swim to jump overboard first and swim ashore; the rest were to follow, holding on to the planks or to some broken pieces of the ship.*

*And this was how we all got safely to shore.* Acts 27:39, 41, 43–44

The crew and the passengers were lucky to have landed on friendly Malta.

*The believers in Rome heard about us and came as far as the towns of Market of Appius and Three Inns to meet us. . . .*

*When we arrived in Rome, Paul was allowed to live by himself with a soldier guarding him.* Acts 28:15–16

In other words, Paul is put under an ancient form of house arrest.

This gives him considerable freedom.
It is a welcome relief
from his imprisonment in Caesarea.
The date is about A.D. 61.

The novel *The Apostle* portrays
hundreds of condemned Christians
in an underground dungeon.
They will not see the light of day again
until they are hauled up through a tiny
trapdoor in the ceiling to be executed.
Suddenly the trapdoor opens and a new
prisoner is lowered into the dungeon.

To everyone's amazement, this prisoner is
singing and praising God. Someone shouts,
"It's Paul!" Paul's enthusiasm is so great
that everyone begins singing.

*I'll never forget a summer canoe trip*
*that I made with some of my friends.*
*We'd looked forward to it all summer.*
*It started great, but then it rained.*
*We became soaked, cold, and miserable.*
*The trip was turning into a huge disaster.*

*Then one of my friends stood up in the canoe*
*and sang "Singin' in the Rain."*
*He got so involved in his song and dance*
*that he tipped over the canoe and*
*we all went flying into the river.*

*My friend kept right on singing,*
*and we all came up laughing.*
*We got back into the canoe and continued*
*down the river laughing and singing.*
*That day I discovered something*
*I'll never forget. We all have the power*
*to change a bad situation into one*
*that is good—even fantastic!*

Paul's sea voyages
took him to ports
like this one at
modern Kavalla
(ancient Neapolis).
Acts 16:11

Such ports were filled
with colorful ships
from faraway lands
and small boats owned
by local residents.

Many ancient seaports
were protected by hilltop
fortifications, like
the ones shown here.

The dungeon is instantly transformed
into a place of joy. It was this kind
of an impact that Paul had
on many Christians in Rome.
How do you account for:
a. The difference between the condemned
Christians' mood and Paul's spirit?
b. Paul's power to rally and lead people?

2. Describe a time when you, or someone
you know, transformed a bad situation
into one like the following:

Explain each of the following, and use
the canoe story to illustrate your point.

a. "Two men looked out through prison bars.
One saw mud; the other stars."   Oscar Wilde
b. "I don't think of all the misery, but of
the beauty that still remains."   Anne Frank
c. "Let's not look back in anger,
nor forward in fear, but around
in awareness."   James Thurber
d. "The speed of the leader determines
the rate of the pack."   Wayne Lukas

### Shipwrecked

On what island did
the shipwreck occur,
and how did the
passengers and crew
get ashore?
How long did they
remain on the island?

2. What happened
when Paul, Luke,
and Aristarchus landed
on the Italian coast?

3. Describe Paul's prison
situation in Rome
and how he spent his
time awaiting his trial.

205

# 99  Paul in Rome

Once Paul got settled in Rome, he met with local Jewish leaders. They were eager to sit down and find out more about his teachings.

*"We would like to hear your ideas, because we know that everywhere people speak against this party to which you belong."*  Acts 28:22

Paul eagerly welcomes the opportunity to talk about "this party" (Christianity).

*From morning till night he explained . . . his message about the Kingdom of God, and he tried to convince them about Jesus by quoting from the Law of Moses and the writings of the prophets.*

*Some of them were convinced . . . but others would not believe. So they left, disagreeing.*  Acts 28:23–25

The Acts of the Apostles ends abruptly with this summary statement:

*For two years Paul . . . welcomed all who came to see him. He preached about the Kingdom of God and taught about the Lord Jesus Christ, speaking with all boldness and freedom.*
Acts 28:30–31

Luke never does tell us what happened at Paul's trial in Rome. One of Paul's own letters suggests he was freed.  2 Timothy 4:16–17

Perhaps he then went to Spain (Romans 15:24), Asia Minor (Titus 3:12), Macedonia (1 Timothy 1:3), and Crete (Titus 1:5).

Once back in Rome, Paul appears to have been brought to trial a second time. This time he is convicted.  2 Timothy 4:6

Tradition says Paul was eventually beheaded in Rome around A.D. 67.

And so the question returns: Why did Luke leave Acts unfinished? One intriguing answer is that Luke left it unfinished on purpose, because its story is still unfinished.

And so the preaching of the Good News about Jesus goes on—and must go on— until the world is fully re-created and Jesus returns in all his glory.

El Greco's famous portrait of Paul highlights his hands and his eyes.

No doubt El Greco was inspired by Luke's reference to Paul's use of his hands in speeches at Antioch (Acts 13:16), Ephesus (Acts 20:34), and Jerusalem (Acts 21:40, 26:1).

And Luke refers to Paul's use of his eyes in speeches at Salamis (Acts 13:9) and Lystra (Acts 14:9).

Britain's Malcolm Muggeridge interviewed Mother Teresa on TV. The verdict was that the interview was hardly usable. Her delivery was too halting, and her accent was too thick.

One TV official, however, sensed it had a mysterious power and decided to air it on prime time one Sunday night. The audience response was incredible, both in letters and money contributions.

Later, in *Something Beautiful for God,* Muggeridge described Mother Teresa's impact on one live audience this way:

*Every face . . . was rapt, hanging on her words; not because of the words . . . but because of her. Some quality came across over and above the words . . . penetrating every mind and heart.*

a. What quality enabled Mother Teresa to move audiences deeply?
b. What message might this hold for you and your future power as a person?

2. There are clues in Paul's letters that suggest he, too, was neither impressive as a person nor dynamic as a speaker. For example, he himself writes:

*Someone will say,
"Paul's letters are severe and strong,
but when he is with us in person,
he is weak, and his words are nothing!"*
2 Corinthians 10:10

Paul explained the source of his power this way:

*My teaching and message
were not delivered with skillful words
of human wisdom. . . .
Your faith, then, does not rest
on human wisdom but on God's power.*
1 Corinthians 2:4–5

a. Explain Paul's point.
b. What is your suggestion for developing more people like Paul and Mother Teresa?

3. Explain the following, and illustrate each with an example if you can.

a. "We must not be content to be cleansed from sin; we must be filled with the Spirit."
John Fletcher

b. "Where the human spirit fails, the Holy Spirit fills." Anonymous

c. "Make sure the thing you're living for is worth dying for." Charles Mayes 🖊

In A.D. 70, shortly after Paul's death, Roman armies, under Titus, leveled the Jerusalem Temple.

This panel from the Arch of Titus, which celebrates the event, shows soldiers taking booty from the Temple.

## Paul in Rome

How did Paul's trial in Rome turn out, and what happened to Paul after it?

2. When, where, and how does tradition say Paul's life ended?

3. What is a possible answer to the question, Why did Luke leave Acts unfinished?

# CHAPTER TWENTY

# Paul's Letters

## 100  1–2 Thessalonians

> I sought my God
> but my God
> I could not see.
> I sought my soul,
> but my soul
> eluded me.
> I sought
> my brother
> and found all three.

Paul's greatest legacy is the letters Paul wrote to churches of his day. Tradition assigns thirteen letters to him, and groups them as follows:

Early:     1–2 Thessalonians
Great:     1–2 Corinthians,
           Galatians, Romans
Prison:    Philippians, Colossians,
           Ephesians, Philemon
Pastoral:  1–2 Timothy, Titus

Paul wrote his first letter about A.D. 50 to Christians living in Thessalonica. Somehow they had gotten the idea that Jesus was coming soon to escort all believers into heaven *alive*.

Then, when some of them began to die, the Thessalonians grew sad and confused, thinking these believers would never see Jesus or be with God forever. Paul sent them a letter to assure them that this was not the case. He writes:

*From Paul, Silas, and Timothy—*
*To the people of the church*
*in Thessalonica, who belong to God*
*the Father and the Lord Jesus Christ:*
*May grace and peace be yours.*

*We always thank God for you. . . .*
*We want you to know the truth*
*about those who have died. . . .*

*Jesus died and rose again, and . . .*
*God will take back with Jesus*
*those who have died believing in him. . . .*
*Read this letter to all the believers.*
*The grace of our Lord Jesus Christ be*
*with you.*     1 Thessalonians 1:1–2, 4:13–14, 5:27–28

Paul's letter cleared up the confusion about those who died, and this brought great joy to the Thessalonians. In fact, it seems to have fueled expectations about Jesus' coming.

Rumors that it was near began to fly. Some members even quit their jobs. This created a flurry of new problems. Thus Paul wrote a second letter in reply to these false rumors.     2 Thessalonians 2:1–10

Paul's reply boils down to this: Certain events must precede Jesus' coming. One of these is a major confrontation between the forces of good and evil. Paul's letter is vague about these events, because he presumes his readers are familiar with the teaching he gave to them orally at an earlier date.     2 Thessalonians 2:5

Some scholars said Luke's reference to politarchs ("city authorities") in Acts 17:9 was wrong. Then archaeologists uncovered a six-foot white marble slab listing the names of six officials who governed Thessalonica under this title. Dating from Paul's time, the slab testifies to Luke's care and accuracy in documenting his narrative in Acts.

Paul's two letters to the Thessalonians illustrate the format that he follows in most of his correspondence:

🍃 *salutation,* containing the sender's name, receiver's name, and a greeting;
🍃 *thanksgiving,* acting as a bridge to the body of the letter;
🍃 *body of the letter,* addressing one or several issues of the Christian faith;
🍃 *conclusion,* containing a personal comment and a blessing.

1 n the novel *Brothers Karamazov,* an old woman begins to doubt God's existence and Paul's assurance that "those who have died believing in Christ will rise to life."   1 Thessalonians 4:16

She asks an old priest to *prove* them. He says, "You can't *prove* these things, but you can *become sure* of them." "How?" she asks. The priest answers, "Love your neighbor from the heart. As your love grows so will sureness of God's existence and life after death."

a.  Explain the difference between "proving" and "being sure" of something.
b.  Why would loving her neighbor "from the heart" strengthen the woman's faith?

2.  *Though my soul may set in darkness,*
*it will rise in perfect light,*
*I have loved the stars too fondly*
*to be fearful of the night.*   Sarah Williams

a.  What is the poet's point?
b.  Why do you think her love of the stars has taken away her fear of the night?

3.  Mount Vesuvius erupted suddenly in A.D. 79, burying people alive. The event recalled Paul's words:

*The Day of the Lord will come as a thief*
*comes at night. When people say,*
*"Everything is quiet and safe,"*
*then suddenly destruction will hit them!*
1 Thessalonians 5:2–3

The decayed bodies of the Vesuvius victims have left cavities in the hardened ash.

By pouring plaster into them, archaeologists are able to reconstruct the position of the victims when they died. One reconstruction shows a mother cradling an infant in her arms.

a.  How is the Vesuvius eruption a kind of preview of the Second Coming?

b.  What are your feelings when you think of Jesus' coming? Explain.

4.  Read 1 Thessalonians 4:13–18. Then pause for two or three minutes to reflect on how the coming of Jesus might catch some people unprepared. Record and share your thoughts. Here is an excerpt from what one person wrote:

*I was in a bar on West 25th drinking*
*beer with this blond. She wasn't so bad*
*and things were getting interesting*
*when all of a sudden the whole joint*
*started coming apart at the seams.*
*There was a real weird light in the sky.*
Thomas A. Blackburn 🍃

V olcanic ash from the eruption of Mount Vesuvius froze these people in the exact position they were in when disaster struck.

*1-2*
*Thessalonians*

L ist Paul's thirteen letters according to the four groups into which tradition puts them.

2. When, why, and to whom did Paul write his first letter? His second letter?

3. Describe the fourfold structure Paul usually followed in his letters.

4. What archaeological evidence supports Luke's reference to politarchs?

Chrxst's body,
the Church, xs
lxke a typewrxter.
X am lxke a key
Xf X fail to do
as X could.
Xts message
faxls to be heard
as xt should.

# 101  1–2 Corinthians

Routinely, Greek dramatists portrayed Corinthians as drunk, depraved, and boisterous. In street Greek, the word *korithiazien* meant "to behave like a Corinthian," that is, in an immoral way. And *kore korinthe* ("Corinthian girl") was an accepted label for a prostitute.

Judging by his letters to the Corinthians, Paul's Corinthian converts fitted this ancient stereotype. Paul writes:

*Few of you were wise or powerful or of high social standing. God purposely chose what the world considers nonsense in order to shame the wise.*

1 Corinthians 1:26–27

Understandably, some of the Corinthians slipped back into their earlier ways. Referring to this, Paul writes:

*There is sexual immorality among you so terrible that not even the heathen would be guilty of it. . . . Don't you know that your body is a temple of the Holy Spirit?*

1 Corinthians 5:1, 6:19

Paul goes on to talk about "divisions" that are present among the Corinthians. To illustrate the unity they should have, Paul reminds them:

*Christ is like a single body, which has many parts; it is still one body, even though it is made up of different parts. In the same way, all of us . . . are Christ's body.*  1 Corinthians 12:12–13, 27

Paul's second letter goes a step further, saying that since the Corinthians are Christ's body, they should help one another lovingly, "not with regret or out of a sense of duty."  2 Corinthians 9:7

Paul ends his letter in a personal way, telling the Corinthians how the Lord has used a personal weakness in his life to help him grow spiritually:

*Three times I . . . asked [the Lord] to take it away. But his answer was: "My grace is all you need, for my power is greatest when you are weak."*

*I am most happy, then, to be proud of my weaknesses, in order to feel the protection of Christ's power over me. I am content with weaknesses, insults, hardships, persecutions, and difficulties for Christ's sake. For when I am weak, then I am strong.*

2 Corinthians 12:8–10

Fifteen years after Paul preached in Corinth, the Romans brought 6,000 Jewish POWs to Corinth to begin cutting this canal through four miles of rock.

The POWs were captured after Titus, a Roman general, destroyed Jerusalem and its Temple in A.D. 70, as Jesus had foretold. Matthew 24:2

*T*erry Anderson of the Associated Press was kidnapped by Muslim extremists and spent seven years in windowless cells, often in chains.

At one point he nearly despaired, banging his head against the wall until it bled. He emerged a deeply spiritual person. Later he said, "I think we come closest to God at our lowest moments."

a. What words of Paul do these words remind you of? Explain both Paul's point and Anderson's point.
b. Record and share a "low moment" in your life and what impact, if any, it had on your relationship with God.

2. Listen to a dramatic reading of 1 Corinthians 1:18–31 ("Foolishness"). Record and share:
a. Two or three sentences that sum up the point of the reading.
b. A question or thought that struck you during the reading.

3. The seminary teachers who taught Saint John Vianney feared he was not bright enough to be ordained a priest. But the bishop understood John better than they did. The Holy Spirit worked through John in such a way that people came from all over to hear him preach and to celebrate with him the sacrament of Reconciliation.

a. What do you look for most in a priest?
b. Why do you think there is such a shortage of priests today?

4. A minister lost both his legs as a result of old war injuries. Unable to continue his normal ministry, he felt useless. Then one day a doctor asked him to minister to patients in tragic situations much like his own.

He soon found himself helping people who needed him far more than his former parishioners did. This helped him understand these words of Paul:

*[God] helps us in all our troubles, so that we are able to help others . . . , using the same help that we ourselves have received from God.*   2 Corinthians 1:4

a. How do you understand these words?
b. Record and share one way God has helped you and, because of it, you are better equipped to help others. ✑

*P*aul compared the life of a Christian to the life of an athlete, saying:

*Every athlete in training submits to strict discipline, in order to be crowned with a wreath that will not last; but we do it for one that will last forever.*
1 Corinthians 9:25

This conception of a discus thrower dates back to the Greek artist Myron of the fifth century B.C.

### 1–2 Corinthians

*H*ow did Greek dramatists portray Corinthians, and how does Paul's first letter to them fit the portrayal? What is one way Paul's second letter goes a step further than his first one?

2. What personal item did Paul share with the Corinthians at the conclusion of his second letter?

3. What is the link between the Corinth canal and Jesus' prophecy about Jerusalem?

# 102  Galatians & Romans

*P*aul's Letter to the Galatians
was prompted by Jewish converts
to Christianity who were telling
Gentile converts in Galatia
that they had to be circumcised.

Obviously, the Jewish converts did not
fully understand the relationship
between the Old and the New Testaments.

They failed to understand that, from a
Christian perspective, the Old Testament and
rites like circumcision might be compared
to the scaffolding of a building.

*A*rt, broadly speaking,
is that which invites
us to contemplation—
a rare commodity in
modern life.
Thomas Moore, *Care of the Soul*

Christianity was like the building.
Once the building is erected,
the scaffolding is no longer needed.
Referring to this new order, Paul says:

*It does not matter at all*
*whether or not one is circumcised;*
*what does matter*
*is being a new creature.*    Galatians 6:15

Paul's final *great* letter
was written around A.D. 58 from Corinth
to the Christians of Rome.

Paul began by reviewing how Jesus
fulfilled the Old Testament prophecies
and is both the son of David and
the Son of God.    Romans 1:2–4

Paul continues by saying that because
we are baptized into Christ, we should have
nothing to do with sin.    Romans 6
This does not mean that
we will not feel an attraction to sin.
Paul himself felt it sharply. He writes:

*I don't do the good I want to do;*
*instead, I do the evil*
*that I do not want to do. . . .*
*Who will rescue me from this body*
*that is taking me to death?*
*Thanks be to God, who does this through*
*our Lord Jesus Christ!*    Romans 7:19, 24–25

And so baptism does not
take away our attraction to sin.
It does something more important.
It unites us with Christ's body,
empowering us—in and through Christ—
to defeat sin.    Romans 6:3–6
Paul concludes his letter, saying:

*If we share Christ's suffering,*
*we will also share his glory. . . .*
*What we suffer . . .*
*cannot be compared . . . with the glory*
*that is going to be revealed.*    Roman 8:17–18

*Music expresses that which cannot be said in words and about which it is impossible to be silent.*   Victor Hugo

*L*eopold Stokowski was conducting the Philadelphia symphony. One overture featured a trumpet, played offstage. Twice the time came for it to sound; twice it didn't sound.

After the overture Stokowski stormed offstage to find the trumpet player. There he was—arms pinned to his sides by a burly security guard, who said, "This nut was trying to play his horn during your concert."

a.  How does this story illustrate the kind of problem some Jewish converts caused Paul and his other converts in Galatia?
b. Explain how the relationship between Judaism and Christianity might be compared to the relationship between a scaffolding and a building.

2.  Referring to what matters when it comes to being saved, Paul says, "Neither circumcision nor the lack of it makes any difference at all; what matters is faith that works through love."   Galatians 5:6

a.  What does Paul mean by the expression "faith that works through love"?

b.  William Sumner says, "I never set aside beliefs deliberately. I left them in the drawer, and after a while I opened it, and nothing was there."
What important point is Sumner making?

3.  Paul writes to Romans, "I don't do the good I want to do; instead, I do the evil that I do not want to do."   Romans 7:19

These words recall a humorous story. A young salesperson approached an old farmer sitting in a rocker on the porch of his rundown farm. He said, "Sir, I have a book that tells how you can farm your land ten times better than you're doing right now."

The old farmer continued to rock. Then, after a long pause, he said, "I know how to farm ten times better than I'm doing. That's not my problem."

a.  Explain the farmer's point.
b.  Explain the difference between sins of omission and sins of commission.
c.  Make a list of things you should be doing better than you are.
d.  Pick out one thing that you should be doing better and compose a prayer to God about it.

*Galatians & Romans*

*W*hat problem triggered Paul's Letter to the Galatians?

2. Cite and explain an analogy that might be used to illustrate the way Christianity sees itself related to Judaism.

3. Explain how baptism affects our relationship to Christ and to sin in our personal lives.

213

# 103  Philippians & Colossians

By moving only two barriers, turn the jail upside down, jailing the jailor and freeing Paul.

A modern peace activist was jailed for hammering, in *symbolic* protest, on an F15 bomber. (It costs $40 million and burns $6,000 worth of fuel a minute while flying.) He describes his prison situation in these terms:

*The jail we are currently in is awful. . . .
The TV blares at full volume all day
and all night. We have no privacy.
We are led around in chains and shackles.
Our mail is censored; much of it is turned away.
We are allowed no books. . . .
I have not been outdoors in over a month.*

John Dear, S.J.

Paul could relate to this *prison* letter. He wrote four letters from prison: Philippians (1:7), Colossians (4:10), Philemon (23), and Ephesians (6:20).

Paul's letter to the Christian community of Philippi contains a meditation on Jesus that follows this twofold focus:

- Jesus' divine nature,
- Jesus' human nature.

*He always had the nature of God, but . . .
took the nature of a servant. He became
like a human being. . . . He was humble
and walked the path of obedience all the
way to death—his death on the cross.
For this reason God . . . gave him the name
that is greater than any other name.
And so, in honor of the name of Jesus
all . . . will fall on their knees, and
all will openly proclaim
that Jesus Christ is Lord.*     Philippians 2:6–11

**W**ith my own hand I write this. Greetings from Paul.
Colossians 4:18

Paul ends several letters with a postscript like this, testifying that he used scribes.

His handwriting would have contrasted sharply with the scribe's, just as the postscript on this ancient letter contrasts with the neat hand-writing of its scribe.

Paul's second prison letter is addressed to the Christian community in Colossae. It, too, has a lovely meditation on Jesus. It, too, has a twofold focus:

- Jesus' role in God's plan,
- Jesus' role in the Church.

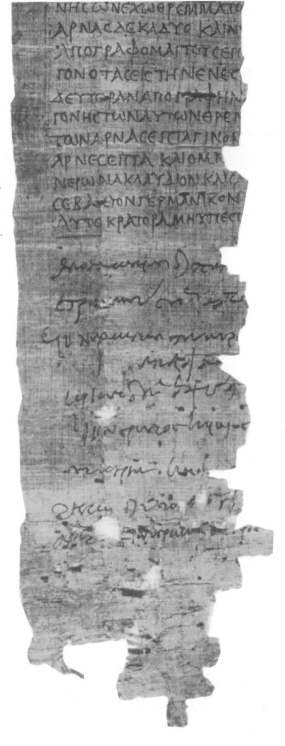

*Christ is the visible likeness of the
invisible God. He is the first-born Son,
superior to all created things. . . .
Christ existed before all things. . . .
He is the head of his body, the church;
he is the source of the body's life.
He is the first-born Son, who was raised
from death, in order that he alone
might have the first place in all things.*
Colossians 1:15, 17–18

7th WAR LOAN **NOW··ALL TOGETHER**

*P*eace activist John Dear, S.J.,
and his associates
were led around in shackles,
had their mail censored, were permitted
no books, and hadn't been allowed outside
in over a month.

a. Why do you think the peace activists
were treated like drug dealers and rapists,
if not worse?

b. How do you feel about the production
of a military weapon that costs
$40 million and burns $6,000 in fuel
each minute it is in flight?

2. Paul writes to Colossians:
*You are the people of God;
he loved you and chose you for his own. . . .
Forgive one another
whenever any of you has a complaint
against someone else.
You must forgive one another just as
the Lord has forgiven you.* Colossians 3:12–13

Father Jenko was one
of the many Westerners held hostage
in Lebanon by Muslim extremists
in the 1980s and the 1990s.
After his release, he recalled
some of his experiences in captivity.

One moving experience was
how the attitude of his Muslim guards
softened noticeably when they saw him
making a rosary from string.

a. Why would making the rosary from
string change the attitude of the guards?
b. What does the "softened" attitude
of the guards say about them?

c. Recall a time when your attitude toward
someone was changed or softened
by something they did. Explain.

3. Television's Phil Donahue says that
commitment is made up of three stages.

First, there is the *fun* stage.
That's when I say, "I love doing this.
Why didn't I get involved sooner?"
Then there's the *intolerant* stage.
That's when I say, "Anyone who's not
involved isn't really Christian!"
Finally, there's the *reality* stage.
That's when I realize my involvement
will probably make only a slight dent
in the war against evil.
It's at that stage that saints are made.

a. What is one commitment (like that of
the peace activist) that you have made,
when it comes to doing what you think
is right, regardless of what it costs you?
b. At which of Donahue's stages are you?
c. Is everyone called to a commitment
like that of the peace activist? Explain. ✎

*H*ow do you hold in
balance loyalty to one's
country and fidelity to
one's conscience?

*Philippians
&
Colossians*

*L*ist and describe briefly
the twofold focus of
Paul's meditation on
Jesus:
a. In his Letter to the
Philippians.
b. In his Letter to the
Colossians.

2. List and briefly
describe the three stages
of Christian commitment,
as summed up by Phil
Donahue.

3. Explain how the
ending of a number
of Paul's letters testify
to his use of scribes.

You find it
once in Philemon,
twice in Ephesians,
in the midst
of every dream,
at the end
of time,
and double in
heaven and eternity.
What is it?

# 104 Philemon & Ephesians

Onesimus was a runaway slave who belonged to a new Christian named Philemon. During his stay in prison, Paul instructed and baptized Onesimus. Paul wrote to Philemon, asking him to forgive Onesimus:

*Here, I will write this*
*with my own hand:*
*I, Paul, will pay you back.*    Philemon 12, 16–19

No other letter reveals Paul's warmth more than this one does, and no other letter expresses more eloquently the love Christians should have for one another because of their unity in Christ.

Paul's last prison letter is to the Christian community at Ephesus. Its style and theology are so distinctive that some suggest it is the work of one of Paul's later disciples. But such speculation is often pointless. Besides, Paul used different scribes, approving and signing what they wrote. Typical of Paul's signature is this one:

*With my own hand I write this:*
*Greetings from Paul.*
*This is the way I sign every letter;*
*this is how I write.*    2 Thessalonians 3:17

A highlight of Paul's Letter to the Ephesians is his concise overview of God's plan.

*This plan, which God will complete*
*when the time is right,*
*is to bring all creation together,*
*everything in heaven and on earth,*
*with Christ as head. . . . God chose us . . .*
*in union with Christ. . . .*

*[God] appointed some to be apostles,*
*others to be prophets . . . evangelists . . .*
*pastors and teachers.*
*[God] did this to prepare all God's people*
*for the work of Christian service . . .*
*to build up the body of Christ. . . .*

*Pray always for all God's people.*
*And pray also for me.*
                    Ephesians 1:10–11, 4:11–12, 6:18–19

"Seize me if I should try to escape and send me back to my master," reads this metal tag that once hung from the neck of a Roman slave.

A similar identification probably hung from the neck of Onesimus.

*I am sending [Onesimus]*
*back to you now,*
*and with him goes my heart. . . .*
*He is not just a slave, but . . .*
*a dear brother in Christ. . . .*
*Welcome him back*
*just as you would welcome me.*
*If he has done you any wrong*
*or owes you anything,*
*charge it to my account.*

Years ago, John Howard Griffin dyed his skin black, shaved his head, and posed as a black man. He wanted to learn firsthand what it was like to be black in the South.

One day he asked for a Catholic church and was told the "colored Catholic church" was on Drysades Street. He replied, "There's no such thing as a colored Catholic church." The person said, "You don't really believe that? . . . This is the South. You're going to find that a lot of white Catholics look on you as a nigger first and a Catholic second, no matter what the Archbishop says."

a. How does Paul's Letter to Philemon refer to a similar cultural barrier that Christians in Paul's time had to wrestle with and overcome?
b. List some other modern barriers that threaten the unity that binds us together into Christ's body.
c. What are some positive, practical steps that your group might explore to help overcome these barriers?

2. Read Ephesians 2:11–22 ("One Body"). Record and share:
a. What cultural barrier is Paul dealing with, and what approach is he using?
b. What earlier highlight of this letter does Paul develop, and in what way?

3. *From Paul . . .*
*To our friend and fellow worker*
*Philemon, and the church*
*that meets in your house. . . .*
*Every time I pray, I mention you*
*and give thanks to my God. . . .*
*I make a request to you on behalf of*
*Onesimus, who is my own son in Christ. . . .*
*Epaphras . . . sends you his greetings,*
*and so do my coworkers*
*Mark, Aristarchus, Demus, and Luke.*
*May the grace of the Lord Jesus Christ*
*be with you all.*   Philemon 1–2, 4, 10, 23–25

a. These excerpts from Paul's Letter to Philemon illustrate the fourfold format he follows in most of his letters.

Review the elements of the format and explain each briefly.
b. Explain the significance of the words "the church that meets in your *house.*"
c. Identify Mark and Luke.

4. Concerning Epaphras, Paul writes to the Colossians: "You learned of God's grace from Epaphras. . . . He has told us of the love that the Spirit has given you."   Colossians 1:7–8
What does this suggest about Paul's connection with the Colossians? ❧

*To sing is to pray twice.*
Anonymous

## Philemon & Ephesians

Who was Onesimus, and what is his connection with Paul?

2. To whom does Paul write concerning Onesimus, and why?

3. A highlight of Paul's Letter to the Ephesians is an overview of God's plan for people. What is that plan? For what purpose does God appoint apostles, prophets, pastors, and the like?

# CHAPTER TWENTY-ONE

# Other Letters

## 106  James

*When things go wrong,
as they sometimes will,
When the road
you're trudging
seems all uphill . . .
When care is pressing
you down a bit,
Rest, if you must,
but don't you quit.*

Author unknown

United States Air Force plane carrying 30,000 letters to soldiers crashed just off Newfoundland. At considerable risk to their own lives, divers recovered the canvas mailbags.

Why the great concern for these letters? Experience shows that combat soldiers cope much better with food shortages than they do with letter shortages.

The leaders of the early Church also knew the importance of letters. They used them to keep in touch with distant brothers and sisters.

Besides the thirteen letters tradition attributes to Paul, there are eight letters by various other church leaders.

Seven are general, or "catholic," letters, so-called because they are addressed to no special congregation. They include James, 1–2–3 John, 1–2 Peter, and Jude.

Take the Letter from James. It treats such practical, down-to-earth topics as

- persevering under trial,            1:2–18
- avoiding discrimination,         2:1–13
- helping the poor.                      5:1–6

The letter's style and tone are more like those of a sermon than a letter. This suggests it may have been a sermon that was converted into a letter.

One passage, especially, deserves note. It discusses the important relationship between faith and action, and reads:

*What good is it for one of you to say that you have faith if your actions do not prove it? Can that faith save you?*

*Suppose there are brothers or sisters who need clothes and don't have enough to eat. What good is there in your saying to them, "God bless you! Keep warm and eat well!"—if you don't give them the necessities of life?*

*So it is with faith; if it is alone and includes no actions, then it is dead.*

James 2:14–17

There is no better summary of this passage than Saint Paul's famous words:

*I may have all the faith needed to move mountains—but if I have not love, I am nothing.*   1 Corinthians 13:2

he happiest people in the world are those who have found the life task to which they have been called. . . .

[The unhappiest] are those who have not even begun to search.

Robert C. Leslie

here is a whole literature of "Texas humor." Its theme is that nothing in Texas is ever done on a small or limited scale.

One story concerns a New Yorker who did a favor for a Texan. The Texan insisted on giving him a gift. Finally, the New Yorker relented, saying, "Oh, a few golf clubs would be nice."

A few days later, the New Yorker got a fax from Texas, reading: "Have six golf clubs for you. Unfortunately only five have outdoor swimming pools." That "Texas humor" is but a faint glimpse of what James has in mind when he says, "God gives generously . . . to all."   James 1:5

a. If God offered to give you anything that would be helpful to you or your family, what would you ask for? Explain.
b. When should/shouldn't you ask God for things?

2. Robert Louis Stevenson wrote the great classic *Treasure Island*. In *Voyage to Windward*, J. C. Furnas says that Stevenson, in his adolescence, carried a formula for summoning the devil.

"What a strange thing to do," we say. "What kind of person would do that?" The truth is we all do it when we fail to resist temptation immediately. The Letter from James puts it this way:

*We are tempted when we are drawn away and trapped by our own evil desires. Then our evil desires conceive and give birth to sin.*   James 1:14–15

Record and share:
a. What advice you would give to a friend who asked you how to resist temptation.
b. A temptation you resisted.
c. A temptation you gave in to and why you failed to resist it immediately.

3. *We are no more responsible for the evil thoughts that pass through our minds than a scarecrow for the birds that fly over the seedplot he has to guard. The sole responsibility in each case is to prevent them from settling.*   John Collins

Record and share:
a. What author John Collins has in mind.
b. Why his words do/don't apply when we knowingly, willingly, and without sufficient reason place ourselves in a situation that previous experience has shown will cause evil thoughts to enter our minds. ✍

*James*

List the seven "catholic" letters, and explain why they are given this name.

2. List two practical topics that the Letter from James takes up.

3. What makes some think the Letter from James didn't start as a letter?

4. Explain James's point about the link between faith and works.

221

> **N**o pain,
> no *palm*;
> **N**o thorns,
> no *glory*;
> **N**o cross,
> no *crown*.
>
> William Penn

# *107  Peter*

**F**ather Brandsma, a Dutch priest, was kept imprisoned in a dog kennel in a Nazi concentration camp. For their amusement, guards made him bark like a dog each time they passed by. Eventually the priest died in the kennel.

Among his possessions was a prayer book. The Nazis failed to notice that between its lines he kept a journal of his prison sufferings. One entry includes this poem.

*No grief shall fall my way, but I*
*Shall see Thy grief-filled eyes;*
*The lonely way that Thou once walked*
*Has made me sorrow-wise. . . .*
*Stay with me, Jesus, only stay;*
*I shall not fear / If, reaching out my hand,*
*I feel Thee near.*    Kilian J. Healy, *Walking with God*

The First Letter from Peter was sent to suffering Christians, who could relate to that poem. The cause and nature of their suffering isn't known for certain, but it may be inferred from these lines:

*The heathen are surprised*
*when you do not join them*
*in the same wild and reckless living,*
*and so they insult you. . . .*
*Happy are you if you are insulted*
*because you are Christ's followers.*
1 Peter 4:4, 14

The letter also addresses the question of Jesus' second coming. Many early Christians believed that Jesus would return in their lifetime. When he didn't, they grew worried. Peter assures them:

*We have not depended on made-up stories*
*in making known to you the mighty coming*
*of our Lord Jesus Christ.*
*With our own eyes we saw his greatness.*
*We were there when he was given honor*
*and glory by God the Father,*
*when the voice came to him*
*from the Supreme Glory, saying,*
*"This is my own dear Son,*
*with whom I am pleased!"*
*We ourselves heard this voice coming*

**W**e saw his greatness. . . . We ourselves heard this voice coming from heaven, when we were with him on the holy mountain.    2 Peter 1:16, 18

Peter's reference is to Jesus' transfiguration, portrayed in this mosaic located in the Church of the Transfiguration atop Mount Tabor.

Who are the five people with Jesus in the mosaic? Explain what you think is the clue to their identity.
Luke 9:28–36

*from heaven, when we were with him
on the holy mountain.*   2 Peter 1:16–18

Peter ends by reaffirming Jesus' return,
adding the same caution that Jesus did:

*"No one knows, however, when that day
or hour will be—neither the angels . . .
nor the Son; only the Father. . . .
I say to all: Watch!"*   Mark 13:32, 37

Tennis star Alice Marble woke up
the day of the finals at Wimbledon
with a terrible pain in her stomach.
The doctor diagnosed it as a torn muscle.
When Alice insisted on playing anyway,
the doctor said she was foolish.

Alice wrote later,
"I shall never forget that first game.
Every swing made me want to scream."
Incredibly, she went on to win,
while the Queen of England and 20,000
unsuspecting spectators watched.

Alice's experience recalls these words
of the First Letter from Peter:
"Christ himself suffered for you and
left you an example, so that you would
follow in his steps."   1 Peter 2:21

Record and share:
a.   What gave people like Alice Marble
and Father Brandsma
the strength and courage to endure pain.
b.   The four kinds of pain there are.
c.   Why you think God permits pain.
d.   How pain and suffering can be
transformed into prayer and grace.
e.   The meaning of these words:
"Be glad . . . of the many kinds of trials
you suffer. Their purpose is to prove
that your faith is genuine."   1 Peter 1:6–7

2.   The Second Letter from Peter begins:
"May grace and peace be yours
in full measure through your knowledge
of God and of Jesus our Lord."   2 Peter 1:2

The biblical idea of *peace* is not so much
the absence of war as it is the presence
of a right relationship with God.
Peace begins in the human soul.
A Chinese proverb explains why.

*If there is right in the soul,
there will be beauty in the person.
If there is beauty in the person,
there will be harmony in the home.
If there is harmony in the home,
there will be order in the nation.
If there is order in the nation,
there will be peace in the world.*

Record and share :
a.   One way your relationship with God
has changed this year.
b.   One reason for the change.
c.   One good result because of the change.

*Be bold—and mighty
forces will come to
your aid.*   Basil King

*Peter*

**W**hat is the situation
of the Christians
to whom Peter addresses
his first letter?

2. What vexing question
does Peter address
in his second letter?

3. What reassurance
and what caution does
Peter give the readers
of his second letter?

4. Identify the following:
a. Father Brandsma
b. Alice Marble
c. Mount Tabor

# 108 John

False teachers began to infiltrate the early Christian community. John refers to them, collectively, as the "Enemy of Christ," or "Antichrist." Who were these people? John says:

*Those who say that Jesus is not the Messiah . . . are the Enemy of Christ. . . . Do not believe all who claim to have the Spirit, but test them to find out if the spirit they have comes from God. . . .*

*Who acknowledges that Jesus Christ came as a human being has the Spirit. . . . Who denies this about Jesus does not. . . . The spirit that he has is from the Enemy of Christ.* 1 John 2:22, 4:1–3

The *Docetists* were one set of false teachers. They taught that Jesus only "appeared" to have a human body and, therefore, was not a true *human being.*

The *Gnostics* were a second set. They taught that all matter is evil and, therefore, Jesus is neither the *Son of God* nor the *Messiah,* because neither of them would be joined to something evil. Thus false teachers denied Jesus to be

- a human being,    1 John 4:2
- the Messiah,    1 John 2:22
- the Son of God.    1 John 2:23

John reaffirms both the humanity and the divinity of Jesus, saying:

*We write to you about the Word of life, which has existed from the very beginning. We have heard it, and we have seen it with our eyes. . . .*

*What we have seen and heard we announce to you also, so that you will join with us in the fellowship that we have with the Father and with his Son Jesus Christ.* 1 John 1:1, 3

John's second letter is only a note. Addressed to "the dear Lady and to her children" (a church in Asia Minor), it exhorts them to love one another and to guard against false teachers.

The final letter is also a mere note. Addressed to a certain Gaius, it warns the local church about a certain leader who has broken with John and threatens to lead the community astray.

John ends his third letter to Gaius, saying:

*I have so much to tell you, but I do not want to do it with pen and ink. I hope to see you soon, and then we will talk personally.* 3 John 13–14

The portrait of this girl, poised with pen and pad, was found at Pompeii. That city was buried under volcanic ash when Mount Vesuvius erupted in A.D. 79— around the time John was writing his own letter to Gaius.

*A*lthough the term *Antichrist,* or *Enemy of Christ,* is unique to John, the gospel idea of *false messiahs* and *false prophets* is similar.   Mark 13:21ff.

Even closer to the idea of the Antichrist is Paul's "Wicked One"—
who will come and "claim to be God."
Paul adds, "Something . . . keeps this from happening now, and you know what it is."   2 Thessalonians 2:3–4, 6
But we don't know! Paul is probably referring to something he said orally.

John L. McKenzie sums up Paul's thought this way in his *Dictionary of the Bible:*

*When this restraining influence is removed, the man of sin [Wicked One] will be revealed. . . .*
*His revelation will be accompanied by signs and powers and many will be deceived* [2 Thessalonians 2:1–10];
*this is the great apostasy [defection] which precedes the Parousia [Christ's final coming]. . . .*

*The figure of the Antichrist has been interpreted in many ways; but there are good reasons for doubting . . . that he signifies a real historical-eschatological [end-time] figure. . . .*

*Antichrist is rather a personification [treated as a person] of the powers of evil which occasionally focus in some individual person and can be expected to do so again.*

Record and share:
a.  What you can do to keep from being deceived by the "Wicked One" and being a part of the "great apostasy" that will preview Christ's final coming.
b.  The probable interpretation of the Antichrist.

2.  Some false teachers denied the idea of sin, saying the body was evil *by nature.* Therefore, only the soul mattered. John corrects this false view, saying:

*If we say that we have no sin, we deceive ourselves. . . .*

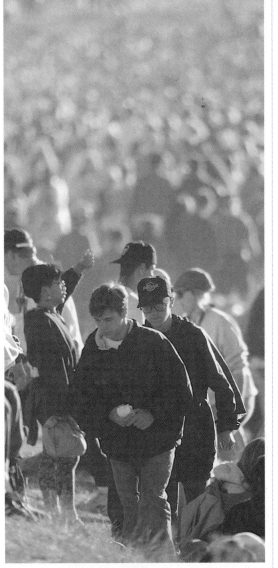

*But if we confess our sins to God, he will . . . forgive us our sins and purify us from all our wrongdoing. If we say that we have not sinned, we make a liar out of God.*   1 John 1:8–10

How do John's words fit in with what Louis Evely stresses in these two statements?

a.  "It is better to sin with sincerity than to lie to oneself in order to stay virtuous."
b.  "Commit straightforward, clear-cut and undeniable sins of which you will later be able to repent with the same sincerity you used in committing them."
*In His Presence* ✍

*M*y saving power will rise on you like the sun and bring healing like the sun's rays.
Malachi 4:2

*John*

*W*hat name does John give to false teachers, collectively?

2. Identify two groups of false teachers and what they taught.

3. List the three truths about Jesus that these false teachers denied about Jesus.

4. Identify:
a. "Wicked One"
b. apostasy
c. Parousia
d. eschatological
e. personification

225

The cost
of being
a disciple
is **big**;
the cost of
not being one is
**bigger**
still.

Author unknown

# 109 Jude

Recall the parable that Jesus told about an enemy who oversowed a farmer's wheat field with weeds. When workers saw the weeds growing, they went to the farmer and asked him if they should pull up the weeds.

*" 'No,' he answered, '. . . you might pull up some of the wheat along with them. . . . Let [them] grow together until harvest. Then I will tell the harvest workers to pull up the weeds first, tie them in bundles and burn them.' "* Matthew 13:29–30

The apostle Jude (Luke 6:16, Acts 1:13) addresses a situation similar to the one that Jesus describes in his parable.

An enemy oversowed a farmer's wheat with weeds. The farmer told his workers not to uproot them:

"You might pull up some of the wheat along with them. . . . Let [them] grow together until harvest.

"Then I will tell the harvest workers to pull up the weeds first, tie them in bundles and burn them."

Matthew 13:29–30

Of special note is Jude's observation that some "godless people" are distorting the message of Jesus (sowing weeds in it) "to excuse their immoral ways." Jude 4

Jude's point is excellent. He is implying that when belief and behavior clash, we can become a Dr. Jekyll and Mr. Hyde. We can split down the middle, believing and behaving differently.

Since living this way is uncomfortable, we try to resolve our conflict. First we try to change our behavior to fit our belief. If we cannot do this, we change our belief to fit our behavior. The "godless people" chose to do this. As a result, says Jude:

*They are like wild waves of the sea, with their shameful deeds showing up like foam. They are like wandering stars, for whom God has reserved a place forever in the deepest darkness.* Jude 13

Jude ends his letter with this moving exhortation to his readers:

*"When the last days come, people will appear who will make fun of you, people who follow their own godless desires." [These people] do not have the Spirit.*

*But you, my friends, keep on building yourselves up on your most sacred faith. Pray in the power of the Holy Spirit, and keep yourselves in the love of God, as you wait for our Lord Jesus Christ in his mercy to give you eternal life. . . .*

*To the only God our Savior, through Jesus Christ our Lord, be glory, majesty, might, and authority, from all ages past, and now, and forever and ever! Amen.* Jude 18–21, 25

*They are like wild waves of the sea . . . for whom God has reserved a place forever in the deepest darkness.* Jude 13

*I*magine you had a close friend who was split down the middle, believing one way but behaving in a completely opposite way.

What advice would you give if your friend confided in you and asked your help?

2. *The Last Days of Pompeii* by Edward Bulwer-Lytton tries to reconstruct what life was like in the city of Pompeii before Mount Vesuvius erupted and buried it under volcanic ash in A.D. 79.

One episode concerns two young friends searching for something to believe in. Eventually, one becomes a Christian and the other casts his lot with a pagan cult. Later on the two young friends meet. The one who cast his lot with the cult is totally disillusioned, saying:

*"My nature has revolted at what I have seen and been doomed to share in! Searching after truth, I have become a minister of falsehoods. . . . I am in the deepest abyss of gloom; I know not if there be gods above, if we are the things of chance. . . . Tell me thy faith. Solve me these doubts, if thou hast indeed the power."*

Record and share:
a. To what extent you think young people today are searching for something to believe in.
b. Five things you believe in profoundly.

3. Recall a time when someone asked you about your faith.
a. How comfortable are you talking about your faith?
b. Where would you begin if a "searching friend" asked you about your faith?

4. The Christian youth in *The Last Days of Pompeii* began talking about his faith this way:

*He spoke first of the sufferings and miracles of Christ— he wept as he spoke: he turned next to the glories of the Savior's Ascension.*

His friend was moved so deeply that he asked to go to an underground Mass.

*Curiosity, too, mingled with his purer stimulants—he was anxious to see those rites of which so many dark and contrary rumors were afloat.*

a. Why begin with the sufferings and the miracles of Jesus?
b. Why an "underground" Mass?
c. Explain the reference to "dark and contrary rumors."

*Jude*

**D**escribe the situation that Jude addresses in his letter.

2. Explain Jude's point about the belief-behavior conflict and how it works.

227

# 110 Hebrews

**N**ovelist Joseph Conrad went to sea when he was little more than a boy. One day he was learning to steer the ship. Suddenly a big storm blew up. The skipper kept him in full control, shouting instructions: "Keep her facing the wind, boy! Keep her facing the wind!"

The author of the Letter to the Hebrews takes a similar kind of an approach with his readers.

First, he tells his readers to imitate Jesus, who experienced temptation and the hatred of sinners:

*Hold firmly to the faith we profess.
For we have a great High Priest
who has gone into the very presence
of God—Jesus, the Son of God.*

*Our High Priest is not one who cannot
feel sympathy for our weaknesses. . . .*

**H**undreds of Christians, like those addressed in the Letter to the Hebrews, were thrown to wild beasts in Rome's Colosseum.

A letter by a Christian, written just before being thrown to beasts, reads:

*I am God's wheat
and shall be ground by
the teeth of wild beasts,
so that I may become
God's pure bread. . . .
My time of birth
is close at hand.*
Ignatius of Antioch (ca. A.D. 100)

We are not sure who the "Hebrews" were, but one proposal is that they were a community of Jewish priests who converted to Christianity and then suffered persecution because of their faith in Jesus.

Whatever the case, the author of Hebrews makes two specific recommendations: imitate Jesus and imitate your ancestors.

*[He] was tempted in every way
that we are, but did not sin.*

*Let us have confidence, then,
and approach God's throne,
where there is grace. There we will . . .
find grace to help us just when we need it.*
Hebrews 4:14–16

*Let us keep our eyes fixed on Jesus,
on whom our faith depends*

*from beginning to end. . . .*
*Think of what he went through;*
*how he put up with so much hatred*
*from sinners! . . .*
*Lift up your tired hands, then,*
*and strengthen your trembling knees!*
*Keep walking on straight paths.*
Hebrews 12:2–3, 12–13

Second, the author of Hebrews counsels his readers to imitate the deep faith of their ancestors:

*It was faith that made Abraham*
*able to become a father,*
*even though he was too old. . . .*
*It was faith that made Abraham*
*offer his son Isaac as a sacrifice. . . .*
*It was faith that made Moses . . . suffer*
*with God's people.*  Hebrews 11:11, 17, 24–25

Frederic Remington is a famous American sculptor who lived in the early 1900s. His art sells today for as much as $100,000 for just one single object.

One of his best works, *The Rattlesnake*, depicts a horse encountering a huge rattlesnake. The horse is reared up on two legs, the horseman is holding on mightily, and the rattlesnake is poised to strike.

This sculpture acts as a parable of how we should react when we encounter temptation. We should react as swiftly and seriously as did the horse.

Record and share:
a.  How firmly do you believe Jesus wants to help you when you are tempted?
b.  How do you explain the times when you ask for help but fall anyway?
c.  How do you understand these words: "We are not tempted because we are evil; we are tempted because we are human"?
Fulton J. Sheen (slightly adapted)

2.  Author Ardis Whitman recalls how as an eight-year-old in Boston she attended her first circus. She says:

*I marveled at the trapeze artists,*
*soaring impossibly through space,*
*always catching the flying swing*
*from each other. "Aren't they scared?"*
*I whispered to my mother.*
*A man in the row ahead turned to answer,*
*"They aren't scared, honey,"*
*he said gently. "They trust each other."*

a.  What is one thing that sometimes makes it hard for you to trust Jesus, the way the author of the Letter to the Hebrews exhorts his readers to do?
b.  What is one thing that sometimes makes it hard for you to trust people?

3.  In a *TV Guide* article, Jane Fonda says her father, Henry, was a "somewhat troubled and distant parent" who didn't know how to reach out to his children. She says that now that she is a parent, she realizes that "blame and judgment are no way to go through life."

In the same spirit as the Letter to the Hebrews (8:12), she says, "Forgiveness is important . . . and it is the child who must usually make the first move."

a.  To what extent do you make the first move to repair a fractured relationship?
b.  What usually happens if the other person rejects your first move? Explain.
c.  How understanding and forgiving are you of the shortcomings of your parents?

*Little love, little trust.*
English proverb

## Hebrews

What is one proposal concerning who the Hebrews were and why they were suffering?

2. Explain the two recommendations that the author of the Letter to the Hebrews makes to his readers.

229

# CHAPTER TWENTY-TWO

# Revelation

## 111 Seven Messages

**P**ersistence of Memory is an
eerie painting by Salvador Dali.
The glow of a never-setting sun
seems to light the background.
Three watches,
looking like slices of melted cheese,
drape over objects in the foreground.

Pondering Dali's surrealistic creation
is like pondering a scene from a dream.

We get a similar impression
when we ponder the Book of Revelation.
It is filled with dreamlike images
granted to "John" during visions
on Patmos, an island in the Aegean Sea.
Civil authorities had banished John there
for preaching about Jesus.

John's visions began on the Lord's Day,
when he heard a voice.
Turning around, he saw Jesus
standing amid seven lampstands,
symbolizing seven churches

**S**alvador Dali's
*Persistence of Memory*
has also been dubbed
"A Dream Captured
on Canvas."

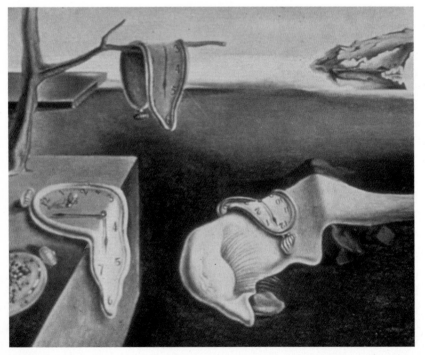

(Ephesus, Smyrna, Pergamum, Thyatira,
Sardis, Philadelphia, and Laodicea).

All seven churches
were facing persecution under Domitian,
the current Roman emperor (A.D. 81–96).

At the sight of Jesus,
John fell to the ground "like a dead man."
But Jesus reached down, touched him,
and said, "Don't be afraid!"    Revelation 1:17

Then Jesus dictated seven messages
to John, one for each threatened church.

They follow a general twofold *format:*
commending the churches on some things
and correcting them on others.
They also follow a general *theme,*
which may be summed up
in this excerpt to the church in Smyrna
(in modern Turkey):

*"This is the message from the one . . .*
*who died and lived again. . . .*
*The Devil will put you to the test. . . .*
*Be faithful to me . . .*
*and I will give you life*
*as your prize of victory."*    Revelation 2:8, 10

After the dictation is completed,
the visions begin to unfold,
somewhat like a stage play in three acts:

Act 1:  Preview visions    Revelation 4:1–8:5
Act 2:  Conflict visions    Revelation 8:6–15:8
Act 3:  Judgment visions    Revelation 16:1ff.

**B**ritish author C. S. Lewis was riding
on a bus. Suddenly, a thought
came to him out of nowhere
and struck him with great force.

*I became aware*
*that I was holding something at bay,*
*or shutting something out. . . .*

*I felt myself being, there and then, given a free choice. I could open the door or keep it shut. . . . Neither choice was presented as a duty; no threat nor promise was attached to either, though I knew that to open the door . . . meant the incalculable. . . . I chose to open.* Surprised by Joy

Lewis's experience recalls Jesus' final message to the seven churches:

*"Listen! I stand at the door and knock; if any hear my voice and open the door, I will come into their house and eat with them, and they will eat with me."* Revelation 3:20

Explain and give an example to show what Lewis meant by:
a. "I could open the door or keep it shut."
b. "Neither choice was presented as a duty."
c. "No threat nor promise was attached."
d. "To open . . . meant the incalculable."

2. Lewis was talking about the door to his heart and about letting Jesus enter it and reign over his life.

a. Record and share some similar door you are, perhaps, keeping shut.
b. Why are you keeping it shut?
c. Why do you think opening it could lead to something "incalculable"?

3. Imagine you are John copying down these words to the church in Smyrna:

*"This is the message from the one . . . who died and lived again. . . . The Devil will put you to the test. . . . Be faithful to me . . . and I will give you life as your prize of victory."* Revelation 2:8, 10

What thoughts come to mind as you copy this passage? Why these thoughts?

4. Read the letter "to the angel of the church in Ephesus." Revelation 2:1–7
a. List the compliments and the criticisms.
b. List the warning and the promise.
c. Imagine your pastor asks you to write a similar, short, unsigned letter to the people of your parish for publication in the bulletin. Compose that letter. ❧

## Seven Messages

To whom were the "seven messages" penned, and what did the recipients have in common?

2. What format and theme did each message follow?

3. Briefly explain the format of the visions that follow the messages.

# *112 Preview Visions*

The *preview* visions (Act 1) open with a voice from heaven telling John, "Come up here, and I will show you what must happen." Revelation 4:1 John goes and beholds God on a throne, holding a scroll with seven seals.

John weeps when he learns that no one is worthy to break the seals. Then a Lamb appears. He is worthy,

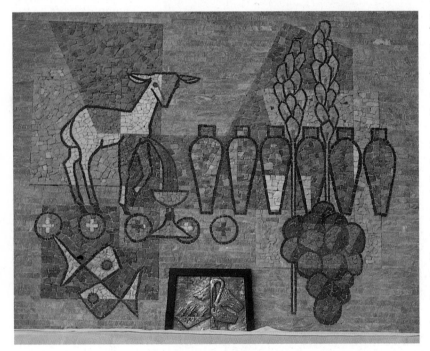

**W**hy is the Lamb an ideal eucharistic symbol? Identify other eucharistic symbols in the photo.

because by his death he "bought for God people from every . . . nation." Revelation 5:9 The first four seals reveal, in turn:

🐚 a white horse, whose rider wears a crown, suggesting *victory;*
🐚 a red horse, whose rider carries a sword, suggesting *conflict* between the forces of good and evil;
🐚 a black horse, whose rider carries a scale, suggesting *judgment* (evil),

reward (good), and punishment; and
🐚 a pale green horse, whose rider is named Death and Hades, suggesting the *fate of the evil forces.*

Then the Lamb breaks the *fifth* seal. It reveals a host of martyred Christians, who are told more will join them soon, suggesting further persecution.

Next the Lamb breaks the *sixth* seal, revealing cosmic catastrophes. They cause people to tremble and shout to the mountains: "Hide us." Revelation 6:16

Then four angels arrive from the four corners of the earth to mark the foreheads of the 144,000 people. (This symbolic number derives from the 12,000 members of each of the tribes of old Israel, suggesting the "new Israel," those who will remain faithful to Jesus.)

"Dressed in white robes and holding palm branches," they have "washed their robes and made them white with the blood of the Lamb." Revelation 7:9, 14

Then the Lamb breaks the *last* seal. As he does, silence fills all of heaven. *Silence* is a biblical code word, symbolizing an awesome moment: "Be silent, everyone, in the presence of the LORD." Zechariah 2:13

Then three things happen, setting the stage for the *conflict visions.*

First, seven angels get seven trumpets. Second, a eighth angel places on an altar a container of prayers and then hurls fire down to earth. Third, the fire triggers thunder, lightning, catastrophes, and earthquakes.

*J*ohn was crying bitterly because
no one in heaven was worthy
to open the scroll with the seals.
Then, suddenly, one of the elders saw
John, turned to him, and said joyfully:

*"Don't cry. Look! . . .*
*The great descendant of David*
*has won the victory, and he can break*
*the seven seals and open the scroll."*

*Then I saw a Lamb*
*standing in the center of the throne,*
*surrounded by the four living creatures*
*and the elders. . . . The Lamb . . .*
*took the scroll from the right hand*
*of the one who sits on the throne.*
*As he did so, the four living creatures*
*and the twenty-four elders*
*fell down before the Lamb. . . .*
*They sang a new song:*

*"You are worthy to take the scroll and*
*to break open its seals.*
*For you were killed, and by your*
*sacrificial death you bought for God*
*people from every tribe, language,*
*nation, and race."* Revelation 5:5–9

Explain your interpretation of:
a. "The Lamb."
b. "The one who sits on the throne."
c. "The four living creatures."
d. "The twenty-four elders."

(How might Revelation 21:12–14
be a clue to the identity of the elders?)

2. Imagine you are John as the curtain falls
on the *preview* visions.
Record and share your thoughts
about the preview you have just watched.

3. Revelation has a number of prayers
such as this one in chapter 15, verses 3–4:

*Lord God Almighty,*
*how great and wonderful are your deeds!*
*King of the nations,*
*how right and true are your ways!*
*Who will not stand in awe of you, Lord?*
*Who will refuse to declare your greatness?*
*You alone are holy.*
*All nations will come and worship you.*

Compose your own prayer to God.
You might wish to model it after this one:

*Lord, how great you are!*
*We ask you for a rose;*
*you give us a rose garden.*
*We ask you for a tree;*
*you give us a forest.*
*We ask you for a star;*
*you give us the Milky Way.*
*We ask you*
*for something to eat and drink;*
*you give us the body and blood*
*of your only Son.* ❧

*T*he sculpture above the
entrance of the Cathedral
of Chartres in France
was inspired by
Revelation 4:7.

Most ancient cathedrals
faced east (rising sun),
the direction in which
they believed
Jesus would appear
at his final coming.

The cathedral's entrance
faced west (setting sun).
Around and over
its doors were symbols
of the Last Judgment.

This reminded people
entering the cathedral
(symbol of heaven)
that they must first
pass through
the Last Judgment
before entering heaven.

## Preview Visions

*H*ow do the
*preview* visions open?
Who is found worthy
to break the seven seals,
and why?

2. List and explain what
the breaking of each
of the seven seals
reveals and suggests.

3. What sets the stage
for the *conflict* visions?

# 113 Conflict Visions

The *conflict* visions (Act 2) open with seven angels sounding, in order, seven trumpets.
The trumpets unleash a series of plagues not unlike those unleashed against the ancient Egyptians.
And like the ancient Egyptians, the evil people on earth remain obstinate.

Then a mysterious woman, dressed in the sun, appears in the sky.
She gives birth to a son.
A dragon leaps forward to kill it.
But like the infant Jesus, who was saved from Herod, the infant is saved from the dragon.

Then war breaks out in heaven.
"The dragon" and "his angels" battle "Michael" and "his angels."    Revelation 12:7
Michael is victorious and hurls them down to earth, where they pursue the woman's descendants: the faithful followers of Jesus.    Revelation 12:17

Next, a sea beast receives power from the dragon and is worshiped by all except the faithful—until he is wounded.

Then a second beast comes forth from the earth and breathes life back into the first beast, whose number is "666."    Revelation 13:18
(This is the symbolic number of Nero, first Roman to persecute Christians, suggesting the second beast is Domitian.)
John continues:

*Then I looked, and there was the Lamb standing on Mount Zion;*
*with him were 144,000 people who have his name and his Father's name written on their foreheads. . . .*

*[Then an angel] flying high in the air . . . said in a loud voice,*
*"Honor God and praise his greatness!*
*For the time has come for him to judge all people. . . ."*

This mural by students portrays the battle in which Michael defeats the dragon.

The vertical painting (separating Michael and the dragon) portrays Adam and Eve (humanity) in the garden.

Satan avenges his defeat by successfully tempting the human race to sin and lose the right to be with God in heaven.

Thanks to the Lamb, humanity defeats Satan in a final battle and is put right with God.
Revelation 12:11

*[Finally,] I looked,*
*and there was a white cloud,*
*and sitting on the cloud*
*was what looked like a human being,*
*with a crown of gold on his head*
*and a sharp sickle in his hand.*

Revelation 14:1, 6–7, 14

The curtain falls on the *conflict* visions
as seven angels appear holding
seven bowls filled with God's anger.
It's time for the *judgment* visions (Act 3).

*M*any identify the woman
who gave birth as Mary; others
identify her as symbolizing Israel.
Both are true mothers of the Messiah.
Like the infants Moses and Jesus,
the infant Church will be saved
from those seeking to destroy her.

Record and share:
a. How Moses and Jesus were rescued
in infancy.   Exodus 2:1–10, Matthew 2:13–15
b. How the infant Church might be compared
to Moses and Jesus.

2. The second beast breathed life
back into the first beast.
"Its number is 666."   Revelation 13:18
Many identify the beast as Nero Caesar
(*nrwn qsr*, in Hebrew). The numerical
value of the letters adds up to 666
(50 + 200 + 6 + 50 + 100 + 60 + 200).
Nero, the first to persecute Christians,
returns to life in Domitian.

Nero's persecution occurred in connection
with a great fire in Rome in A.D. 64.
Rumor said Nero wanted to burn much
of the old city, rebuild it, and rename it
for himself. To shift blame from himself,
he blamed Roman Christians.
The historian Tacitus (A.D. 110) says:

*Unusual brutality attended their execution:*
*they were dressed in animal skins*
*and torn to pieces by enraged dogs;*
*they were put on crosses,*
*and at nighttime burned as torches*
*to light up the darkness.*

Record and share:
a. Similarities between Nero and Hitler.
b. Examples of recent mass atrocities.
c. The reason behind such atrocities.
d. Why you do/don't think such atrocities
are possible in our own country today.

3. Early Christians didn't have to puzzle
over the strange imagery in Revelation.
They learned the meaning of the images
almost as another language. For example,
Revelation contains some 400 references
and 100 allusions to the Old Testament.
Consider four examples:

| | |
|---|---|
| lion of Judah | Revelation 5:5, Genesis 49:9 |
| seven lampstands | Revelation 1:12, Zechariah 4:10 |
| six wings | Revelation 4:8, Isaiah 6:2 |
| seven eyes | Revelation 5:6, Zechariah 4:10 |

Team up with another, check the references,
and explain the link between the way
the Old Testament and the Book of Revelation
use the images. ✍

*T*his wood sculpture
is an artist's prayer:

*May Mary's motherhood*
*extend to a united*
*Christianity.*

*Conflict*
*Visions*

*D*escribe briefly:
a. how the start of the
conflict visions parallels
the start of Israel's flight
from Egypt.
b. how the births of
Moses and Jesus parallel
the birth of the Church.
c. two suggestions
about the woman's
identity.
d. the war in heaven
and what the defeated
army did.
e. the symbolism "666"
and its link to Domitian.

# COME LORD JESUS

## 114 *Judgment Visions*

The *judgment* visions (Act 3) open with the seven angels pouring out the seven bowls of God's anger on the earth.    Revelation 16:1–21 The first five bowls trigger a series of terrible plagues. Then John says:

*[When] the sixth angel*
*poured out his bowl . . .*
*I saw three unclean spirits . . .*
*go out to all the kings of the world,*
*to bring them together for the battle*
*on the great Day of Almighty God . . .*
*in the place that in Hebrew*
*is called Armageddon.*

*Then the seventh angel poured out*
*his bowl in the air. A loud voice came*
*from the throne in the temple, saying,*
*"It is done!"*    Revelation 16:12–17

*Then [John] saw heaven open,*
*and there was a white horse.*
*Its rider is called Faithful and True;*

*it is with justice that he judges. . . .*
*The armies of heaven followed him. . . .*
*[He bears the name]*
*"King of kings and Lord of lords."*
                    Revelation 19:11, 14, 16

Then they engage the armies of earth. The battle is swift and decisive.

The dragon—"the Devil, or Satan"— is chained "a thousand years."    Revelation 20:2 (This symbolic time designates the era of the reign of Jesus' Church on earth from the end of the Roman persecution to the Last Judgment.) At the end of this era, Satan is freed and leads a final assault against the just. It ends with Satan being "thrown into the lake of fire." John concludes:

*I saw a great white throne*
*and the one who sits on it. . . .*
*All were judged. . . .*
*Those who did not have their name*

**W**hen I die,
God won't measure
my head to see
how clever I was.
God will measure
my heart to see
how loving I became.
                    Anonymous

*written in the book of the living*
*were thrown into the lake of fire.*
*(This lake of fire is the second death.)*

Revelation 20:11, 13, 15, 14

*Then the one who sits on the throne said,*
*"And now I make all things new! . . .*
*I am the first and the last. . . .*
*I am coming soon!"*    Revelation 21:5–6, 22:7

And so, saints enter into eternal life
(book of life); and sinners,
into eternal death (lake of fire).

The curtain falls with John praying,
"Come, Lord Jesus!"

Some people feel the "decisive battle"
between God and Satan is not far away.
For example, TV shows and magazines
are beginning to ask the question,
Is the end near?
What are your thoughts about this?

2.  At the end of the 1,000-year period,
Satan went about on earth and assembled
an army, "Gog and Magog,"
to war against God's people.    Revelation 20:8
The strange names *Gog* and *Magog*
are borrowed from Ezekiel 38–39 and
symbolize here the pagan nations arrayed
against the Church in the end times.

This tabernacle door
on a church in Germany
portrays seven images
from Revelation.

Going from top to
bottom on the left door
(3:4, 5:1, 7:1)
and from top left
to bottom right
on the right door
(5:6, 11:15, 14:14, 14:3)
identify as many images
as you can without
using the Bible.
(You may, however,
use your textbook.)

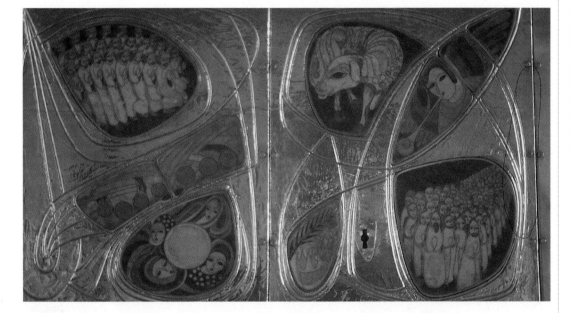

The writing style of Revelation
is often called *apocalyptic.*
This means it uses visions and
symbolic images to speak of the future.
Apocalyptic writing is also found
in the last half of Daniel and, occasionally,
in the Gospels.    Matthew 24:29–31

Apocalyptic writing was used, especially,
to address future "crisis" situations.
The "crisis" situation of Revelation
is the persecution of the early Church.
Revelation presents it as a preview
of the decisive battle between God and
Satan that will usher in the world's
end and the completion of God's kingdom
("re-creation" of the earth).

Some images in the Book of Revelation
are not only strange but also grotesque
to the eyes and ears of modern readers.
For example, Jesus is portrayed
as "a Lamb" having "seven horns and
seven eyes."    Revelation 5:6
This image simply affirms that
the fullness (seven) of power (horns) and
knowledge (eyes) dwells in Jesus.
In some cases, even scholars are not sure
of the meaning of a *particular* symbol.
But the book's *general* message is clear.

a.  In one sentence, what would you say
the *general* message of Revelation is?
b.  What special application
might this *general* message have
for Christians today? Explain.

*Judgment*
*Visions*

Explain the meaning of:
a.  Armageddon
b.  dragon
c.  thousand years
d.  book of life
e.  lake of fire
f.  Gog and Magog
g.  apocalyptic writing
h.  seven horns
i.  seven eyes

# 115 Interpreting Revelation

"Christ has conquered; so will you!"

Three different ways to interpret the Book of Revelation have emerged over the centuries. We may label them:

 - the early-history approach,
 - the sweep-of-history approach, and
 - the end-of-history approach.

The *early-history* approach regards the book's primary audience to be persecuted Christians of the first century.

To these Christians it says, "There will be times of testing and suffering, but persevere; the re-creation of the world will take place according to God's plan."

Finally, the *end-of-history* approach regards the primary audience to be Christians who will be living when the world ends. To them it says:

*"Then the Son of Man will appear, coming in a cloud*

Young people from all the nations of the world gathered with the Holy Father on World Youth Day in Denver, Colorado.

Here they reenact the "Way of the Cross." Why did this reenactment have a "special" meaning for certain young people?

To these Christians the book says, "Persevere and remain faithful in your time of suffering! Christ has conquered; so will you!"

The *sweep-of-history* approach regards the book's primary audience to be Christians of all times.

*with great power and glory. When these things begin to happen, stand up and raise your heads, because your salvation is near."*
Luke 21:27–28

Each of these three approaches has profound merit and value.

The first approach makes Revelation, primarily, a guide for Christians of *early times.*
The second approach makes it, primarily, a guide for Christians of *all times.*
The third approach makes it, primarily, a guide for Christians of the *end times.*

Perhaps the best approach is to realize that the Book of Revelation, as the inspired word of God, has a message for every Christian— regardless of time or place.

*J*ames Cone's book *God of the Oppressed* describes the Sunday worship service of black people in early America.

*On Sunday morning,*
*after spending six days of struggling*
*to create meaning out of life,*
*the people of Braden would go to church*
*because they knew*
*Jesus was going to be there. . . .*

*When the pastor would say,*
*"I know the Lord is in this place!*
*Can I get a witness?" the people*
*responded with shouts of praise,*
*saying "Amen" and "Hallelujah." . . .*

*How could black slaves*
*know that they were human beings*
*when they were treated like cattle?*
*How could they know*
*that they were somebody*
*when everything in their environment*
*said that they were nobody? . . .*

*Only because they knew*
*that Christ was present with them*
*and that his presence included*
*the divine promise*
*to come again and to take them*
*to the New Jerusalem.*

a. How does the situation of these black slaves parallel the plight of the seven churches referred to in the Book of Revelation?
b. To what extent is the situation of modern Christians approaching, slowly but surely, the same situation as that of the early Christians described in the Book of Revelation?

2. *The few little years*
*we spend on earth*
*are only the first scene*
*in a Divine Drama*
*that extends into eternity.*    Edwin Markham

a. What is the poet's point, and why do so few people live according to it?
b. Write out a brief prayer to Jesus, stating what you understand to be the message of Revelation for you, personally, right now— and ask his help to put it into practice. ✍

This ancient Roman coin lists two Jesus symbols:

(χ) Chi and (ρ) Rho, Greek initials for Jesus Christ, and (Λ) Alpha and (ω) Omega, first and last letters of the Greek alphabet.

Jesus identified himself by these letters at the conclusion of the Book of Revelation:

*"I am the Alpha and the Omega."*
   Revelation 22:13 (NAB)

Why are Alpha and Omega fitting symbols for Jesus?

*Interpreting Revelation*

**L**ist and briefly describe the three different approaches to interpreting the Book of Revelation.

2. State briefly the merit and value of each of the above three approaches.

3. What is perhaps the best approach?

# REFERENCE NOTES

## PART I

Roland de Vaux, "The Qumran Story," *The Bible Today Reader* (Collegeville, Minn.: Order of St. Benedict, 1973), p. 42.

*Popular Science,* as reported in "Geiger Counters Prove Age of Biblical Scrolls," *Catholic Universe Bulletin,* December 7, 1951.

Watch Tower Bible and Tract Society, *Is the Bible Really the Word of God?* (Watch Tower and Tract Society of Pennsylvania, 1969), pp. 21–22.

Charles Clayton Morrison, "Protestant Misuse of the Bible," *The Christian Century,* June 5, 1946.

Ronald Kotulak, "Deadend for Expanding Universe?" *Chicago Tribune,* 1973.

"The Stars, Where Life Begins," *Time,* December 27, 1976.

George Higgins, "Sin Comes Back on the Scene" (Washington, D.C.: National Catholic News Service, 1974).

"The Ten Biggest Challenges," *Newsweek,* March 29, 1993.

Arthur Snider, "Man's a Born Killer . . . ," *Chicago Daily News,* September 1–2, 1973.

Dorothy Thompson, "The Lesson of Dachau," *Ladies' Home Journal,* September 1945.

*Time,* November 28, 1977.

## PART II

J. Peter Schineller, "Promises to Keep . . . ," *Review for Religious,* January 1979.

*Everyday Life in Bible Times* (Washington, D.C.: National Geographic Society, 1967), p. 179.

David S. Boyer, "Geographical Twins a World Apart," *National Geographic Magazine,* December 1958, p. 852.

Carl Sandburg, as quoted by Ralph McGill in "The Most Unforgettable Character I've Met," *Reader's Digest,* May 1954, p. 110.

## PART III

Philip Yancey, "Fire," *Campus Life* Magazine, September 20, 1970.

"History by Computer," *Time,* April 27, 1962.

Howard LaFay, "The Years in Galilee," in *Everyday Life in Bible Times* (Washington, D.C.: National Geographic Society, 1967), p. 328.

## PART IV

Doug Alderson, "Why Drive When You Can Walk?" *Campus Life* Magazine, August–September 1976.

"The Exorcism Frenzy," *Newsweek,* February 11, 1974, p. 74.

Kenneth Clark, *The Other Half: A Self-Portrait* (New York: Harper & Row, 1978).

## PART V

Dietrich Bonhoeffer, "Night Voices in Tegel," from *I Loved These People* by Dietrich Bonhoeffer (Louisville, Ky.: John Knox Press, 1965).

George Seaver, *The Faith of Edward Wilson* (London: John Murray, 1948), p. 44.

Ardis Whitman, "The Courage to Trust," *Reader's Digest,* December 1968, p. 141.

# INDEX

# PHOTO CREDITS

Argus Communications    156B

Bill Aron    2

Bettmann Archive    10B, 11, 16T, 30, 35, 40T, 49, 65, 149, 152T, 183, 215, 230

Biblical Archaeology Society    Werner Braun 58,188/ Stanley Houston 239/ Ze'ev Meshel 57/ Garo Nalbandian 70, 124, 125, 142, 162B, 166B, 226, 228/ Zev Radovan 39T, 68T, 68B, 69, 77, 78, 79, 106, 155, 180 (courtesy of Nahman Avigad), 201/ John Trevor 82

Courtesy of the Trustees of the British Library    8B

Courtesy of the Trustees of the British Museum    4T (#K6752), 13 (#K853), 32B (#K108,244), 80T, 93 (#K6822), 95 (#K806), 105 (#K63,492), 208 (#K120357), 216 (#GR1975.9-26)

Syndics of Cambridge University Library    214

Courtesy of the Trustees of the Chester Beatty Library, Dublin    6B (scroll fragment)

Ecole Francaise d'Archeologie    196

FPG    Alun Crockford 113/ LPI 197/ Art Montes de Oca 31/ John Taylor 12/ Telegraph Colour Library 121

Dennis Full    15, 16B, 21, 25, 26L, 33, 34, 37, 43, 54, 71, 76, 83, 85, 89, 99, 110, 114B, 115 (courtesy of American Bible Society), 135, 138, 145, 146T, 147, 148, 151, 159, 164T, 167, 168T, 175, 187, 189, 191, 193, 195, 217, 218, 221, 225, 236, 238B

Sonia Halliday    COVER, 4B, 186 (with Laura Luchington), 231

Marlene Halpin    17, 47

Image Bank    James Carmichael 14/ John Kelly 173/ Alberto Incrocci 132T/ Steven E. Sutton 95

Israel Museum    3

John Rylands Library    112/ Andrew Sacks 185

Leo De Wys    Sipa 61, 181, 203/ Bachmann 7

Erich Lessing/Art Resource, NY    22, 24, 38, 80B, 98, 224

Mark Link    5, 10T, 18T, 18B, 26R, 27, 32T, 42T, 46, 72T, 72B, 81, 86, 87, 90, 92, 94T, 94B, 101, 104, 117, 119, 126T, 126B, 127, 128T, 131, 132B, 134T, 134B, 136, 137, 140B, 143, 144, 146B, 150T, 150B, 153, 154, 156T, 157, 158, 161, 162T, 164B, 166T, 168B, 169, 172, 174T, 176, 182T, 182B, 184, 200, 202, 232T, 232B, 233, 234T, 234B, 235, 237, 238T

Courtesy of the Metropolitan Museum of Art    6B (figures), 52

Notre Dame De Sion    133

Courtesy of the Oriental Institute, University of Chicago    39B, 88

Peter Arnold Inc.    NASA 19/ Jim Olive 9

Picturepoint, London    174B, 205, 210

Robert Harding Picture Library    55, 63

Raymond Schoder, courtesy of Loyola University, Chicago    viii, 6T, 8T, 28T, 36, 40B, 41, 42B, 44, 50, 51, 53, 60, 62, 66, 73, 84, 91, 97, 100, 102, 114T, 116, 118, 120, 122, 130, 140T, 152B, 160, 163, 165, 170, 179, 190, 192, 194, 198, 204, 206, 209, 211, 219, 222

Sonia Halliday Photographs    Barry Searle 129/ Jane Taylor 48, 128B

The Stock Market    Andrew Holbrooke 23/ Michael Keller 20, 141/ Tim McKenna 64/ Mary Ellen Meyer 59/ Jose L. Palaez 220/ Sanford & Agliolo 29/ Robert Wagoner 213

Superstock    229/ Kai Chiang 139/ Gerald Fritz 212/ Catherine Gockley 177/ Dennis Junor 75

Tony Stone Images    199, 227/ Bruce Ayres 123/ Dan Basler 109/ David Madison 223/ Charles Thatcher 103/ Tom Walker 56

Werner Forman Archive/Art Resource, NY    28B, 207